"Dr. Charles Theisler has written a new book, *Maximum Malpractice Protection: A Physician's Complete Guide.* I have been a medical malpractice expert witness for plaintiff and defense work for 20 years. I am in a well-qualified position to review this new book. It is an incredibly well-written and extremely thorough review of the entire medical malpractice subject. This is a must-read for all doctors, especially new physicians who have just finished their residency and fellowship. I even go so far as to suggest that all medical practices and malpractice carriers provide this book to all new associates and new hires. Every section shines; the mock deposition is spot on."　　　— Jason Brajer, MD
Board Certified Anesthesiology and Pain Management

"This is an outstanding book on malpractice that provides a comprehensive review of the topics that are most relevant to practicing physicians interested in this field. Although this book is written from the perspective of American Jurisprudence, including an excellent review of the legal principles that underlie our court system, the information presented would be of interest to physicians practicing nationally as well as internationally. By virtue of its broad perspectives and detailed recommendations, the book is likely to be helpful to health care providers involved in a variety of capacities in the medico-legal system, be it as a defendant or expert witness for plaintiff or defense, or as a risk manager. Bravo to Dr. Theisler for his outstanding work!"
— Jonathan D. Marmur, MD, FACP, FACC

"Dr. Theisler has produced a truly comprehensive guide for understanding the medical malpractice process; he adeptly explains how medical care providers can reduce their own risk *and* keep their patients' safe. His work is equally applicable to physician extenders such as physician assistants and advanced practice nurses. Chapters are written with clarity and practicality. Legal theory and recommendations are well-referenced in addition to being based on years of personal experience with clinical case review and court testimony. *Maximum Malpractice Protection* is an essential read for all providers who wish to be the best clinicians they can be for their patients and to help ensure lengthy satisfied careers free of litigation."
— Jeffrey G. Nicholson, PhD, PA-C
Medical Malpractice Researcher and President
The PA Experts Network

"Very detailed and comprehensive. It gives great insight, is very easy to read, and follows a straightforward order. The real-life examples help break up the technical information and make the book more personal and relatable. There is a lot of very clear and concise advice here that will hopefully help keep a few more docs out of trouble! The rules listed to prevent malpractice were great and I am sure something most doctors would love to have as a quick reference."

— Eoin M. Halpin, DMD

"Dr. Theisler's book for physicians on how to navigate a malpractice case is a thoughtful and accessible introduction to the topic. He starts with a brief summary of the U.S. legal system with emphasis on medical malpractice. He next goes into the legal and ethical contract between physicians and patients in great detail so that the reader really understands what this means, how it applies to law, and the traps to avoid. This first section should be required reading for all new and established physicians. The next section is the primary focus of the book on how to avoid a malpractice suit, how to succeed in winning a lawsuit if one is filed, and how to learn from such a lawsuit in the future for yourself and colleagues. The book contains sections on how to deal with specific situations in the course of clinical practice, how to preserve assets before a suit is filed, and what to do if an error occurs to minimize risk. This should also be required reading for all new physicians, both to minimize risk of malpractice suits and to provide high-quality, compassionate care. Dr. Theisler has done an excellent job in helping physicians through this stress-inducing part of clinical practice. It isn't heavy in legal jargon and is written in a way that is applicable to all specialties."

— Ankush K. Bansal, MD

Maximum Malpractice Protection

A PHYSICIAN'S COMPLETE GUIDE

Maximum Malpractice Protection

A PHYSICIAN'S COMPLETE GUIDE

Charles Theisler, MD, JD, Editor

CRC Press
Taylor & Francis Group
Boca Raton London New York

CRC Press is an imprint of the
Taylor & Francis Group, an **Informa** business

Designed cover image: © Shutterstock

First edition published 2023
by CRC Press
6000 Broken Sound Parkway NW, Suite 300, Boca Raton, FL 33487-2742
and by CRC Press
4 Park Square, Milton Park, Abingdon, Oxon, OX14 4RN

CRC Press is an imprint of Taylor & Francis Group, LLC

© 2023 Charles Theisler

This book was previously published by Ayer Publishing in 2020 and is now being republished by CRC Press with minor modifications.

ISBN: 9781032403175 (hbk)
ISBN: 9781032403168 (pbk)
ISBN: 9781003352464 (ebk)

DOI: 10.1201/9781003352464

Interior design: Pamela Beaulieu

Table of Contents

Dedication

This book is gratefully dedicated to physicians and health care professionals everywhere who have sacrificed their personal lives and have devoted their skills, time, and energies to help those suffering and in need. It is also dedicated to those medical instructors who have nurtured and developed the seeds of interest in their eager students who did not yet comprehend the positive potential and importance of the careers they had chosen.

The second part of this dedication is to my family. As such, I remind my grandchildren, as well as their parents before them, that they were well-loved even before they were born, and that this love has only grown daily since. Each of them continues to be a source of joy and enduring delight in their facing challenges, persevering, overcoming obstacles, developing new skills and capabilities, and in their continued personal growth and maturity.

A special dedication is for my wonderful wife who has always managed to be supportive while possessing the sweetness and grace to not flaunt the fact that she's always been out of my league.

Acknowledgment

This is a book for physicians in every specialty, doctors of every discipline, and health care students in any educational allied health care program.

Everything in this book came from someone else by way of appropriation. I freely acknowledge and credit the legal and medical scholars who have made such a complex topic so understandable. As usual, I feel that I have benefited most from the scholars I have borrowed from.

Doctors are a special breed. They work harder and play harder than most people I know. They want to not only know, but to understand. They also have a need to share their knowledge and understanding for the betterment of others. That is why this book is important for medical professionals in general and physicians specifically. A general understanding of the law can pay real dividends in every aspect of life and doctors should not shy away from this vital and highly beneficial knowledge.

Introduction

I found this publication by Dr. Theisler to be compact, on the mark, and extremely informative. It is a must-read primer for any physician who is unfamiliar with the workings of the medicolegal arena from business, expert witness, and defendant standpoints. I have many years of experience as a practicing anesthesiologist, as a pain management physician, and as an expert witness in both specialties, plus an experience as a defendant.

This book is compact, no-nonsense, and concise, with excellent headings and simple explanations. He makes an excellent point with respect to anesthesia malpractice, with which I totally concur, when he states that "facts underlying anesthesia malpractice are almost never contained in anesthesia records."

Physicians often do not recognize the risks. The author talks about this "clinical blind spot" with an excellent emphasis on the under-reporting medical mistakes. He says that medical mistakes are the "third leading cause of death in the U.S."

The chapter on practice structure, Chapter 7, is very well written, concise, to the point, and is valuable to physicians deciding on their practice structure. I wish I would have had this information years ago. He does fail to mention the state-to-state variations in the support of the corporate practice of medicine (not permitted here in Nevada), but this is an issue which usually can be fixed by your local attorney.

His cut/paste warning is very timely; he quotes Allen Block, MD, that "cutting/pasting is rarely a good idea" and that "[regulators look at] large blocks of texts." I loved the creating of the "monster note, a creation of auto-filled blanks with vital signs and test results that tell you very little about what's really going and there is an overall lack of a good impression." These points are spot on.

As has been my own experience in multiple cases, he emphasizes that "a significant number of med mal suits are rendered indefensible because of poor medical records." In my experience with interventional pain management, the lack of a fluoroscopy or ultrasound image is very detrimental to the defense of a possible misplaced needle in an interventional pain management case.

The chapter on consent and release forms, Chapter 9, is very useful. I'm going to have my office review our forms and compare to these examples.

The chapter on plaintiff attorney depositions, Chapter 11, is very useful for the non-expert witness physician, whether you are a physician defendant or are new to being an expert witness.

The chapter on cross-examination, Chapter 12, is riveting; it reads as if from a movie, but is probably not that helpful since 99% of physicians would have gotten the EKG that the defendant physician did not get and was trying to justify. This doctor should have settled.

Dr. Theisler makes one of his most important points: "Too many doctors suffer from the misconception that malpractice cases are often brought thoughtlessly on a whim or on impulse… If doctors had any idea of the amount of time and money attorneys risk losing in this type of litigation, they would have a better understanding of the high degree of careful screening, diligence, and investigative work that is completed before filing such an action. No sensible attorney will spend hundreds of hours and $30,000–$60,000 for records, experts, depositions, transcripts, etc., on a case without significant potential for a recovery. One or two [losses in] malpractice claims like that could easily put an attorney out of business."

His metaphoric humor about a zebra defense is poignant and entertaining. The chapter on making your testimony shine in deposition and in court, Chapter 14, is valuable for novice experts, defendant physicians, and experienced experts like myself.

The Latin word for doctor means "to teach." The author correctly emphasizes that the jurors see you as a teacher, even if you are the defendant. The author advises the physician defendant to listen [to an objection] from his own attorney; your attorney may be giving you an important clue. There is also good advice for experienced expert witnesses in Chapter 14.

All in all, this monograph is packed with basic and clearly-written definitions, well-thought-out advice, and practical tips, all framed by common sense. For all of this, you will not have to pay an expensive attorney. Dr. Theisler is to be congratulated on an excellent, concise guide.

— Robert H. Odell, Jr., MD, PhD
Diplomat, American Board of Anesthesiology
Diplomat, American Board of Pain Medicine
Fellow of Interventional Pain Practice
American Academy of Pain Management

Gateway Essentials
Why This Book Is Needed and What It Means to You

It is said of medicine that the work brings us as close to God as man can be. I agree. I'm a physician by training and a malpractice attorney by trade. I deeply respect the medical education I received for its quality and values; I also have the highest regard for my dedicated mentors and for all that they shared with me and my colleagues, despite my brief time with them. In my opinion, medicine's goal of providing relief from human suffering is the result of the most benevolent human urge in history.

Unfortunately in this world, troubles are universal and inevitable. Medicine for all its nobility has its own unique set of problems. Not least among them, just the thought of malpractice lawsuits with all of their negative consequences rightfully strikes fear into the hearts of most physicians. As someone who has been on both sides of the table, I've witnessed those fears and faced oncoming legal horrors firsthand. I'll share my story below as an example of the kinds of unexpected things that can go wrong.

The primary purpose of this book is to arm physicians with practical working knowledge. This is accomplished in two steps: 1) by providing straightforward facts and commonsense explanations of legal concepts underlying medical malpractice in everyday terms, and then 2) by combining those clarifications with solid practical advice regarding how best to prevent malpractice allegations, minimize liability, properly and efficiently manage charges of malpractice that are brought, improve testimonial skills, better protect assets, and minimize personal and professional losses. These are all critical informational pieces that are missing from a standard medical education.

It is my hope that this book can serve the greater good by helping others become better, more efficient, and more caring practitioners.

The Rest of the Story

Not long after I graduated from medical school, I became embroiled first-hand in a legal matter involving well-intended but vaguely written and conflicting laws and have suffered the consequences of misguided attempts to enforce them.

I was working part-time at a pain management clinic, while I also practiced law. This experience gave me a unique and painfully intimate understanding of the extent to which things can go wrong. It could have been anyone. Life happens to us all, but this time it was me.

Although I always believed for good and sufficient reasons that I acted in complete conformity with the law, I was unable to protect myself from being ensnared in a maze of regulations applying different standards arising from the same events. My life was changed in unexpected and fundamental ways that were initially devastating.

Like countless other survivors of medical and law school, I had worked long hours, sacrificed much, and was truly passionate about my new profession. In an instant, the future I had envisioned and strived mightily to obtain for myself and my family was gone.

The clinic that employed me was managed by two medical specialists whose patients all had thorough histories in addition to extensive physical examinations with pertinent diagnostic documentation. Every patient underwent regular monitoring and appropriately prescribed treatment from the licensed physicians.

After initially consulting one of the specialists at the medical facility, patients returning for follow-up appointments would often see me. My job was to examine established patients and to dictate the results in a SOAP notes format. My medical assignments were taken seriously and performed cautiously, meticulously, and considerately. I took great satisfaction in this job, which provided daily opportunities to learn and grow and help people.

I was taken completely by surprise when the DEA suddenly swept in one day and closed down the office. The reasons for this unexpected shutdown sounded like a story ripped from the tabloids: The ex-girlfriend of one of the managing physicians had leveled prescription drug abuse allegations against him. Although her charge was later shown to be accurate, her accusation was wholly unrelated to the actual care of patients at the clinic.

Unfortunately, her actions had significant negative ramifications for me. During my short time at the pain clinic (a matter of a few weeks), the physician who had originally hired me was mostly out of the office recovering from a heart attack. This should not have posed a problem, however, because the other medical specialist ran the entire office during that time.

To the casual observer, it probably looked like I was directly caring for patients in the one specialist's absence. For the authorities, that was apparently close enough. Using classic $2 + 2 = 5$ logic, prosecutors somehow charged me, a part-time employee, with running a full-time professional practice without supervision. No one seemed the least bit concerned or interested in how anyone could possibly run a medical practice without possessing any prescription pads.

Like most states, my home state had enacted a law (OAC 4731-23-01 to 04) regarding delegation of medical tasks. That law prohibits the prosecution of any medical assistant who is not licensed as an MD or DO and who is following the medical instructions of a supervising physician in the care of patients. Nonetheless, the proceedings went forward.

My employers could easily have affirmed that I had always been supervised, I had performed only assigned medical tasks, and that I had never run the clinic myself. In fact, they were the only individuals who possessed that specific knowledge and could do so.

In another stroke of misfortune, both my employers were also facing possible charges for their billing practices and personal drug use. This effectively eliminated the only two witnesses who were capable of corroborating my innocence, because those pending charges meant that their attorneys would not allow them to testify in another trial. I was on my own legally, deprived of firsthand accounts that should and would have exonerated me. It was the worst of all possible scenarios.

To my surprise, on the last day of presenting their case, the prosecution called one of the specialists (who had just settled his legal case) to the stand. Indeed, he testified that he had run the entire clinic during the other doctor's convalescence and had supervised everything himself.

For the briefest moment, I felt relief and hope that his admissions were my salvation and the answer to my prayers. By testifying to that one basic yet critical fact, the medical doctor provided the needed "supervision" under the law for my complete legal defense. That should have ended the case and exonerated me.

I believed that justice, fairness, and truth would prevail, and that his testimony would end the apparent insanity of this case. Indeed, the judge could have issued a directed verdict, or at least instructed the jury that if the medical specialist had supervised and directed my medical tasks as he testified, that criminal charges should not have been brought and that I was innocent under the law.

Unfortunately, none of that happened.

The facts that the jury wasn't informed or instructed about the law cited above or the significance of the managing partner's testimony under that law, that the judge didn't bother, and the jury didn't ask, made all the difference in my case. The scales of justice cannot always be evenly weighed, but whether through judicial indifference, or a prosecuting attorney's misjudgment of the law, participants in the process should never be allowed to put their thumbs on those scales.

The reward for my diligent, painstaking efforts, and professional clinical evaluations, along with the honest, reliable performance of assigned medical duties for my employers was prison.

Life isn't always fair. Sometimes the innocent pay or the guilty go free. It takes time to learn that the truth of a matter will not always come to light in a courtroom.

Despite the outcome of the case, I believe that our justice system is still without equal on the planet or in history. It is a prescription for order and social stability, and is indispensable for protecting the public, dispensing justice and mercy to the deserving, community growth, and success. Of course our legal system has its flaws, but I fully embrace it without reservation. I regularly remind others that lawyers often stand between the abuse of governmental power and the individual, and that they also defend the rights of individuals against corporate abuses of power.

This author continues to practice law with a sharp focus on medical malpractice. I believe that the experience of my ordeal has strengthened my faith, persistence, resolve, patience, and dedication to strategic planning, which are not bad attributes to have—Thank God!

Everyone in the medical professions needs the tools in this book to better protect and defend themselves against claims of malpractice to the maximum extent possible. If this book can prevent others from having to learn life lessons in malpractice the hard way, I will have accomplished my goal. I thank you for reading and wish you all the best.

=

Malpractice— Knowledge Is Power

CHAPTER 1

Physicians and the Law
– An Overview –

INTRODUCTION

The average physician sees medicolegal proceedings as a dark and foreboding aspect of practice that would preferably be ignored and forgotten. However, interactions with legal processes are an inescapable part of every physician's professional and personal life and, in fact, many aspects of these medicolegal proceedings are already built into medical practice. Doctors are often called upon to give evidence for workers' compensation cases, personal injury disputes, eligibility for social security benefits, missed time from work, insurance coverage issues, limited work duties, and qualification for automobile, airplane, or trucking licensures via the department of transportation. Medicolegal matters also extend to evidence in criminal actions, child custody cases, domestic disputes, and the military services, as well as medical malpractice lawsuits and conflicts with state boards.

Responsible doctors attempt to educate their patients about their medical condition. This way, medical advice is not generated in a vacuum where it is more likely to be ignored by the patient, to their own detriment. In the same fashion, it is incumbent on doctors to possess more than a distant familiarity with legal concepts. Physicians should strive for a higher level of legal sophistication and take full advantage of the professional and personal benefits therein.

Legal knowledge is power! That knowledge gives medical professionals command and control over aspects of their practice that extend from medicolegal proceedings to tax strategies and to the complexities of obtaining maximum malpractice protection.

OVERVIEW OF AMERICAN LAW

"The life of the law has not been logic; it has been experience."

—Oliver Wendell Holmes

More than two thousand years ago Aristotle observed, "It is more proper that law should govern than any one of the citizens."[1] Today, every modern society has laws that govern and protect its citizens. After all, the only realistic alternative to violence and chaos is some system with rules of order. Such a system is needed to keep the behavior of society's members within reasonable limits. One legal dictionary defines law as "the legislative pronouncement of the rules which should guide one's actions in society." The rules that make up the law are, in fact, legal duties imposed on people requiring them to behave in a certain way. It has been properly observed that the individual can do anything except that which is forbidden by the law. In the real world, the law binds and guides our whole society and to a great extent it defines our everyday lives.

Most of us are well aware of our rich Judeo-Christian heritage in the form of the Ten Commandments. The first five commandments define our proper relationship with and our duties to our creators, God and parents, while the last five describe our obligations and duties to each other.

In a similar fashion, the law first defines our relationships to the higher secular authority of government in all its forms and secondly describes legal relationships between individuals. The law then goes on to detail the obligations in those relationships of each to the other. Selected examples of legal relationships include:

- the United States and a citizen
- a state and a resident
- a city or town and its inhabitants
- the military and armed services members
- the Social Security Administration and a beneficiary
- the IRS and a taxpayer
- a married couple
- corporation and stockholder
- lender and borrower
- employer and employee

---

[1] Aristotle, *Politics: A Treatise on Government* (A&D Publishing, 2009).

- insured and insurer
- doctor and patient
- bailor and bailee
- principal and agent
- parent and child
- master and servant
- guardian and ward
- creditor and debtor
- attorney and client
- seller and purchaser
- landlord and tenant
- shipper and common carrier
- trustee and beneficiary

Ordinary relationships with neighbors, classmates, co-workers, or the general public carry no specific legal duties, obligations, or responsibilities other than avoiding doing harm to others through one's own conduct.

PUBLIC AND PRIVATE LAWS

Another way to look at the law is to divide the legal world into public laws and private laws.

Public Laws

Public laws are aimed at protecting society at large and encompass:

- constitutional law, which involves the legal interpretation of state and federal constitutions
- administrative law where legal principles are applied to government agencies, e.g., state boards
- criminal law that deals with all aspects of crimes ranging from the trivial to the most serious, e.g., from littering to torture and murder

Private Laws

Private laws allow a party to recover money damages from a wrongdoer and include:

- tort law that allows an injured individual to recover damages for negligence

- property law which deals with land (mortgages and leases), goods, copyrights, trademarks, and patents
- contract law which addresses agreements that can be enforced by courts, i.e., the doctor-patient contract

MEDICINE IN THE EYES OF THE LAW

Medicine falls under the general legal heading of business law. Business law is not a separate branch of the law; rather it is the part of the legal system that deals with business activities through public and private laws. It comprises the laws that deal with business and commercial transactions, business organizations, administrative agencies, negligence, and contracts. Medicine requires a special and unique blending of both public and private laws to properly function.

The Business of Medicine

The medical industry broadly comprises medical and surgical equipment, as well as drug development, approvals, safety, and manufacturing. These issues are of vital public importance, hence it is no surprise that they are regulated and controlled by public laws through administrative agencies like the federal Food and Drug Administration. These agencies, often referred to as the fourth branch of government, oversee complex matters of governmental concern and public interest that are beyond the expertise of legislators.

The business of medicine also embodies physician qualifications, licensure, discipline, continuing education, scope of practice, and interactions with the general public.

Medical boards are the state administrative agencies that formulate applicable licensing and professional standards through rules and regulations. These directives governing medical business operations have three broad purposes:

1. to protect the public against unqualified practitioners and unsafe practices
2. to ensure that businesses compete fairly with each other
3. to make sure practitioners and businesses don't take advantage of consumers

Society as a whole does not want health care providers to confuse, mislead, or misdirect the public.

State boards also investigate and adjudicate rule violations. Do not underestimate an agency's formidability, since its rules and regulations have the full force and effect of law, giving them far-reaching power. Anyone who has crossed swords with a state medical board has learned this lesson in a way that will not fade or dim with time.

The Practice of Medicine

The law does not see the practice of medicine as a healing art. Legally, the practice of medicine is a **service commodity**. Unlike commodities such as a car, a can of peaches, or box of detergent, doctors do not generally deal in tangible goods where the right of ownership transfers with the purchase. Instead, doctors deal in commodities comprising **intangible services**. Intangible in this context means that the characteristic of the service is one the individual cannot touch, see, or otherwise sample prior to obtaining that service.

There is no transfer of ownership rights for the medical services performed. For example, no patient owns their history or examination results, tests, or other health care services, including x-rays. That information belongs to the patient, whereas the record of it, e.g., test results, x-rays, and the patient's file, belongs to the record's creator who is legally bound to keep and store these records for a period of years.

The practice of medicine in restoring and preserving health within the doctor-patient relationship is controlled by the private laws of negligence and contracts.

THE COURT SYSTEM

The court system is how courts have the authority to resolve disputes between parties. State constitutions provide the general framework, legislation through laws adds to that framework, and the courts establish rules that are the finish work to the system. The end result of this process provides the guidance and authority by which courts can hear and resolve disputes between parties.

There are state courts and federal courts to hear disputes, depending on the circumstances. A federal court presides over state civil law controversies when the legal dispute presents a federal question or is between citizens of different states and is for an amount more than $75,000.00. State courts can adjudicate some federal claims, but most often hear state law issues.

Filing a Complaint

For any lawsuit to be initiated, a complaint must first be filed in the proper court and that court at plaintiff's request will then issue a summons for the person to appear. The complaint and summons from the court must be delivered to the defendant so that person can read and be aware of the lawsuit—this is called service, or service of process. Once the defendant is served, the suit can move forward under the court's direction.

After service is obtained, usually by mail or personal service, the court requires the defendant to file an answer or plea to the charges, after which the case can then proceed further through motions, discovery (depositions, written interrogatories, requests for production of documents, requests for admissions), and eventually mediation, arbitration, or a trial with the court making its final decision based on the evidence.

Demonstrating Standing to Sue

The one bringing a civil lawsuit under private law is called the plaintiff. That person must demonstrate that he or she has standing to sue. Standing is a legal term that has three requirements:

1. The underlying issue must involve an actual legal case or controversy, since courts are prohibited from issuing advisory opinions based on hypothetical situations.

2. The individual must have a personal stake in resolving the matter. This means that the controversy or dispute has touched upon the legal relationship between the parties and damaged the party filing the suit.

3. The court must have the power and authority to hear the case. The power to hear a case is called "subject matter jurisdiction." Some courts have limited subject matter jurisdiction such as a family court, probate court, or the court of claims that hears private claims against the state. Courts must also have authority over the parties in the case, which is known as "personal jurisdiction." Personal jurisdiction is usually obtained through a summons or notice to appear in court.

Settlement

This section, no doubt, looks misplaced. Why is settlement listed here? It is to remind the reader that malpractice cases can and do settle at every stage of the litigation process[2] and the vast majority will settle prior to trial.

---

[2] Margaret Dean, BSN, JD, *The Jurisprudent Physician* (Phoenix, AZ: Legis Press, 1999), 283.

Discovery

In this stage of the process, both sides discover what they can about their opponent's case.[3] There will likely be interrogatories, or questions, for the defendant doctor to answer under oath. Requests for production of documents will ask for relevant materials like the case records, the doctor's CV, etc. There may also be requests for admissions where the doctor will admit or deny the truth of certain statements. Finally, the most damaging weapon in the plaintiff attorney's arsenal is the deposition.

Motions

"The parties often file written motions when they want the judge to take certain actions with respect to the case. For instance, if the defendant doctor's attorney believes that all, or part, of the lawsuit file…is without merit, he may file a motion asking the judge to dismiss those claims."[4]

Settlement Conference

Many jurisdictions require the "litigants in all types of civil claims to participate in a formal settlement conference before proceeding to trial."[5]

Trial

The trial is the pinnacle of the legal process, but not necessarily the end of the case.

At trial, the first order of business is selecting the jurors. Next, opening statements are made and then witnesses are presented. Finally, there are closing arguments before the case goes to the jury for their verdict.

Appeals

After a trial, it is possible to have that court's decision be reviewed by an appeals court and thereafter by either a state supreme court or a federal court of appeals and even, in a tiny fraction of cases, by the United States Supreme Court. Opinions issued by the United States Supreme Court are said to represent the "law of the land" because that court is the highest authority and has the final word on the meaning and application of federal law. Supreme Court opinions may have far-reaching implications and, therefore, often receive national attention.

---

[3] Ibid., 287.
[4] Ibid., 292.
[5] Ibid., 293.

CONCLUSION

From medical records to malpractice suits, the law has a bearing on all aspects of professional health care, including reinforcing the ethical principles at the core of the doctor-patient relationship. Laws emphasize the importance of maintaining professional competence, good practice management, and patient autonomy by guiding professional conduct. This includes but is not limited to licensure, obtaining consent to diagnostic and treatment procedures, continuing medical education, confidentiality, peer review, limits on professional negligence, expert witness testimony, as well as other health-related issues.

COMMENT

Physicians' views of attorneys tend to be shaped by their fears of medical malpractice litigation. Physicians tend to dislike trial attorneys and are often none too happy with attorneys in general. The result of this uneasy relationship is that physicians do not make effective use of legal services and may take unnecessary legal risks. This is unfortunate. The law exists for everyone's benefit. Why not let the law assist and help protect physicians in their medical practices and personal lives?

Consider the following quote from Stephen King regarding the consolation of having your own attorney.

> "There's something oddly comforting about talking to a legal guy once the billable-hours clock has started running; you have passed the magical point at which a lawyer becomes your lawyer. Your lawyer is warm, your lawyer is sympathetic, your lawyer makes notes on a yellow pad and nods in all the right places. Most of the questions your lawyer asks are questions you can answer. And if you can't, your lawyer will help you find a way to do so. Your lawyer is always on your side. Your enemies are his enemies."
>
> —*Bag of Bones* (1998), pp. 167–168

Prudence in life, as well as in general or specialized practice, requires that doctors, like all professionals, be proactive, not reactive, in avoiding and preventing repeated mistakes. As stated by John Foster Dulles, "The measure of success is not whether you have a tough problem to deal with, but whether it is the same problem you had last year." The goal of this work is to give doctors all the tools they need to achieve that success with respect to malpractice.

BIBLIOGRAPHY

Aristotle. *Politics: A Treatise on Government.* A&D Publishing, 2009.

Beatty, J.F. *Business Law and the Legal Environment: Standard Edition 6.* Cengage Learning, 2013.

Cheeseman, Henry R. *Business Law.* 7th ed. Prentice Hall, 2009.

Dean, Margaret. *The Jurisprudent Physician.* Phoenix, AZ: Legis Press, 1999.

Gifis, Steven H. *Law Dictionary.* 4th ed. Barron's Legal Guides, 1996.

Goldman, A.J., and W.D. Sigismond. *Business Law Principles and Practices.* 9th ed. NY: Houghton Mifflin Co., Cengage Learning, 2014.

Locke, John (1632–1704). *The Second Treatise of Government.* Edited by C.B. Macpherson. Indianapolis, IN: Hackett Publishing Co., 1980.

Mann, R.A., and B.S. Roberts. *Smith and Robertson's Business Law.* 16th ed. Cengage Learning, 2015.

CHAPTER 2

The Doctor-Patient Contract
– It's Legally Valid and Binding –

INTRODUCTION

Contract law lies at the heart of our legal system and serves as a foundation for the rules of society. In that same vein, the doctor-patient contract serves to establish the rules of conduct for both the physician and the patient. It is the legal essence of the doctor-patient relationship. The contract involves every patient that a doctor treats and is a valid, legal, binding agreement in all fifty states. It is also a core issue in many malpractice lawsuits. Contracts are serious legal matters. Because there is little formality to the doctor-patient contract, its importance is too often underestimated.

In a malpractice claim, lawyers typically try to show that the doctor failed to meet the professional and ethical duties required by that contract. That is why a deeper understanding of the concepts and obligations that make up the fundamentals of this special contract is essential to help win malpractice suits.

THE INS AND OUTS OF CONTRACT LAW

Contracts are an integral part of everyday life and are entered into whenever an individual:
- writes a check
- purchases satellite or cable TV services
- subscribes to a magazine
- insures a car or home
- borrows money
- acquires concert or sporting event tickets
- secures electrical or natural gas service
- owns a cell phone
- procures any item with a warranty
- buys or leases equipment
- purchases property or rents
- sells or obtains services, including those of a physician

Contract law is the framework in which many personal and all commercial transactions take place. Most simply, contract law is about agreements, whether written, spoken, or implied. In each of the preceding examples there is an agreement and promises are exchanged. When agreements and promises are enforceable in a court of law, they are considered to be contracts. Each person or "party" to the contract obtains certain rights and assumes certain binding obligations or duties in the contract.

The Inner Workings of Contracts

Doctors routinely enter into commercial contracts for the purchase of goods or services, including employment services, on a regular basis. In clinical practice, doctors with increasing frequency are entering into so-called contracts with patients. These include opioid contracts, suicide prevention contracts, addiction treatment contracts, healthy living contracts, transplant substance abuse contracts, and safe treatment contracts.[1] Medical releases, informed consents, HIPAA notices, etc., help round out the medical contract landscape. For these reasons, contracts are playing an ever more important role in medicine.

If goods or services are not delivered or maintained, or agreements are not complied with as promised, some doctors may assume that no further obligation on their part is owed because the other side has failed to keep their promises. Unfortunately, the law of contracts does not always work that way. Doctors must understand when a representation or commitment to do something is: (a) a mere promise, (b) a counteroffer or negotiation, or (c) part of a proper legal contract with rights and binding obligations.

Forming a Contract: The Big Picture

It's been said that "contract law is firmly built on the triad of offer, acceptance, and consideration."[2] In addition, two other elements are in play and are ultimately required for a contract to be legal and enforceable in a court of law. The legal components comprising a valid contract are:

- offer
- acceptance
- consideration
- capacity
- legal purpose

---

[1] Sarah R. Lieber, Scotty Y. Kim, and Michael L. Volk, "Power and Control: Contracts and the Patient-Physician Relationship," *Int J Clin Pract* 65, no. 12 (Dec. 2011): 1214–1217.
[2] Scott Turow, *One L* (G.P. Putnam's Sons, 1977).

1. An **offer** is simply a promise by one person to do or not to do something. The offer typically contains a specific promise and a specific demand. For instance, I promise to examine patients for the ABC Clinic if they will pay ninety ($90.00) dollars per hour and will also provide health care benefits.

2. **Acceptance** of the offer indicates a willingness to be bound by the terms of the offer. An acceptance can be made in one of two ways: 1) by a return promise to perform an act or service or 2) by performing the act or service described in the offer, such as paying the agreed upon price for medical equipment or examining patients at ABC Clinic.

    Regarding the offer to ABC Clinic appearing above, assume that ABC Clinic responds by saying, "We accept. You will start at eighty ($80.00) dollars per hour." Since the acceptance does not mirror the original offer requesting $90.00 per hour and providing health insurance, ABC's reply is considered to be a rejection of the original offer with a counter proposal that the doctor can freely accept or reject in return.

3. **Consideration** is the glue that seals an offer and acceptance into a legally binding contract. The principle behind consideration is that one party to an agreement should not be bound by it if the other party is not also bound. Each party must promise to do something of value for the other. A mere promise to make a gift does not obligate the person receiving the gift to do anything of value. Therefore, it is not a contract and cannot be enforced by a court.

    To illustrate, assume that Dr. Wilson tells Ms. Davis, the office nurse, that if he wins the lottery he'll share his winnings with her. He makes this statement in front of several witnesses. That week Dr. Wilson hits the winning numbers, but instead of giving a share of the winnings to Ms. Davis, he pays off all his student loans and his practice start-up debts, then he goes house shopping with his wife.

    Ms. Davis sues to recover her promised share of the winnings. However, the question becomes, what did Ms. Davis do or give up of value in order to bargain or negotiate for a share of those winnings? Answer: nothing. Since Ms. Davis was never obligated to do anything of value or perform additional duties to obtain a share of the winnings, this is a mere promise by her employer and not a valid contract. Dr. Wilson cannot be legally forced to give any of his winnings to Ms. Davis. Case dismissed!

> **NOTE:** The consideration must induce both parties to act. It demonstrates that the deal or transaction is a positive exchange, i.e., a bargained-for agreement and not a gift. Perhaps that is why consideration has also been described as "the price of the promise."

Example #1. Mr. Thompson says, "Doctor, I'll pay you one thousand dollars because you saved my nephew's life." Legally, the doctor cannot enforce collection. The offer to pay one thousand dollars did not induce the doctor to save Mr. Thompson's nephew, so there is no consideration. The thousand dollars was never bargained for.

Example #2. The Mayo Clinic offers to hire the doctor for one year at a competitive salary. The doctor is eager and accepts. However, the final paragraph of the contract states, "The Clinic reserves the right to cancel this contract at any time." The contract is not binding on the hospital since the Clinic is not bound to hire the doctor for a full year, so there is no consideration. Neither party is restricted from terminating the contract, so the doctor can leave or quit at any time without legal liability.

Example #3. Your office receives a check for four hundred dollars on an account with a balance of over nine hundred dollars, but the words "Paid in Full" appear on the check. There is concern that if the office cashes the check the account will be settled for a fraction of its worth. If the amount owed by the patient is not in dispute, the office can cash the check and still pursue collection on the remaining balance. Why? Because the patient gave no additional consideration to accept less than the full amount owed. However, if any part of the debt were in dispute, then the account would be completely settled by accepting the amount offered as payment in full.

4. **Capacity** is the legal term for possessing adequate mental competence to engage in a contract. With a noble eye toward protecting the public's welfare and maintaining social stability, courts will *not* enforce otherwise valid contracts if **one party is a minor, mentally incompetent, or temporarily impaired** from being under the influence of drugs or excessive alcohol, thus limiting their full understanding of the agreement's responsibilities and obligations.

Legally speaking, such a person cannot develop the intent to enter into a binding contract, let alone comprehend the duties to which they are agreeing.

5. **Legality:** Courts also will not compel one party to comply if the contract's purpose is not a legal one. This includes contracts that:

- Charge excessive interest.
- Are against public policy, e.g., that injure others financially, physically, or psychologically, or that damage the government, or violate the law.
- Are harmful to marriage or family relationships. Example: a doctor offers his or her spouse $50,000 and a new car for a divorce. The divorce is now final and the ex-spouse insists on the agreed payment. A contract or agreement to harm a marriage is illegal and will not be enforced by a court of law. Therefore, the spouse cannot legally collect the promised payment.
- Interfere with the administration of justice. Example: paying a witness to give false testimony or to conceal evidence.
- Have non-compete clauses that unreasonably restrain or limit competition and trade, e.g., restrict a current employee from being employed in the same line of work within a relatively large geographic area and for more than a six to twelve-month period of time.
- Are unconscionable, i.e., grossly unfair or too harsh.
- Shift liability through exculpatory clauses attempting to avoid or limit liability for negligence. This is done by excusing a party in advance for injuries or damages caused by their acts.

Example of an illegal exculpatory clause:

I understand that Dr. A. Schweitzer does not carry malpractice insurance and, therefore, I agree to hold the doctor harmless in the event of a medical mistake or error in judgment resulting in injuries or damages to myself or a family member.

_____   _____
Patient Signature   Date

Thus, a contract is not a contract if its purpose is not legitimate.

A Contract Needs a Signature, Right?

Engaging in a contract may not be as formal or complex as one might think. Placing a signature on a piece of paper is no longer necessary to enter into a binding contract. There are many different means to enter into a contract electronically to buy services and goods, take out a lease, obtain a loan, or enter into a doctor patient-relationship. Pressing "1" on a phone, entering a pin number, clicking a box on a web page such as "Yes" or "Agree to Terms," or the last 4 digits of your social security number are all ways to form binding contracts. In fact, typing in your name as an electronic or digital signature (e-signature) is considered acceptable and legally binding under the Electronic Signature in Global and International Commerce (E-SIGN) Act of 2000. This Act applies and is valid in all commercial contractual transactions in the United States.

It is important to realize that for all these reasons a physician's website can be an unintended source for establishing unwanted yet legally binding doctor-patient contracts.

Is the Contract Unilateral or Bilateral?

By and large, the business community is dominated by bilateral contracts. In a bilateral contract, both persons or parties exchange promises, one in the offer and the other in the acceptance. This is the most common type of contract and is legally binding on both parties when adequate consideration is present. Each person or party has made promises with duties and obligations to the other.

Another type of contract is created when an offer is made for a completed act or undertaking. The acceptance happens when a person seeking to collect on the offer performs the required assignment. This is a unilateral contract. A unilateral offer is often made to the public at large, such as offering a reward for the return of a lost item or pet.

A prime example of a unilateral contract in the medical field is the malpractice insurance policy. The insurance company offers to pay legal fees and a judgment up to the policy limits if the doctor is sued. The doctor makes no promises, but must first perform the act of paying a premium, and that payment must be paid in full (which then counts as acceptance of the offer) before the insurance company is obligated to perform its duties.

In another example, let's assume that Dr. Drew offered a patient $1,000 if he refrained from drinking for the next six months. If the patient performed the requested act of abstinence, then Dr. Drew owes him $1,000.

Is It an Express or Implied Contract?

Most of us think of contracts as being formed in writing and signed by both parties. It is well understood that in some contracts the terms can be set out and agreed upon through spoken words instead. Both of these types are express contracts.

In other cases, a contract is formed by the actions of the parties. Under these circumstances, the terms are not written down or spoken but are implied from the circumstances. For instance, when someone empties their shopping cart at the checkout of the grocery store, they imply their willingness and ability to pay for those items selected. When a customer is in a barbershop or a nail salon, it is implied that they want the service and are willing to pay for it. The same is true for a patient who keeps an appointment by arriving in the doctor's reception room. His actions indicate that he seeks professional help for the treatment of a complaint and will pay the doctor's fee. Implied contracts, like the doctor-patient contract, bring order and clarity to business transactions that may otherwise seem ill-defined and chaotic.

THE NUTS AND BOLTS OF THE UNWRITTEN PHYSICIAN-PATIENT CONTRACT

The doctor-patient relationship has a unique role in the context of the history of medicine because it goes back to the time of Hippocrates. That relationship is governed commercially by state medical boards and in direct medical practice by the courts under state negligence law and the physician-patient contract. The physician-patient contract was not created by doctors or patients, but is required by the law as a matter of reason and justice.

The doctor-patient contract is also not a bargained for agreement, but rather it is an unspoken business agreement that involves the exchange of services, money, and obligations. Perhaps most important, it is one of the cornerstones of good medical care.

Once the doctor consents to enter into this relationship by advising or treating the patient, the physician-patient contract is formed. The contract represents a consensual agreement that creates a relationship where both parties agree and are willing to enter into it, similar to two people who consent to abide by a marital contract.

What Type of Contract Is It?

The doctor-patient relationship is an **implied bilateral contract** for the purchase of intangible clinical services. (See also "The Practice of Medicine," p. 7.)

What Is the Offer and Acceptance?

A person offers to become a patient by making an appointment or otherwise seeking the doctor's professional services and advice.

A physician, as a rule of thumb, has the right to accept or reject any individual as a patient. If he chooses to reject a patient, he must do so prior to or after the first appointment, or at the conclusion of the physician's evaluation process.

Once care or treatment has begun, the doctor has fully accepted that person as a patient. As such, a bona fide physician-patient relationship and a doctor-patient contract clearly and unarguably exist at that time.

Likewise, the patient confirms acceptance of the contract by complying with the treatment recommendations on the basis of a genuine informed consent and understanding of the recommended treatment involved.

What Is the Consideration?

The inconvenience and risks undertaken by the patient in both seeking and undergoing treatment and paying the fee, as well as the time and professional efforts expended by the doctor in evaluating the patient, comprise adequate consideration from both parties to seal the contract.

What Duties and Obligations Exist?

Like all implied contracts, the doctor-patient relationship includes promises and obligations by the parties that have not been specifically set out, written, or talked about, but that nevertheless exist. In other words, there is no express agreement, yet the binding legal effect is no different from having a notarized signed written contract with the patient.

PHYSICIAN DUTIES

Every physician owes a duty of care to their patients. In the traditional patient-physician relationship, the central principle of that duty is that the patient's interests come first. The rationale is as follows:

By entering this relationship, the patient has displayed the utmost in trust and confidence in the physician by putting their body, their well-being, and potentially their life in the doctor's hands. Therefore, the physician, in fairness, must reciprocate by not doing anything to take advantage of his trusting patient. That means putting the patient's best interests and welfare above the physician's self-interests and obligations to other groups.

In the legal world, prioritizing and placing the patient's interests first is known as a fiduciary relationship. The essence of such a relationship is that the professional knows more than the person who seeks his help. Therefore, the physician is under a positive duty to disclose all relevant facts, i.e., to obtain informed consent before rendering care. It further requires physicians to take care to avoid conflicts of interest and to advocate for their patient's welfare as part of good faith and fair dealing.[3]

The doctor, as a condition of his or her employment, is also under a legal duty to utilize ordinary diligence and reasonable skill and judgment in detecting, diagnosing, and managing the patient's problem.

The physician-patient contract further demands that physicians agree to give timely attention to their patients' needs and exercise due care and caution in avoiding undue risks and dangers. As such, physicians have an obligation to stay current in medical knowledge and to keep informed of the latest patient care protocols and medical advances.

Doctors also accept the responsibility to provide continued treatment or care to the patient as long as necessary, promise not to abandon the patient, and acknowledge a duty to promote patient understanding. Advancing patient understanding entails sharing material medical information and obtaining consent, as well as giving proper instructions for further care to the patient or others who may be responsible for administering or overseeing that care.

Finally, the trusted physician pledges to keep the patient's medical condition and information in the strictest confidence. (See Table 2.2, p. 21.)

PATIENT DUTIES

The patient agrees to give an honest and accurate medical history, consents to physical or other examination procedures, makes himself available for treatment or management by keeping scheduled appointments, and otherwise complies with the physician's instructions and recommendations to the best of his ability. Patients also consent to pay the doctor's reasonable fee for the services provided. The patient may accept or refuse any recommended medical treatment or procedure for any reason.

---

[3] AMA Code of Ethics Opinion 10.015, Dec. 2001.
    See also the AMA's Council on Ethical and Judicial Affairs Opinion 8.03.

ADDITIONAL DUTIES

All contracts, including physician-patient contracts, include the implied obligations of good faith and fair dealing in its performance from both parties to each other. "Good faith" basically means being faithful to the purpose and terms of the contract. "Fair dealing" means that neither the doctor nor the patient will break their word or use underhanded means to avoid their obligations or to deny what the other party obviously understood.

TABLE 2.2: DOCTORS' OBLIGATIONS IN THE PHYSICIAN-PATIENT CONTRACT

Doctors' Duties to Their Patients

1. Put the patient's interests first and avoid conflicts of interest.[4]
2. Inform the patient of the nature, purpose, and material risks/dangers, etc., in a recommended, but complicated, procedure or treatment. Also, disclose any interests the physician may have that might cause the patient to reconsider that procedure.
3. Obtain the patient's consent prior to rendering care and ensure that the patient is competent to invoke their absolute right to accept or refuse that medical care.
4. Render competent/reasonable medical care using the application of ordinary skills, knowledge, and judgment. Employ accepted methods while using due care and caution to avoid unreasonable risks and dangers.
5. Give timely attention to the patient's medical needs.[5]
6. Provide continuing care as long as necessary.[6]
7. Keep current on recent medical developments and knowledge.
8. Promote patient education and understanding.
9. Give proper general and follow-up care instructions.
10. Advocate for the patient's welfare.[7]
11. Keep patient information private and confidential.[8]
12. Give advance notice of an impending end to the doctor-patient relationship and give reasonable assistance to the patient so he or she has sufficient opportunity to secure alternative arrangements for care.[9]

---

[4] AMA Code of Ethics 10.015, adopted June 2001.
[5] AMA Code of Ethics 10.01(3), *JAMA* 262 (1990): 3/33; updated 1993.
[6] AMA Code of Ethics 10.01(5), *JAMA* 3/33; updated 1993.
[7] AMA Code of Ethics 10.015, adopted June 2001.
[8] AMA Code of Ethics 10.01(4), *JAMA* 262 (1990): 3/33; updated 1993.
[9] AMA Code of Ethics 8.115 (June 1996).

At all times, ethics, communication skills, honorable motives, sincere efforts, and principled conduct must underlie the terms of the doctor-patient contract.

How Can the Contract Be Ended?

The patient is free at any time to terminate the contract. The doctor is also free to terminate the relationship. However, the physician must advise an existing patient ahead of time of an approaching end to the relationship. This allows a practical amount of time for the patient to engage another physician's services in the interim.

Notice to the patient typically includes an understanding via a written notice that, except for emergencies in the interim, the termination of the relationship will be effective 30 days from the date of the notice. The notice should specify whether the patient's medical condition requires continued physician supervision and, if so, should instruct the patient to select another physician as soon as possible. The notice should be printed on the doctor's or facility's letterhead and sent via certified mail with return receipt requested.

The physician must also help support the transition, which may include providing records or having a discussion with the new doctor. Otherwise, the doctor, as a practical matter, may have wrongly abandoned the patient and can be sued for that action.

It is usually more difficult for physicians with a managed care contract to terminate a patient enrolled in the program. In this case, doctors should review their HMO/MCO contract before giving notice of ending the relationship and should always seek legal advice as to the proper form and specifics needed to give the required form of notice.

THE INSIDE SCOOP ON THE MODERN PHYSICIAN-PATIENT RELATIONSHIP

Recent years have seen a decline in perceived physician credibility and patient trust. In large part this can be attributable to insurance cost-containment strategies that have eroded and conflicted with the doctor-patient relationship. In some managed care settings, the clinical encounter is deliberately managed so that it puts the physician's interests at odds with the patient's interests. The expectation is nevertheless that the physician will continue to put the needs of the patient first over the interests of a third party (e.g., an insurance company, HMO, PPO, etc.). Certainly, the relationship between physicians and patients must be held to a higher standard of loyalty, good faith, and trust than that of an ordinary business partnership.

Conclusion

The doctor-patient contract is legally binding everywhere in the United States and applies to each and every patient who is receiving care or advice and to each licensed doctor giving that care or advice.

Checklist

✓ Malpractice grows out of a violation or breach of the physician-patient contract. It is crucial to review Table 2.2 because these duties are vital to the safety and well-being of both the patient and the doctor. This core concept must be fully understood and embraced by the medical provider.

✓ The patient's adherence to or non-compliance with their portion of the contract, e.g., keeping appointments, taking medications, and following recommendations, should be accurately and objectively reflected in the medical record. Evidence of the patient's non-compliance can usually be presented even in the absence of a contributory negligence or comparative fault defense.[10]

✓ If objective evidence of non-compliance can be presented without the appearance of resentment, ill-will, animosity, or in an attempt to blame the patient, then it should be done.[11] Under such circumstances, the jury cannot help but compare and contrast the doctor's clinical caution, attempts at patient education, and attention to detail with the patient's apparent indifference and inaction. "Proof of patient non-compliance may well result in a defense verdict."[12]

---

[10] "Prove Patient's Non-Compliance: A Defense Verdict Might Result," *Physician Risk Management* (Nov. 2012), AHC Media.

[11] Ibid.

[12] Ibid.

BIBLIOGRAPHY

ACP Ethics Manual. 6th ed.

AMA Code of Medical Ethics. 2014.

Emanual Law Outlines: Contracts. 10th ed. 2012.

Li, James T.C., MD, PhD. "The Patient-Physician Relationship—Covenant or Contract?".

Mayo Clinic Proceedings 71, no. 9. (Sept. 1996).

Murphy, Edward J., and Richard E. Speidel. *Studies in Contract Law: University Casebook Series.* Mineola, NY: The Foundation Press, Inc., 1977.

Woodside, Frank C., Nancy A. Lawson, and Deborah R. Lydon. *The Law of Medical Practice in Ohio.* Rochester, NY: The Lawyers Cooperative Publishing Company.

CHAPTER 3

Negligence Principles
– The Underpinnings of Malpractice –

INTRODUCTION

"Negligence, including medical negligence, is the failure to use reasonable care to avoid harming others and is part of tort law. The term 'tort' is derived from the Latin verb 'tortere' = to hurt."[1] A tort causes one to unfairly suffer injury or harm. Tort law evolved into our current civil laws and determines which hurts, wrongs, or injuries to people and their property should be compensated. Torts first emerged as an important branch of law in the late nineteenth century as a type of compensation system, so to speak, in response to the epidemic of injuries that resulted from unsafe upstart factories during the industrial revolution.

The general purpose of tort law is to secure compensation and to protect people against certain forms of loss or harm to their person, reputation, property, business, or social relationships, not because the losses are morally wrong, but because they cause unreasonable harm.[2]

There are six areas of tort law, but it is unnecessary to explore them all in detail here. In order to analyze and understand malpractice effectively, however, it is essential to have a basic working legal knowledge of negligence concepts.

TORT LAW AND NEGLIGENCE ARE FOR PRIVATE WRONGS

"Mistakes take place, things go wrong, and accidents happen; that's the nature of life. Sound policy in the law typically allows such losses to lie where they fall, except where a person or party is clearly to blame. Negligence law does not seek to compensate a person for all harms but applies only to those harms that are carelessly committed and where the risk of an injury or a loss was plainly foreseeable."[3]

---

[1] http://ceaccp.oxfordjournals.org/content/11/4/124.full.
[2] Oliver Wendell Holmes, *The Common Law* (Little, Brown, and Company, 1881).
[3] Ibid.

For example, if the wind causes the neighbor's healthy oak tree to fall and it lands on your car, you must bear the loss since your neighbor did nothing wrong and those types of things naturally happen. This is generally referred to as an "act of God." There is no liability.

However, if the neighbor botches the job of cutting down that tree and it falls on your vehicle, then the neighbor is clearly at fault for this mishap and, therefore, is the person legally liable to pay for those damages.

The guiding principle behind negligence law is that all of us have a right to go about our daily activities and routines without being thoughtlessly injured by others. The law presumes and requires that persons possess an ordinary capacity to avoid harming those around them. When a person should reasonably be expected to know that an act is likely to harm another or their property, he or she is legally accountable for the resulting harm. Why?—Because he or she nevertheless carried on and performed the careless act despite this knowledge.

The term "negligence" is derived from the Latin "to neglect." It means a neglect to take care to avoid foreseeable harm. Generally, negligence is harm accidentally caused to another from either:

a) **the failure to perceive a risk** to others through one's own conduct

b) **the failure to avoid** foreseeable injury to others

Whether one didn't see the harm coming but should have, or didn't do anything about the potential damage they did see coming, it's all negligence. (See examples below.)

Example of Failing to Perceive a Risk

Assume that an avid golfer is chipping some balls near a neighbor's home but toward an open field to the side of that home. Human nature allows us to tell ourselves that we're not chipping directly at the neighbor's house, that we're experienced and somewhat skilled as a golfer. Besides, there's no wind and the open field is large, which leaves plenty of room for error on our part. There's no real problem. However, as certain as Phil Mickelson golfs left-handed, a ball will eventually slice sharply toward the house with seemingly laser-guided accuracy, shattering the neighbor's new custom-made extra-large triple-pane picture window.

Like most of us, the golfer in our scenario likely never seriously considered the amorphous possibility, or risk, of a shattered window actually materializing, even though he or she should have. Nevertheless, if an individual of ordinary intelligence should perceive a danger or risk, then that individual is blameworthy if he or she continues to pursue that risk-laden course of action and it results in harm. Because the golf fan acted without taking care to avoid that harm, he or she must surely pay to replace the damaged window.

Despite the obviousness historically of an abundance of repeated personal mistakes, miscues, blunders, and accidents, people never seem to anticipate a negative outcome to any activity in which they are engaged. Perhaps this is one reason why emergency rooms and court dockets are always so crowded.

Example of Failing to Take Care to Avoid Injury to Others

In the previous example, a man decided to cut down a tree. The tree clearly leaned toward the neighbor's driveway and the neighbor's car was also parked in that driveway within reach of the tree's span. The man could have hired a professional or used a wedge or ropes to alter the direction of the tree's fall, or waited until the parked car was no longer under the tree. Unfortunately, he did none of those things.

It is undeniable that this individual either failed to perceive a risk or failed to prevent or stop harm from happening due to that risk. He must, therefore, be held legally responsible for the ensuing damages he should have known were likely to result.

The wisdom and time-honored concepts of negligence and liability are woven deeply into the fabric of our history, legal system, and society. The bottom line is that the law intends to impose liability when it is fair, just, and reasonable to do so. In this way, negligence and fault are the cornerstones of tort law.

PROVING NEGLIGENCE

In the legal arena, the following four separate elements are needed to prove negligence.

Duty

Under the law, each person owes a duty to other people and their property to refrain from injuring them. It is a bedrock social obligation for adults to act responsibly and with care.

Duty is judged by the "reasonable person" standard. That is, a reasonable person has a duty to follow rules of caution when interacting with others, the same way the safety rules of the road must be followed on our highways and streets. Individuals are expected not to drive their vehicle on the wrong side of the road, into another vehicle, through a stop light, or drive the wrong way down a one-way street, etc.

Likewise, a reasonable property owner should not allow their stairs and porch to rot or crumble or a railing to fall into disrepair; no one should leave live electrical wires exposed at a work site or in a public building; and front sidewalks should not be dug up because this would create a hazard for pedestrians and bicycle riders. In all of the examples above, it is obvious that the risk of harm to others is greatly increased. As such, the owner has a duty to refrain from causing harm through such carelessness, or at the very least to give warning of the danger.

On the other hand, individuals have no legal duty to the general public, neighbors, or even close relatives to warn them about or prevent harm from any danger that they did not cause. For example, one has no legal duty to warn the public of hazardous road conditions such as a washed-out bridge ahead. There is no duty to warn a non-patient that they have cyanosis, pallor, or jaundice or that they should seek care; nor is there any legal duty to warn a neighbor that you saw a large snake or an alligator on their property. Likewise, a person has no duty to avoid injuring others through non-conduct or by standing idle. In the previous examples, we are guided by moral and ethical imperatives, not the law.

Breach of Duty

The failure to act responsibly is a breach of one's duty not to injure another or their property. This applies to every adult. Jurors apply the "reasonable person standard" to judge whether the accused failed to live up to that standard. The standard is defined as conduct below the level required for the protection of others against unreasonable harm. In other words, someone is legitimately at fault.

For example, "Clueless Joe" is driving well over the speed limit and is texting at the same time. Because of his recklessness and inattention, he careens over the curb and onto the sidewalk and clips a food cart, injuring its owner and a customer. Joe has breached his duty to society by not acting responsibly and failing to use care in avoiding injury to others, even though it would have been easy for him to do so. Hence, Joe is blameworthy and will be liable for any harms his carelessness caused to the owner, customer, and hot dog stand.

Proximate Cause

"Proximate cause" is a confusing term that needs clarification because proximate cause has little to do with proximity of either time or distance.

Proximate cause is better understood as a foreseeable harm. When the type of harm is the kind that would normally be anticipated from the carelessness or mistakes made, it is termed foreseeable harm. In a negligence case, the law will not compensate every possible outcome, but only those outcomes with a sound cause and effect that relate directly to the carelessness and the resulting type of damage.

The legal rationale for proximate cause is straightforward. The law imparts a legal duty to only prevent *foreseeable harm* to others. Therefore, those engaged in a harmful activity are legally liable only for harms that are reasonably anticipated from that activity. This is why proximate cause in the form of a foreseeable harm is the third essential element of proving negligence.

Both proximate cause and foreseeable harm as defined under the law have much to do with fairness and justice because, at some point, it becomes unfair to hold a defendant responsible for all the possible results of his or her negligence.

Example 1: A husband and wife in a Chevy Cruze are accidentally struck in a highway accident. Two days after the accident, while taking their car for a repair estimate, they are struck again by a hit-and-run driver. It seems unfair to hold the first driver responsible for the second driver's irresponsibility, even though the first driver started this chain of events.

In addition, let's assume that the loud and sudden sound from that initial accident startled a woman in a nearby supermarket parking lot. As a result, she let go of her grocery cart, which rolled into another shopper and injured that shopper's leg. Is a shopping cart mishap the kind of result one would naturally expect from a car accident? Of course not, so the negligent driver of the car should not be held responsible for the shopper's injured leg.

Example 2: A builder uses too few supports when adding a deck onto a restaurant, causing the deck to collapse. The builder should be responsible for property damage or injuries to persons caused by the cave-in, as well as for lost business revenue to the owner. Those harms can all be reasonably anticipated in the wake of the builder's careless conduct.

A short-order cook in a neighboring diner claims that in witnessing the collapse, he lost concentration and spilled boiling water, which scalded his torso. A claim for this burn injury takes the principle of foreseeable harm too far and exceeds what would be considered an expected type of injury or harm from a deck collapsing.

Example 3: A property owner throws a bucket of dirty mop water onto the sidewalk in the middle of winter. A pedestrian falls on the icy walkway and shatters their wrist. Compensation from the owner should be forthcoming for the related injuries.

If, shortly after falling, the victim also needs to have their gall bladder removed, it is neither a natural or direct result of the fall, nor was it foreseeable. Therefore, this type of harm cannot be charged to the owner.

If the harm was not foreseeable that means there is no negligence case. If the facts underlying the claimed injuries or harms in a claim are vaguely reminiscent of a bad storyline from *The Twilight Zone*, it's probably too far-fetched for court consideration.

Damages

Those who believe they have been wronged want to extract their pound of flesh in vengeance. This is human nature. In medieval times individuals might have destroyed the transgressor's crops, burnt his barn, taken his wife, sold his children into slavery, and/or killed the offender. Today this behavior is properly seen as excessive and cruel.

Even the Bible's admonition in *Exodus* 21: 23–27 of taking "an eye for an eye" may seem to some like a harsh standard and an excuse for payback, rather than an equitable means of settling a wrong. Is it considered just when a man who accidentally causes another to lose an eye must remove his own eye in return? After all, the fact that the perpetrator has now also lost an eye is no real compensation to the victim or the family.

What value or social good to anyone is brought about by such an action? Another way of interpreting this Bible verse, however, is that the responsible party should, in fairness, pay the cost of the loss of an eye. In other words, it seems the wronged individual and the family suffering the loss should receive some kind of useful and fair compensation. This approach establishes a path to meaningful justice and attempts to minimize the urge for vengeance.

So, what is modern justice? In reality, after an injury or loss, no judge or jury can award true justice. The bottom line is that public decency, morals, and ethics through the *Rules of Civil Procedure* demand that money be the only remedy a court of law can provide to an injured party. This is true even when money is a poor substitute for unrelenting pain, disfigurement, lost function, or loss of a loved one.

Money damages are established by producing evidence such as medical records and doctor bills, impairment, disability, witness statements, lost wages, and/or reduced earning capacity.

CONCLUSION

"Under negligence, the rule that you are to love your neighbor has become law. You must not injure your neighbor."[4] This rule brings legal order out of social chaos.

Negligence principles are embedded in the Bible and laws allowing compensation date back at least to the Romans in the third century B.C. when the *lex Aquilia* was enacted and provided compensation if a slave or animal were accidentally killed.[5] These rules of human conduct have evolved over the years but have never been abandoned since their inception.

ASSESSMENT

1. Under what circumstances should a person be liable for harm to another? (See p. 26.)

2. What duty do we have to each other? (See pp. 27–28.)

3. How can people violate that duty? (See p. 28.)

4. What is proximate cause? (See p. 29.)

5. What types of damages can a court deliver? (See pp. 30–31.)

---

[4] Donoghue v Stevenson (1932) AC 562.
  http://sixthformlaw.info/01_modules/other_material/tort/1_duty/1_duty.htm.
[5] https://www.britannica.com/topic/Lex-Aquila.

BIBLIOGRAPY

Epstein, Richard A., and Catherine M. Sharkey. *Cases and Materials on Torts.* Tenth Ed. Aspen Publishers, 2004.

Hodgson, John, and John Lewthwaite. *Tort Law Textbook.* Oxford University Press, 2007.

Holmes, Oliver Wendell. *The Common Law.* Little, Brown, and Company, 1881. http://www.gutenberg.org/files/2449/2449-h/2449-h.htm.

Prosser, William L., John W. Wade, Victor E. Schwartz, Kathryn Kelly, and David F. Partlett. *Cases and Materials on Torts.* 12th Ed. University Casebook Series.

Robertson, David, William Jr. Powers, and David A. Anderson. *Cases and Materials on Torts.* St. Paul, MN: Westlaw Publishing, 1989.

CHAPTER 4

Malpractice
– What It Is, and Is Not –

INTRODUCTION

As a legal matter, malpractice is a tort and an extension of negligence law. Like all torts, malpractice causes loss or harm for which compensation may be sought in a court of law. Although the dereliction arises from a violation of the doctor-patient contract in failing to exercise ordinary care to avoid harm, malpractice is governed in chief by negligence law.

There is no appreciable difference between negligence and medical malpractice. The principles are identical in all vital respects. It is only in their application that there are minor differences between the two. Malpractice basically involves rules of negligence that are put into practice regarding medical care.

As we have seen, under the umbrella of negligence each adult has a duty to exercise reasonable care to avoid doing harm to others. How much more important is it then for doctors to use caution to avoid injuring their trusting and vulnerable patients? Stated another way, in negligence there is a reasonable person standard; in malpractice there is a reasonable doctor standard. The law is not concerned with a best doctor standard or even a good doctor standard; all that is required is for a reasonably prudent doctor to apply ordinary skills. Nonetheless, the principles remain the same.

A BRIEF HISTORY OF MALPRACTICE

The earliest writings on malpractice can be traced back to the Code of Hammurabi (ca. 1750–1790 B.C.). This code is one of the earliest records of a legal system and includes a list of laws, crimes, and penalties for medical malpractice. It is named for the Babylonian King Hammurabi who reigned at the time. Medical malpractice has been recognized as a violation of law since Roman times. After the Romans this concept was adopted by English Common Law, which heavily influenced and gave rise to the common law in the United States.

MALPRACTICE: SEARCHING FOR A PRACTICAL DEFINITION

One legal definition for malpractice is that the doctor in the performance of his service either did some particular thing or things that physicians and surgeons of ordinary skill, care, and diligence would not have done under the same or similar circumstances, or that the defendant failed or omitted to do some particular thing or things which physicians and surgeons of ordinary skill, care, and diligence would have done under the same or similar circumstances.

Another legal definition is that a health care provider rendered services that were below the accepted standard of care in the medical community.

The definitions of the law are not very helpful here because they fail to clarify, enlighten, instruct, or inform as to what specifically in a physician's misconduct constitutes malpractice.

A more practical working definition of malpractice would include taking any action that exposes the patient to unreasonable or unnecessary risk that results in additional harm to the patient. This concept is central to the various descriptions and examples of malpractice which follow below.

For instance, if a physician fails to anticipate the potential harmful consequences of prescribing an antibiotic such as streptomycin for a gram-positive bacterial infection, the patient may experience irreversible hearing loss, vertigo, or kidney damage when another safer antibiotic could and should have been used instead. It follows that, if any of these potential side effects develop, it would be considered malpractice. The patient could legitimately claim that the doctor did not employ ordinary judgment to protect the patient's safety and well-being, which in turn caused an unreasonable increased risk of harm and damages.

Also, if an ER doctor or surgeon failed to respond to a large and acutely symptomatic abdominal aortic aneurysm in a timely fashion, i.e., as an emergency, and if another reasonably cautious physician would have responded promptly in the same situation, the failure to act in a timely manner would be unreasonable in terms of patient safety because it would needlessly expose the patient to likely catastrophic consequences such as the loss of life or limb. As such, this scenario is likely to be termed malpractice because it would be seen as a departure from the standard of safe care.

What Malpractice Is

It could reasonably be considered malpractice, or practicing below the standard of care, if any of the following actions result in additional injury or harm to the patient:

- Exposing the patient to unnecessary or unreasonable risk of harm, e.g., risks are increased without justification or medical risks exceed potential benefits.

- Unreasonable failure to consider or implement other safer available courses of care.

- The unreasonable failure to properly diagnose, treat, or monitor a medical condition.

- Careless or sloppy practice.

- Making a decision or taking an action that is not reasonably cautious or prudent—in other words, the failure to use ordinary care.

- A material departure from the safety zone of good and accepted medical practice.

- An unreasonable omission of something that ordinarily should be done or doing something that a reasonable physician would not have done under the circumstances.

- Ignoring or overlooking established guidelines, accepted methods of practice, or protocols.

- Failing or choosing not to make use of the available resources on hand to care for an ailing patient.

- Anticipating a potential injury, but nonetheless proceeding without reasonable precautions.

- Failing to take reasonable steps to avoid plainly foreseeable harm or further injury.

- Unreasonable failure of properly planned actions to be completed as intended, e.g., a procedure was ordered but not performed, medication was prescribed but never given, a care plan was only partially implemented, or a lab test was requested or ordered, but not accomplished.

- Utilization of the wrong plan or scheme to diagnose, care for, or monitor the patient.

- Failure to warn/failure to advise of potential negative effects/consequences.

A second more egregious level of malpractice exists when a provider's conduct is considered to be highly unreasonable. This is known as gross negligence. Gross medical negligence is worse than not using ordinary care; it is a complete disregard for the life or safety of another person, for example, performing surgery while inebriated. Another example might include a preventable mix-up in which a healthy right arm is amputated instead of performing necessary surgery on the left arm due to peripheral artery disease. Fortunately, such events are relatively rare.

WHAT MALPRACTICE IS NOT

Although malpractice cases are typically initiated due to an adverse outcome or injury from a medical mistake, not all medical mistakes or errors in judgment cause injury, and not all bad outcomes are the result of medical malpractice. Malpractice does not include:

- Imperfection in patient outcome, i.e., an undesirable development or a poor result.
- 20/20 hindsight of what should have been done.
- A difference in opinion as to what would have been the best or better approach in managing the patient.
- An error in judgment or mistaken diagnosis.
- The fact that a different or atypical approach was used.
- What the majority of doctors would have done or the most widely accepted practice.[1] (What the majority of doctors would do is called the "customary practice." It is not always the same as the standard of care. In some instances, current customary practice may not be sound or good practice.)

In summary, if a practicing doctor's actions are deemed relatively safe, reasonable, or necessary, and alternatives were considered, then it is almost certainly not malpractice.

---

[1] Victor Cotton, MD, JD, "Defining the Standard of Care," *Law & Medicine* 1 (2001): 4.

TABLE 4.1: LEGAL FRAMEWORK FOR A MALPRACTICE CASE

Every malpractice lawsuit is comprised of the exact same four legal elements listed below. The plaintiff must prove each of these components to win at trial.

1. **Duty**: The plaintiff was the doctor's patient; therefore, the doctor had a legal obligation to use due care and caution in avoiding unreasonable risk and injury to that patient.

2. **Breach of Duty**: The doctor failed to take reasonable care not to increase risk or injure the patient.

3. **Causation:** The harm was foreseeable and had a solid cause and effect relationship to the careless act.

4. **Damages:** The patient is entitled to the reasonable value of the additional injury or loss.

MALPRACTICE REQUIRES FOUR LEGAL ELEMENTS (SEE ALSO TABLE 4.1 ABOVE.)

The following legal elements are required as a baseline level of sufficient evidence for a court to proceed in a case of medical negligence.

Duty of Care

The duty of care owed to patients arises in part from the fact that there can be substantial potential harm to patients as a result of the doctor's advice or treatment recommendations. This is why for thousands of years doctors have been asked to be careful and cautious regarding their recommendations and interventions. A physician has a specific duty to the patient before him and any failure to give that patient adequate and judicious care is not excusable.[2]

Therefore, **a legal duty is imposed on doctors** that obligates them to conduct themselves with caution and due care in their treatment of and attention to their patients. Because doctors only owe that duty of care to their own patients, the plaintiff must first show that he or she was in a doctor-patient relationship with that physician. Whether there is a duty of care is very easy to determine: an individual was either a patient of that doctor or they were not.

A doctor has no duty to treat or advise any person who is not already a patient. As a representative illustration of this point, if a non-patient in a restaurant starts to choke, a doctor who is dining at the next table has no legal obligation to take any action whatsoever.

---

[2] V.F. Colon, J. Scheper, and N. Bunch, *Medical Malpractice Risk Management* (An ACPE Publication, 2001), 35.

When Does the Duty Begin?

The duty of care begins immediately when a doctor-patient relationship is formed. How specifically is a doctor-patient relationship formed? First, in most states a potential patient cannot create a doctor-patient relationship merely by scheduling an appointment, any more than a person can create a marriage by offering a proposal. Making an appointment demonstrates only the patient's offer to be in the potential relationship. It is the physician who must accept the patient in order to create a doctor-patient relationship. (See also "Chapter 2: The Doctor-Patient Contract.")

As a rule, physicians in private practice are not required to accept everyone who seeks treatment. Doctors may choose whom they wish to treat. It is only when the physician undertakes a professional service, e.g., orders tests, performs an examination, gives advice, writes a prescription, etc., directed toward the diagnosis, care, or treatment of the patient's condition that the patient is deemed to be accepted and the doctor-patient relationship is conclusively formed. At that juncture the physician-patient contract is also in force and the duty of care is well-established.

Once the relationship is formed, "[t]he doctor takes the patient as is and is legally bound to manage the disease process in the context of the patient's ability to comply. If that is not possible, the doctor is free at any time to terminate the doctor-patient relationship."[3]

Determining the exact moment when a doctor-patient relationship begins is relatively straightforward in a clinical setting. However, it can be more difficult to ascertain when and if such a relationship started in a social setting. For instance, at a dinner party or a golf outing, simple inquiries to a physician may be interpreted by the inquirer as the beginning of a doctor-patient relationship. According to standard rules, however, no doctor-patient relationship is created from casual questions at a social function or if a doctor supplies basic information.

Nevertheless, even at a social gathering, anyone can become a patient if that doctor gives a medical opinion or judgment in the care of the patient's condition, and if the person accepts and relies on that advice. Clearly, the best course of action in this situation is to recommend that the individual soliciting medical advice should seek medical attention at an appropriate health care facility or make an appointment that allows for a complete medical history and a thorough evaluation.

---

[3] Victor Cotton, MD, JD, "Defining the Standard of Care," *Law & Medicine* 1 (2001): 4.

Today, the most likely scenario in which an unexpected doctor-patient relationship may begin is on the internet. Such a relationship could be started with the mere click of a mouse. Therefore, it is vital that websites containing medical information or advice should have large, easily-seen, clear, and specific language that sets forth the specific circumstances under which a doctor-patient relationship, if any, is established through the website.

In summary, a duty of care is established and demonstrated if a doctor-patient relationship existed at the time of the alleged medical malpractice.

Breach of Duty

Proving that a physician violated the core duty to provide the full standard of care requires a dual demonstration of:

a) the standard of care

b) a breach of that standard, i.e., that the doctor failed to follow the standard of care

THE STANDARD OF CARE

Somewhat surprisingly, there is no medical definition for the standard of care. Instead, the standard of care is firmly established in the law.

The legal rationale for having a standard of care is that physicians are the guardians of their patient's health and safety. As such, doctors have a legal duty to take reasonable steps to avoid harming those under their care. It means that physicians are not allowed to needlessly endanger patients. The standard of care does not exist for doctors, but rather for the benefit and protection of patients.

The standard of care thus serves to establish a minimum safety standard that describes the degree of prudence and caution required by physicians on behalf of their patients. (See also Table 4.2, p. 43.) It does so by requiring physicians to make every clinical decision in a reasonably sensible, careful, and cautious manner.

As a rule, *the standard of care is what a cautious physician would do to avoid unnecessary or unreasonable risk and injury to a patient.*

What Is Included in the Medical Standard of Care?

Standards of care set out well-established paths in the evaluation and care of patients. Therefore, the standard of care includes every course of assessment and care that is *reasonable, necessary,* relatively *safe* (good benefit to risk ratio), *expert recommended*, e.g., review articles or clinical studies in the medical literature, or *accepted*,[4] e.g., consensus and/or evidence-based clinical practice guidelines[5] which improve patient care and are recommended because they are considered safe, effective, and current, if published within the last five years.

As Victor Cotton, MD, JD, recommends, "A physician should not deviate significantly from these clinical resources without careful consideration and justification."[6]

Variations in the Standard

All the clinical courses of care described above are good medical practices and thus are understood to be standards of care. It is also clear that the fields of medicine, pharmacy, and all the health care sciences are highly complex. Practicing in these professional areas requires not only a depth of knowledge in terms of the general rules that apply, but also an understanding that these rules or standards must, at times, accommodate, or give way, to individual circumstances.

Thus, as a result, the standard can vary depending on an individual patient's needs and other factors, making a course of care ordinarily outside the guidelines acceptable for an individual patient.[7]

Every doctor is fully expected to know the standard of care for his or her own specialty. However, if a doctor cannot follow practice protocols, guidelines, or other trustworthy sources, or if there are reasons for an inability to cooperate with the treatment plan (such as patient intolerance to certain medications or drug allergies, or the patient's refusal of a treatment method), then the decision-making process and these facts should be well-documented in the medical record.

---

[4] Victor Cotton, "What Every Physician Should Know," *Law & Medicine* 1, no. 2 (Oct. 2001): 2–3, as well as seminar materials 2003.

[5] It must be said that modern scientific health care should be grounded firmly in evidence-based medicine for use of the current best evidence in making health care decisions. It means that clinical decisions and patient policies should be based on scientific evidence and individual clinical experience, not empirical beliefs. See D.L. Sackett, W.M. Rosenberg, J.A. Gray, et al. "Evidence Based Medicine: What It Is and What It Isn't," *BMJ* 312 (1996): 71–72.

[6] Victor Cotton (supra).

[7] See *Heinrich v. Sweet*, 308 F.3d 48,59 (1st Cir. 2002), Applying Massachusetts Law.

Deciding Which Standard Course of Care to Follow

Which course of care to choose for a patient is a decision doctors make with regularity. For example, in a patient needing DVT prophylaxis after major orthopedic surgery, medical care may take different forms, such as low molecular weight heparin, warfarin, fondaparinux, dextran,[8] graded compression stockings,[9/10] and/or early mobilization after surgery. Each of these methods is the standard of care because they are supported by the scientific literature, recommended by experts, are accepted, and have a good benefit-to-risk (safety) ratio. All are considered to be reasonably prudent. Which of these courses of care to follow is ultimately dependent upon the individual patient's needs under his unique circumstances as judged in light of the doctor's experience.

It goes without saying that health care decisions, such as which course to follow in a specific case, can have profound effects on human life. Doctors are expected to approach those decisions seriously, deliberately, and cautiously to ensure their patients' well-being to the greatest extent possible.

Updating Standards of Care

The guiding principle underlying the progression of the legal standard of care is as follows: "[When] certain dangers have been removed by a customary way of doing things safely, this custom may be proved to show that [the one charged with negligence] has fallen below the required standard."[11]

When this rule is applied to the field of medicine, it means that if other medical professionals are commonly practicing in a certain way that reduces or minimizes certain risks, then this practice can be used to define the current standard of care, or course of care the patient should have received. In other words, newer and reasonably safe methods of medical management or patient care that are more risk-free automatically become the contemporary standards.

---

[8] Frederick A. Anderson and Anne-Marie Audet, "Best Practices Preventing Deep Vein Thrombosis and Pulmonary Embolism," UMass Medical School Center for Outcomes Research. http://www.outcomes-umassmed.org/dvt/best_practice/.

[9] "Deep Vein Thrombosis," American Academy of Orthopedic Surgeons (New Clinical Treatment Guidelines). https://orthoinfo.aaos.org/en/diseases--conditions/deep-vein-thrombosis/.

[10] "Preventing Venous Thromboembolic Disease in Patients Undergoing Elective Hip and Knee Arthroplasty," along with all supporting documentation and workgroup disclosures, is available on the AAOS website: www.aaos.org/guidelines.

[11] See *Garthe v. Ruppert* 264 N.Y. 290, 296, 190 N.E. 643 (1934).

How Is the Standard of Care Established?

Ordinarily, standards set by the medical profession are generally accepted by the courts. However, under certain circumstances, the standard of care as it applies to the patient at hand is determined by the court and may ultimately be a matter for the judge and jury.

In order to determine whether the standard of care was or was not met, courts may in some circumstances consider scientific proof in addition to expert testimony such as evidence-based clinical practice guidelines, practice parameters, or published principles and protocols.

"The use of clinical practice guidelines (CPGs) to define the standard of care is allowed by some courts, but not others. Normally, a document like a CPG would be considered 'hearsay' in the courts, as the author is not available to testify or be cross-examined. However, the court cases dealing with CPG use have suggested that if the guidelines are of some scientific validity, that they may be used as 'learned treatises' and bypass the hearsay rule."[12]

Some courts are reluctant to admit CPGs, in part because guidelines do not have the regulatory effect of statutes or regulations and doctors do not legally have to comply with them. Also, practice guidelines are not conclusive evidence of the standard of care. Furthermore, guidelines do not necessarily represent customary practice and more than one set of guidelines may exist regarding a medical matter.[13]

In court, "CPGs may be used to lend credence to an expert witness, to impeach an expert witness, to defend a physician for following the document as the standard of care, or to suggest physician deviance from the document as deviance from the standard of care."[14]

Recently, a New York court allowed guidelines from the American Heart Association and the American College of Cardiology into evidence.[15] Although the guidelines represented direct evidence of the standard of care, the court admitted them into evidence, not as practice guidelines, but to show

[12] Peter Moffett, MD, and Gregory Moore, MD, JD, "The Standard of Care: Legal History and Definitions: The Bad and Good News," *West J Emerg Med* 12, no. 1 (Feb. 2011): 109–112.

[13] Clark C. Havighurst. "Practice Guidelines as Legal Standards Governing Physician Liability," *Law and Contemporary Problems* 54, no. 2 (Spring 1991): 87–117. Duke University, http://scholarship.law.duke.edu/lcp/vol54/iss2/5.

[14] Moffet supra.

[15] See *Hinlicky v Dreyfuss*, 848 NE2d 1285 (NY 2006).

the physician's decision-making methodology or practice.[16] Some courts allow guidelines as evidence of the specific legal standard of care, but the court is not obligated to accept or apply the guidelines to determine the standard of care.[17] The ramifications for future cases are yet to be determined.

BREACH OF THE STANDARD

Either the doctor complied with the standard or he did not. A breach means the doctor did not use a reasonable degree of ordinary prudence and caution. Unless there is a disputed factual question about what the defendant doctor did, proving the standard of care most often also proves the physician's compliance or noncompliance with the standard.

TABLE 4.2: HOW TO COMPLY WITH THE STANDARD OF CARE

The following is a checklist of 10 steps that physicians typically follow in order to comply with the standard of care and to avoid unreasonable risk and harm to their patients.

1. **Stay abreast** of new developments in their specialty.
2. **Routinely adhere** to established practice guidelines, evidence-based protocols, or expert recommended advice.
3. **Act in accordance** with current medical literature, weighing the medical and scientific evidence against the patient's individual needs.
4. **Implement** a reasonable, relatively safe course of care whenever possible.
5. **Consider** alternative courses of care.
6. **Conduct a risk-benefit (safety) analysis** for the courses of care considered.
7. **Not increase the risk of harm** without sound reasoning.
8. **Pay attention** to known risks and make reasonable attempts to minimize them, if possible, before proceeding.
9. **Remain alert** for adverse effects, their appearance and any rapid medical intervention required in the case.
10. **Follow core clinical concepts** that are based on medical and professional training and demonstrated knowledge, skill, and experience in

---

[16] Valarie Blake, JD, MA, "Medicine, the Law, and Conceptions of Evidence," *Virtual Mentor* 15, no. 1 (2013): 46–50.

[17] See generally, Rinella, "The Use of Medical Practice Guidelines in Medical Malpractice Litigation," *64 UMKC L. Rev* 337 (1995).

these concepts, e.g., the medicolegal rules set out in Chapter 5, that pertain to the following:

- medical history
- examination
- diagnostic tests
- differential diagnosis
- diagnosis
- medical procedures and treatments
- monitoring
- record-keeping
- obtaining patients' consents

Causation/Proximate Cause

Causation is the demonstration that a doctor's actions, e.g., failure to use ordinary caution, caused the patient's injury. As simple as that sounds, proving causation can be complicated and difficult. It is worth noting that causation can be a legal dilemma for the patient who is suing a doctor. For example, it may be difficult for a plaintiff's lawyer to prove that the patient's condition would not have deteriorated even if the physician had taken a different clinical course. Also, it can be argued that any misstep by the doctor would not have altered the end result or inevitable outcome of the patient's condition. This is why expert testimony is required in these cases.

To demonstrate proximate cause, a direct cause-and-effect relationship is needed between the alleged failure to use reasonable caution and the patient's injury. Causation does not extend to every possible harm from a negligent act. Nor does the causation concept include the bizarre, the unusual, or unexpected harms. If the doctor's missteps cannot be directly connected with the alleged injuries as a foreseeable harm, then causation is not demonstrated and there is no liability. (See also "Chapter 3: Negligence Principles.")

Damages

Damages are the monetary value of the victim's injuries. Damages cannot be speculative, mere possibilities, or contingent; they must be proven. The ultimate question here is, how much compensation for the injured person can be considered fair? It falls entirely to the jury to make this decision.

Three types of damages can be awarded:

- **Economic:** Both past and future losses of wages and medical care expenses and future loss of earnings capacity are included in this category. Funeral and burial expenses are also typically available in a wrongful death action. Economic damages are based on actual and projected reasonable costs.

- **Non-economic:** This includes physical pain and suffering, mental and emotional suffering, physical impairment, inconvenience, disfigurement, loss of enjoyment of life, loss of consortium (the loss of a personal relationship with one's spouse, parent, or child), increased risk of future harm, and curtailment of life expectancy.

  The total amount of non-economic damages is usually determined only by what is just and reasonable in light of the evidence. Several states have capped the dollar amount of non-economic damages an injured person can collect.

- **Punitive:** Although rarely requested, punitive damages are requested when there are allegations of intentional misconduct, gross negligence (deliberate disregard for another's safety), or specific types of negligent conduct such as elder abuse. In medical malpractice, punitive damages are almost never granted.

How Is Malpractice Proven?

Malpractice cases can be demonstrated or proven to a jury or judge through:

- Witnesses.
- Expert testimony.
- Authoritative medical or professional literature—jurors believe that these publications including CPGs contain legitimate information that both they and doctors can rely on. This includes medical books that demonstrate normal vs. abnormal such as *Emergency Radiology* by D.T. Schwartz and E. Reisdorff, McGraw-Hill Companies (2000).
- Some states allow hospital rules and procedures, flow charts, algorithms, CD-ROMs, e.g., for use in emergency medicine, etc., and/or medical staff bylaws into evidence.
- Private agency standards, such as those promulgated by The Joint Commission on Accreditation of Healthcare Organizations.

DEFENSES TO MALPRACTICE

See Chapter 13, The Physician's Defenses.

SOCIAL OBJECTIVES OF MALPRACTICE LITIGATION

Three social objectives are in play when it comes to malpractice litigation: (a) to deter unsafe practices, (b) to properly compensate persons injured through carelessness, and (c) to exact corrective justice.

MOST MALPRACTICE SUITS END IN THE DOCTOR'S FAVOR

Tort law is both fair and, in some ways, favorable to doctors. There is no need to fear the law because it is truly a fault-based standard. If a physician has acted in a way that is considered reasonable by his or her colleagues, even by a minority of such colleagues, it is likely that the physician will have nothing to worry about. It is important to note that malpractice lawsuits that go to trial are overwhelmingly won by doctors regardless of actual culpability.

Nonetheless, the specter of destructive malpractice lawsuits haunts every practicing doctor and there remains a great deal of fear over such accusation. In large part, this is due to a lack of understanding of certain medical and legal principles. Sensational stories in the press or on television contribute to the mystification and misperception of medical malpractice.

The law has always sought a fair and workable balance between promoting public safety, and engendering and maintaining public trust and confidence in the medical field, while allowing physicians to exercise their medical judgment freely. The law not only provides physicians with ample advantages, legal shields and protections, but also aids in advancing medical interests, research, patents, and ethics. The law works!

CONCLUSION

In very general terms, it is the doctor's duty to follow good and accepted practices and standards of care so that no patient is unnecessarily exposed to an increased risk of harm. Doctors might be in real danger of being involved in a medical malpractice lawsuit if their judgment strays too far from accepted practices or scientific evidence.

The fact remains that, as in other responsible professions, medicine seeks to be progressive and continues to raise safety standards for those who place their trust in medical professionals to safeguard their well-being and provide their needed care.

Personal Assessment

Define malpractice. (See pp. 34–35.)
A: Malpractice is the failure to use due diligence or caution in avoiding harm to the patient. It results from exposing a patient to unnecessary risk that results in additional harm.

What is the standard of care? (See pp. 39–40.)
A: The standard of care is what a reasonably competent physician would do to avoid unnecessary risk and injury to a patient. Standards of care set out well-established paths in the diagnosis and care of patients. Therefore, standards of care include every clinical course of evaluation and care that is reasonable, necessary, relatively safe, expert recommended, and/or based on consensus or evidence-based practice guidelines.

How is the standard of care established? (See pp. 42–43.)
A: Expert witnesses, evidence-based clinical practice guidelines, practice parameters, or published principles and protocols help to establish the standard of care. Ultimately, the standard is determined by the court.

How do doctors comply with the standard of care? (See pp. 43–44.)
A: See the checklist of steps in Table 4.2.

Define proximate cause. (See p. 44.)
A: A direct cause and effect connection between an injury and a doctor's inattentiveness or carelessness. The alleged injury must be a foreseeable harm.

BIBLIOGRAPHY

Cotton, Victor, MD, JD. "Defining the Standard of Care." *Law & Medicine* 1, no. 2–3 (2001), as well as seminar materials (2003). Also see Victor Cotton's website at www.lawandmed.com/.

Gladwell, Malcolm. *Blink*. Little, Brown and Company, 2005.

Holmes, Oliver Wendell, Jr. *The Common Law*. Little, Brown and Co., 1938.

King, Joseph. *Law of Medical Malpractice in a Nutshell*. Nutshell Series, 1986.

Mello, M.M., and C.H. Williams. "Medical Malpractice: Impact of the Crisis and Effect of State Tort Reforms." *The Synthesis Project*, Issue 10. Robert Wood Johnson Foundation.

Moffet, Peter, and Gregory Moore. "The Standard of Care: Legal History and Definitions: The Bad and Good News." *West. J. Emerg Med*. Feb. 2011, 12(1): 109–112.

Schoenbaum, Stephen C., MD, MPH, and Randall R. Bovbjerg, JD. "Malpractice Reform Must Include Steps to Prevent Medical Injury." *Annals of Internal Medicine* 140, no. 1 (Jan. 2004): 51–53.

Shandell, Richard E. *The Preparation and Trial of Medical Malpractice Cases*. 1981.

Sonny Bal, B., MD, MBA. "An Introduction to Medical Malpractice in the United States." *Clin Orthop Relat Res* 467, no. 2 (Feb. 2009): 339–347.

Strauss, Dirk C., and J. Meirion Thomas. "What Does the Medical Profession Mean by 'Standard of Care?'" *Journal of the American Society of Clinical Oncology*. (Sept. 2009).

The Talmud, tractate Baba Kamma 85a.

Walston-Dunham, Beth. *Medical Malpractice Law and Litigation*. West Legal Studies, CENGAGE Delmar Learning, 2005–2006.

Wojcieszak, D., J. Saxton, and M. Finkelstein. *Sorry Works!: Disclosure, Apology and Relationships Prevent Malpractice Claims*. 2008.

CHAPTER 5

How to Commit Malpractice Without Trying
– Clinical Avenues to Avoid –

INTRODUCTION

Whether it is labeled as improper, unskilled, careless, or negligent care, malpractice is the failure to use ordinary caution to avoid harming the patient. Physicians fail their legal duty when they expose patients to an unreasonable increase in risk or harm instead of using a safer available alternative. An example of this might be prescribing NSAIDs in significant amounts to a patient with mild arthritis who also has chronic liver disease when, according to some experts, acetaminophen at half the recommended daily dose (< 2 g/day) and well below toxicity levels would likely be as effective and much safer.[1]

Another example would be increasing patient risk by omissions, such as not effectively communicating important information to other members of the medical team or by not reading or reviewing available information in the record, such as the nurse's notes.

Fortunately, not all allegedly careless acts are tantamount to a full-blown case of malpractice. It is important to remember that most cases of negligence do not result in significant harm, if any, to the patient. To be actionable, a careless act or negligence must also cause all of the below:

a) injury to the patient

b) the patient to seek legal help

c) legal help to be sought within a specific and limited time frame (typically within one year of the harm) or the suit is forever barred

d) severe enough injury to warrant the expense of obtaining medical records, an expert's opinion and report, and filing and pursuing a lawsuit

---

[1] Sina Menashehoff, DO, et al. https://www.practicalpainmanagement.com/issue/1309.

e) verification via the timing and causation of injury or at least revealing facts that do not contradict the patient's version of events

f) relatively compelling evidence that the doctor was careless, given that doctors win more than 80% of actual cases brought to trial

MALPRACTICE IN CLINICAL MEDICINE

As Glen Joshpe, MD, emphasizes, "In the practice of medicine, one can never predetermine the simple from the complex cases. A sore throat in a child may turn out to be a post-pharyngeal abscess; a seemingly routine headache may be temporal arteritis leading to blindness; a child with leg discomfort may have undiagnosed Ewing's sarcoma; a belly ache can be an acute abdomen; a benign looking mole can be malignant melanoma."[2] Doctors must act accordingly.

The Medical History—Making the History Defensible

Taking a patient's history is the most important skill in clinical medicine; it is the keystone of clinical diagnosis and is an essential component of clinical competence. A complete history is often the most important single item in establishing both a diagnosis and proper management. Standard questioning protocols exist for many different presentations.

Although nothing can guarantee a completely accurate history that leads to an accurate diagnosis and effective treatment, here is a list of rules to follow and steps to consider to diminish your exposure to malpractice claims.

MEDICOLEGAL RULES TO REDUCE THE RISK OF MALPRACTICE CLAIMS

Rule 1: Each patient complaint must be worked up until it is resolved or a referral is obtained.

Rule 2: In medicine, the depth and detail of the medical history for a symptomatic patient will vary according to the chief complaint. The medical history must be strategically conducted to help:

a) **identify relevant organ system(s)** likely responsible for the patient's symptoms

b) **begin analysis** regarding the nature of the pathological processes

c) **assess** risk factors in appropriate cases such as heart disease, stroke, diabetes, DVT, osteoporosis, cancer, etc.

---

[2] Glen Joshpe, MD, and Kent Joshpe, *Pearls and Pitfalls of Medical Malpractice* (2010), 41.

d) **focus the examination process**

e) **formulate a differential diagnosis**

f) **expedite the diagnosis** and indicate proper treatment

Rule 3: The patient's problem must be clearly identified. As such, the doctor must, with reasonable accuracy, document what is troubling the patient and how the symptoms have evolved over time.

Rule 4: History taking must be logical, organized, relevant, and thorough. Doctors have spent considerable time in medical school and residency learning how to take a thorough, concise, and clear medical history to facilitate gathering all the important information that can affect a patient's diagnosis and treatment. For every doctor, this process should become second nature.

Rule 5: The doctor must make reasonable efforts to obtain all the information needed to provide an expeditious and accurate diagnosis and the best care.

The rules of collecting a patient's medical history dictate that it is poor practice to:

- **Take an incomplete or superficial medical history.** This includes failing to obtain a careful, relevant, and meaningful history. For example, let's take the case of a hospitalized adult patient with an acute medical illness. Such patients can be at significant risk for thromboembolic complications such as pulmonary embolism (PE). PE is the most common reason for preventable hospital death and has a high risk of lethal outcome.

  Therefore, it is careless for the doctor and risky for the patient not to gather historical information regarding DVT risk factors in such a patient. Risk factors include being over 40 years of age, obese, pregnant, using oral contraceptives, being inactive/immobile, having had recent surgery (especially pelvic surgery), having inflammatory bowel disease, heart failure, or a history of COPD or some forms of cancer. Should the patient develop unexplained dyspnea, tachypnea, or chest pain, the history can lead the way to the right diagnostic tests and rapid diagnosis that is vital for improving chances of survival.

- **Failing to develop an appropriate history** on reported symptoms and signs. For example, not determining the location, duration, description, severity, aggravating or mitigating factors, and radiation, as well as associated symptoms and symptom evolution regarding pain complaints.

It further applies to not reviewing or expanding upon the patient's written responses for requested information on the facility's intake form.

- **Not communicating vital historical information** to other members of the medical team.
- **Not having every reported symptom explained by a diagnosis.**
- **Failing to use an electronic health record (EHR)** or failing to document the same information typically found in an EHR.[3] (There are no known cases at the time of this printing regarding this evolving standard of practice. See also Chapter 8.)
- **Ignoring alerts and guidelines** in the electronic health record's clinical decision support (CDS). (See also "Chapter 8: The Medical Record.")

The Examination—Performing a Defensible Examination

The importance of the physical examination in a medical malpractice case should not be underestimated. The complaint-directed physical examination is critical in establishing an accurate diagnosis and paving the road toward early and effective treatment. Basically, the examination is to determine and document the nature of the problem. The examination should indicate how serious the problem is and how quickly the doctor must act. A carefully performed examination is fundamental to providing competent and comprehensive care to patients in every age group.

MEDICOLEGAL RULES TO REDUCE THE RISK OF MALPRACTICE CLAIMS

Rule 1: The physician should render a focused examination that is as thorough and careful as the complaints require and the attending circumstances will permit.

Rule 2: Every abnormal physical finding must be followed-up and resolved or the patient referred.

Rule 3: As with obtaining the medical history, doctors should employ a well-ordered, methodical, and sequential examination process with standard components. This helps to establish baseline data and to identify and assess relevant objective signs while avoiding the exclusion of important assessment areas. Furthermore, it gives key information about the patient's current overall health and clinical status.

Rule 4: During any examination, doctors must observe and attempt to elicit relevant objective signs while adapting to the urgency of the medical

---

[3] "8 Malpractice Dangers in Your EHR," *Medscape Business of Medicine* (Aug. 21, 2014).

situation. Medical judgment is a significant factor in the interpretation of signs that involves recognizing and differentiating not only normal from abnormal findings but differentiating variants of normal from variants of abnormal.

Rule 5: The examination process evaluates body systems and thus helps localize any disease process. More serious presentations require further focus on suspected pathology within those systems. This process is vital, especially in emergency rooms where evaluating the severity of symptoms is required to determine whether this is an emergency medical condition. If so, the absence of immediate medical attention could reasonably be expected to result in placing the individual's health in serious jeopardy.[4]

It may be carelessness and inconsistent with good and accepted practices when there is:

- **Failure to properly and thoroughly examine.**
- **Failure to observe,** detect, record, or recognize the significance of warning signs and symptoms and/or important clinical signs and symptoms, e.g., chest or epigastric pain especially coupled with shortness of breath, or the triad of cough, weight loss, and hemoptysis. Other examples may include failure to recognize a new type of headache in an adult, or sudden severe back pain with fever in which the symptoms and signs were not appropriately followed up.
- **An inadequate response** in investigating and evaluating a patient's symptoms and signs, e.g., failing to adequately work-up the patient by not performing a thorough examination or ordering appropriate tests.

Performing a Defensible Differential Diagnosis

Presenting symptoms and signs may suggest several logical diagnostic possibilities because a number of different processes may account for a patient's condition. This is the primary reason for performing a differential diagnosis.

Differential diagnosis is not an academic exercise. It is direct evidence of the physician's clinical analytic process. Chest pain, for example, could be due to angina, myocardial infarction, cardiac trauma, unstable angina, pericarditis, cardiomyopathy, aortic dissection or rupture, mitral valve

---

[4]COBRA—Consolidated Omnibus Budget Reconciliation Act 42 USC 1395dd.

prolapse, pleurisy, pulmonary embolus, musculoskeletal pain or chest wall trauma, pneumonia, pneumothorax, gastroesophageal reflux, esophageal spasm or rupture, cholecystitis, and cholelithiasis.

The differential diagnosis forces the doctor to consider all the possibilities, rule out the most serious disorders first, and then use the science of medicine to further narrow the list down to determine which disease or condition is actually responsible for patient's signs and symptoms. A differential diagnosis is designed to allow the physician to reach an accurate diagnosis quickly and efficiently and is the safest and most proper method to arrive at a clinical diagnosis.

MEDICOLEGAL RULES TO REDUCE THE RISK OF MALPRACTICE CLAIMS

Rule 1: Differential diagnosis is a standard scientific technique for identifying the cause of a medical problem.

Rule 2: Knowing the clinical significance of why certain signs or symptoms are present is vital to perform a competent differential diagnosis leading to swift and proper treatment in the interests of patient safety.

Rule 3: In accomplishing a differential diagnosis, the most serious potentially life-threatening or limb-threatening disorders must be excluded first. This is consistent with the medical aphorism of "rule out the worst first." Next, potential diseases with the highest risks of morbidity as well as those requiring more immediate attention are ruled out in descending order of severity. This is achieved by analyzing additional historical data, physical findings, and/or diagnostic tests.

Rule 4: In order to select the most likely diagnosis, the physician must incorporate any new information that changes the relative probability of an illness being present or rules out some conditions.

Rule 5: In performing a differential diagnosis, doctors routinely employ a standardized systematic approach that uses algorithms, mnemonics, or checklists. Textbooks, CD-ROMs, and computer programs on this subject are readily available.

Rule 6: Where a physician employs differential diagnosis to rule out other potential causes for the diagnosis at issue, he must also "rule in the suspected cause" and do so using scientifically valid methodology.[5]

---

[5] Ruggiero v. Warner-Lambert Co., 424 F.3d 249, 254 (2d Cir. 2005).

The doctor may be accused of negligence if there is:

- **Too narrow a diagnostic focus** that fails to establish a legitimate differential diagnosis.

- **A failure to accomplish a differential diagnosis.** The differential is performed in order to rule out the most serious potential causes of the patient's signs and symptoms. It is easy at times to anchor on a suspected diagnosis early and dismiss other serious, potential causes.

  In the "chest pain" example above, the majority of patients presenting to the emergency department (ED) with that chief complaint are found to have a noncardiac cause for their symptoms, but myocardial infarction, pulmonary embolus, and aortic dissection should typically be ruled in or ruled out first because they are life-threatening conditions.

  If the physician does not rule out one of these serious causes and the patient is harmed as a result, then the doctor may be sued for failure to properly accomplish a differential diagnosis or include the correct diagnosis on the differential diagnosis list.

  Other examples may include the failure to rule out melanoma in an atypical mole, an epidural abscess in a patient with fever and back pain, or abdominal aortic aneurysm in a male over the age of 60 with sudden onset of severe low back pain.

- **A misdiagnosis or delayed diagnosis** that represents a dereliction to reasonably recognize and consider or rule out other likely conditions as the cause of the patient's problems, or failing to confirm the presumptive diagnosis. This also includes a doctor's failure to recognize the urgency of one of the possible medical problems, to timely order appropriate tests, or to seek a specialist's opinion to verify the viability of the diagnosis.

Ordering Defensible Diagnostic Tests

Inadequate assessments are a common factor in malpractice claims. Accurate diagnostic tests play a key role in patient management and in the improvement of patient care.

MEDICOLEGAL RULES TO REDUCE THE RISK OF MALPRACTICE CLAIMS

Rule 1: Tests should not be ordered in a shotgun pattern with no forethought. The specific purposes of diagnostic tests are to:

- **Rule out, clarify, or confirm** a disease process or pathology in establishing an early diagnosis in symptomatic patients.
- **Screen** for disease in asymptomatic patients.

- **Determine** or estimate the stage, or activity of disease.
- **Provide** prognostic information for an established disease.
- **Discover** occult disease.

Rule 2: Order or perform appropriate and proper diagnostic tests in a timely fashion. Once a patient seeks medical advice and reports a symptom that could be caused by a life or limb threatening condition, the doctor must perform certain diagnostic tests without delay.

Rule 3: Random screening can never replace good judgment. Tests should initially be ordered to narrow the differential diagnosis.

Rule 4: It's better to test than to guess. Performing additional relevant tests can give the doctor a real advantage in making an accurate diagnosis.

Rule 5: Since the accuracy of the diagnosis is only as good as the tests performed, those tests should be necessary, objective, valid, verifiable, and have predictive value.

Rule 6: The doctor should never allow the cost to override a decision on proper testing.

Rule 7: The physician is responsible for acknowledging all abnormal test results including laboratory tests in addition to responding to the same. That includes advising the patient of the abnormality and its significance.

The following are *not* good and accepted practices:

- **Failure to order,** or perform, appropriate tests or studies, including follow-ups, within a meaningful time frame, despite sufficient clinical indication.

    For example, mammography may fail to show breast cancer in approximately 15% to 30% of cases. If symptoms and findings warrant it, e.g., the existence of a palpable, hard, and irregular lump in the upper outer quadrant, then the mammogram should not be relied upon exclusively and a sonogram and/or biopsy should likely be performed as well.

- **Failing to respond quickly and correctly** to the patient's complaints may unfairly deprive the patient of a chance for a cure.[6] If the doctor fails to do so, the patient may suffer terrible consequences, such as in a case of possible bacterial meningitis in an infant or a young child who is febrile, lethargic, and anorexic. This is not the time for procrastination. Early detection can lead to an early cure.

---

[6]Richard E. Kessler and Patrick Trese, *Bitter Medicine: What I've Learned and Teach About Malpractice Lawsuits and How to Avoid Them* (Create Space Independent Publishing Platform, 2012), 77.

- **Misinterpretation/negligent interpretation** of laboratory or pathology specimens, imaging, or other diagnostic studies. Examples might include (1) improper staging of cancer, (2) failure to recognize pathology on chest x-rays leading to delayed diagnosis of squamous cell carcinoma of the lung, or (3) a patient with sudden onset of LBP and positive blood tests for bacteria is misdiagnosed with a likely UTI instead of considering the more serious diagnosis of spinal infection.

- **Wrong test.** Examples include follow-up testing for clostridium difficile and *H. pylori*. Following clostridium difficile infection (CDI), laboratory stool assays can remain positive because many patients with no symptoms shed spores for up to six months. This follow-up test is inadequate to diagnose recurrent CDI.

  For evaluation of *H. pylori* eradication, serologic testing is inappropriate since the test typically remains positive even after successful treatment. (Recommended testing is for stool antigen for *H. pylori* and urea breath tests performed at least one month after a proton pump inhibitor is discontinued.[7])

- **Neglecting to promptly read,** properly interpret, or understand the meaning of tests and studies performed.

- **Not comparing** and putting prior tests in context with current results.

- **Failure to follow up** on abnormal test results or perform repeat studies, e.g., electrocardiogram and cardiac enzymes when indicated.

- **Failure to follow through** on recommended tests.

- **Not documenting a reasonable explanation** for abnormal results where no further action is deemed warranted as a result.

- **Failure to consider** the real possibility of false positive results and rule them out, e.g., for uterine cancer leading to hysterectomy.

- **Failure to weigh the possibility of and to exclude false negative results,** e.g., for malignant melanoma or overreliance on a negative cardiac stress test, which can fail to detect pathology approximately 15% of the time.

- **Failing to properly perform a diagnostic procedure,** e.g., failure to extract targeted abnormal cells via fine needle aspiration.

- **Improper collection or preservation** of specimens obtained for testing.

---

[7] David Johnson, MD, "5 Diagnostic Errors to Avoid: The Patient with GI Symptoms," *Medscape* (Feb. 20, 2016). https://www.medscape.com/slideshow/diagnostic-errors-gastroenterology-6007495.

- **Mislabeled samples**, e.g., blood tubes, tissues, slides, or specimens including samples that did not come from this patient.
- **Failure to identify risks**, e.g., of dystocia from ultrasonography.
- **Failure to report** any critically high or low lab values or imaging results to the treating physician or patient in a timely manner, e.g., when positive margins remain after a lumpectomy.

Developing a Defensible Working Diagnosis

A medical diagnosis must be timely, accurate, and reliable. A timely and accurate diagnosis is the best path to early treatment or cure. Unfortunately, diagnosis errors are a leading cause of malpractice litigation. Additionally, diagnostic errors tend to be the most common, most catastrophic, and most costly of all medical errors.[8]

Clinical judgment factors such as a failure or delay in ordering a diagnostic test, inadequate examination or testing, failure to appreciate and reconcile relevant symptoms or test results, failure or untimely delay in obtaining a consultation or referral, and misinterpretation of diagnostic studies account for many of the diagnostic errors.[9]

MEDICOLEGAL RULES TO REDUCE THE RISK OF MALPRACTICE CLAIMS

Rule 1: Securing a correct diagnosis is the brass ring in medicine and is the essential preliminary to rational treatment of the patient. Therefore, every working diagnosis or clinical impression must be confirmed or refuted.

Rule 2: Remember that doctors can become focused on the diagnosis they first suspect. So-called diagnostic impressions are inherently unreliable and thus provisional. A provisional diagnosis may conform to the doctor's preconceived beliefs about predicting the diagnosis rather than actually confirming it.

Rule 3: When reasonable, the working diagnosis should be amended, clarified, or changed by subsequent tests, examinations, historical data, or another doctor.

Rule 4: Every female (between the ages of 11 and 45) is assumed to be pregnant until proven otherwise.

---

[8] https://www.mdedge.com/cardiology/article/204514/practice-management/third-serious-malpractice-claims-due-diagnostic-error?utm_source=News_MDedge_Evening_071219_F&utm_medium=email&utm_campaign=2633&pu=ea01daad 18be3b2959a941a9159b4ebd. Accessed July 17, 2019.
[9] Ibid.

Rule 5: Doctors should follow their patients' complaints to a full diagnosis. They need to investigate every significant complaint and ideally should have a diagnosis to explain each patient symptom in the history.

Rule 6: Conditions do *not* always appear in standard textbook fashion. Thus, recognizing various presentations of potentially serious cases is critical to making an accurate diagnosis. This skill set is facilitated by medical education, training, and experience.

Rule 7: Treatment directed toward the working diagnosis is with the knowledge that failure of that treatment will lessen the likelihood that the provisional diagnosis is correct.

Rule 8: Treatment success will tend to confirm the diagnosis, but the fact that the patient gets well does not prove the diagnosis was correct.

Carelessness may be alleged if there is:

- **Failure to diagnose.** This encompasses any number of conditions such as cancer, pulmonary embolism, heart attack, or tuberculosis. And no reasonable or careful doctor would prescribe a medication potentially harmful to a fetus without first ruling out pregnancy. During pregnancy, a failure to diagnose or test for pre-eclampsia, Rh incompatibility, anemia, hypoglycemia, fetal abnormality, fetal macrosomia, gestational diabetes, or any other maternal illness that affects the fetus may be considered carelessness.

- **Delayed diagnosis.** This cause of action, in addition to cancer cases, can frequently be the result of an urgent or emergency care visit when there is a failure to recognize, accurately diagnose or treat disabling, life threatening, or limb threatening conditions promptly. These types of maladies require more immediate intervention and may include cardiac distress, TIA's, hemorrhagic stroke, impending embolic stroke, DVT, pulmonary embolus, acute abdomen, impending heart attack, cauda equina syndrome, ruptured spleen, compartment syndrome, meningitis, diabetic acidosis, cancer, spinal cord injury, sepsis or septic shock, necrotizing fasciitis, fracture, dislocation, postoperative bleed or spinal hematoma, fat embolism, perforated colon following colonoscopy, Stevens-Johnson syndrome, etc.

- **Wrong diagnosis.** An early error in assessment can lead to a host of wrong turns and much suffering. Clearly, a wrong diagnosis is not by itself malpractice, but the failure to stop and reassess the problem in the wake of altered or worsening symptoms and signs or treatment failures may be.

Oftentimes, "misdiagnoses happen when doctors settle on a benign, statistically common diagnosis before ruling out a serious condition."[10] To minimize wrong diagnosis cases, doctors should accomplish a differential diagnosis and confirm or refute the working diagnosis.

In a recent Alabama case, for example, a wrong diagnosis that purportedly identified rectal cancer led to an unnecessary colostomy. A small bowel obstruction ensued and the patient died. As the result of that wrong diagnosis, the patient encountered multiple risks and devastating consequences with no possible benefits from the colostomy procedure.

• **Improper or inadequate investigation,** or work-up of a significant complaint or examination finding. The work-up should lead to a definite conclusion or a referral. The most common disease for this version of a delayed diagnosis allegation is breast cancer. A main reason is that mammograms are a suitable screening device, but a poor diagnostic tool due to a false negative rate of nearly 20%. Standard practice is to follow any patient with a palpable breast lump for 30 days (one menstrual cycle) and if the lump does not resolve, needle aspiration or excision may be necessary to establish a diagnosis. The leading cause of delayed diagnosis for breast cancer is unwarranted reassurance that a mass is benign without biopsy.[11] For this reason, physicians should not risk over-relying on negative mammograms.

• **Failing to identify** a condition known to be associated with the established diagnosis in a significant percentage of patients, e.g., malnutrition or infection in patients with severe alcoholic hepatitis or thymoma in 10–15% of patients with myasthenia gravis who report the new symptom of difficulty swallowing.[12]

• **Failure to confirm or refute** a working diagnosis. This means that the patient is diagnosed as having the wrong condition and not the actual condition for which they need care. Examples include diagnosing the flu when the patient actually has Lyme disease or sending a woman to a gastroenterologist for stomach symptoms, when she actually has underlying ovarian cancer and requires treatment by a gynecologist. In addition,

[10] Michael Koskoff and Sean McElligott, *The Medical Malpractice Trial*.

[11] W.H. Goodson and D.H. Moore, "Causes of Physician Delay in the Diagnosis of Breast Cancer," *Arch Int Med* 162 (2002): 1343–1348.

[12] *Decision Support in Medicine: Alcoholic Liver Disease* (Aug. 31, 2016).

illnesses such as systemic lupus erythematosis or sarcoidosis can mimic infections and are often misdiagnosed as such. In these types of cases, the patient is exposed needlessly to the consequences and potential ill effects of antibiotics, while damage from the disease process continues unabated.

- **Failure to properly or promptly recognize complications** such as the possible development of any inherent risk associated with a procedure or condition. An example would include a perforated bowel following a colonoscopy.

Developing Defensible Treatments/Procedures

The treatment plan depends on the totality of the presenting signs and symptoms, patient history, diagnosis, the doctor's experience, and the patient's preferences. The goals of medical treatment are to accomplish one or more of the following: prevent death and disease, restore health where possible, alleviate pain and suffering, and stop or delay deterioration in health, i.e., disease management to include maintaining quality of life and maximizing function.

MEDICOLEGAL RULES TO REDUCE TREATMENT MALPRACTICE CLAIMS

Rule 1: Doctors should always choose the safest and most effective course of care available.

Rule 2: No treatment at all may be better than misdirected treatment. At times, watchful waiting, i.e., non-intervention, can be the most effective and safest intervention. First, do no harm.

Rule 3: In an emergency, treatment delayed is treatment denied. Doctors must attend to each of their patient's medical needs in a timely fashion and begin necessary emergency procedures without undue delay. The patient must not be neglected.

Rule 4: Health care providers are expected to be familiar with safe practices and treatment guidelines and to follow those recommendations. Good medical judgment is important in deciding how to use and interpret this information. The physician's approach to health care should be based on the best scientific evidence available in combination with the doctor's experience.

Rule 5: The treatment or procedure must be medically indicated and any known risks and contraindications regarding nonemergent care addressed before that procedure or treatment is undertaken.

Rule 6: Physicians must not unduly delay or deny their patients access to appropriate medical services due to inaction, costs, personal beliefs, not advocating for needed care, insurance coverage disputes, etc.

Rule 7: Temporary symptomatic improvement can occur, even when the treatment is aimed at the wrong disease.

Rule 8: Physicians should use caution, particularly when phoning in instructions for the treatment of hospitalized patients. Telephone conversations concerning care are inherently deceptive. Any impersonal and hands-off care without listening to or examining the patient is not good medicine and increases the likelihood of additional harm. Even relatively benign diagnoses such as a migraine or a tension headache should not be made over the phone, as each diagnosis is dependent upon a normal neurological examination. Extra caution must be taken regarding "calls concerning abdominal or chest pain, fever, seizure, bleeding, head injury, dyspnea, the onset of labor, complaints that a cast is too tight, or neurological alterations."[13]

The following may violate the rules listed above and may represent **unreasonable medical conduct** in the care of patients:

- **Improper/inappropriate/inadequate treatment**, wherein diagnosed conditions are mismanaged, e.g., inadequate course, dosage, or type of antibiotic therapy; and use of a circular cast for a non-displaced supracondylar fracture, causing unnecessary danger from compromised blood supply. This represents a failure to provide continuous quality medical care.[14]

- **Delayed treatment** is the failure to perform a needed procedure in a reasonably timely manner. This is associated with the triad of failure to assess, diagnose, and intervene. This is a common allegation particularly in cases of delayed surgery for acute abdomen whether due to ischemic bowel, perforated ulcer, peritonitis, or a ruptured appendix, gall bladder, cecal diverticulitis, ectopic pregnancy, or bowel obstruction.

- **No treatment** is synonymous with the failure to appropriately treat or to intervene.

---

[13] Richard E. Anderson, *Medical Malpractice: A Physician's Sourcebook* (Totowa, NJ: Humana Press, 2005), 71–72.

[14] James Beaty and James Kasser (editors), *Rockwood & Wilkins' Fractures in Children*, 6th ed. (Lippincott, Williams & Wilkins, 2006), 552.

- **Misdirected treatment.** This directly implies that the diagnosis was wrong, although a missed diagnosis would not necessarily be a breach of the standard of care. It also likely means that prescribed procedures and treatments performed were not indicated or needed, and that the actual disease process continued unabated. In short, the patient was unnecessarily exposed to multiple medical risks without the prospect or hope of any benefit.

- **Nonmitigation of known risk factors** for CAD, MI, stroke, or PE, etc., which from a preventive standpoint is likely to result in a more favorable outcome per national guidelines.

- **Failure to recognize or mitigate complications** known to be associated with a procedure or accompany certain conditions such as obesity, alcoholism, diabetes, pregnancy, labor or delivery, e.g., a failure to anticipate birth complications due to a baby's size, unnecessary exposure to communicable diseases, or a failure to follow preoperative precautions as in the case of pheochromocytoma to help prevent a hypertensive crisis.

- **Inadequate performance** of a treatment procedure. This includes the wrong surgical site, the wrong patient, the inappropriate or negligent positioning of the patient or hardware, e.g., feeding tube, which may lead to respiratory arrest and brain damage, or the failure to establish and maintain an adequate airway via the improper placement of a breathing tube. Negligent performance of a surgical procedure also falls into this category.

    Examples may involve the misidentification and severance of the common bile duct during laparoscopic cholecystectomy or the failure to identify the ureter, which may be severed during a hysterectomy. The surgeon must seek and identify any anatomical structure before cutting.

- **Disease management failure.** When certain chronic diseases, e.g., CHF, COPD, and diabetes, are not properly managed via coordinated strategies, the course of the disease process often deteriorates, resulting in medical complications and hospitalizations.

- **Treatment and care not aggressive enough** in the face of a potentially debilitating or deadly, but otherwise curable, disease. Examples may include endocarditis, osteomyelitis, or sepsis.

- **Failure to initiate preventative treatment,** e.g., for impending or developing myelopathy, stroke, or MI. An example may include neglecting to prescribe aspirin or other antiplatelet medication after a TIA.

- **Not preparing or implementing** an adequate and appropriate care plan. However, just because a plan in hindsight appears to be inadequate does not necessarily mean it was substandard when formulated.

- **Neglecting to recognize** and promptly treat complications.

- **Failure to transfer** the patient to the appropriate department in a timely manner, e.g., ICU.

- **Performance of unnecessary medical procedures.** Some surgeries may expose the patient to potential risks without conferring any meaningful benefit. Some common unnecessary surgeries may include tonsillectomy, appendectomy, hemorrhoidectomy, herniorrhaphy, hysterectomy, and cholecystectomy. Others, such as cardiac angioplasty and stenting, cardiac pacemakers, back surgery (including spinal fusion), hysterectomies, knee and hip replacements, and C-sections, may also be included.[15]

  Fortunately, recognition that some surgeries are not necessary can lead to changes in medical guidelines. For instance, many experts maintain that most tonsillectomies are of little or no value to the patient. In response, the Academy of Otolaryngology has changed its guidelines and no longer recommends surgery for moderate tonsillitis.[16]

- **Failure to consult** or unwarranted delay in either consulting with a specialist or obtaining the assistance of a more experienced or more highly skilled physician/surgeon.

- **Not providing needed and timely emergency care.**

- **Premature or improper discharge/release from care.**

- **Improper use of medical equipment,** including braces, straps, or restraints.

- **Use of the wrong or outdated medical equipment** and/or failure or malfunction of equipment from inadequate maintenance, calibration, or inspection.

- **Unsanitary practices** or improper or inadequate sterilization of medical equipment.

- **Improper positioning,** e.g., during surgery.

- **Attempts at procedures or treatments** beyond the training, experience, and skill of the practitioner/surgeon.

---

[15] L.L. Leape, "Unnecessary Surgery," *Health Serv Res* 24, no. 3 (Aug. 1989): 351–407 and Peter Eisler, "Six Common Surgeries Often Done Unnecessarily," *U.S.A. Today* (June 19, 2013).

[16] https://www.aafp.org/dam/AAFP/documents/patient_care/clinical_recommendations/aaohns-tonsillectomy-in-children.pdf.

- **Anesthesia errors.** Anesthesia negligence is often suspected when death, brain damage, postoperative blindness (ischemic optic neuropathy), or paralysis (nerve injury) occurs after surgery without obvious cause. Errors often include misplaced endotracheal tube, excessive administration of medication, improper use of an anesthetic, failure to monitor, failure to reverse the action of certain anesthetics, or aspiration of gastric contents in patients with a full stomach. Pregnant patients, the morbidly obese, trauma victims, and patients with bowel obstruction are all considered to have a full stomach.

  Another significant area of liability involves issues regarding proper management of cardiac arrest and resuscitation.

  The facts underlying anesthesia malpractice are almost never contained in the anesthesia records. These cases most often engage the use of early depositions taken of the physician defendants, CRNA, PACU nurses, and others in an attempt to uncover evidence of possible negligence.

MEDICATION MALPRACTICE

Medication error is the most common type of medical error and denotes a preventable adverse event. It is "the failure of a planned action to be completed as intended or the use of a wrong plan to achieve an aim."[17]

Medication malpractice may be reflected by:

- **Negligent drug treatment**, e.g., improperly prescribing contraindicated drugs or drugs that are known to have adverse side effects for the patient's medical conditions and/or adverse interactions with other prescribed medications.
- **Improper administration** of a drug, e.g., wrong patient, wrong medication, wrong timing, wrong route and improper monitoring procedures as well as the wrong dosage. Drugs with a narrow therapeutic window like warfarin and acetaminophen dominate this list.
- **Failure to anticipate or recognize** the development of known risks, complications, or side effects from medications, e.g., heparin-induced thrombocytopenia, hyponatremia from large doses of oxytocin, or severe internal bleeding from thrombolytics.
- **Dereliction of duty to consult** the *Physicians' Desk Reference* (*PDR*) or another authoritative source for contraindications and adverse effects. The *PDR* can be used as evidence of, but does not firmly establish, the standard of care.

---

[17] Institute of Medicine, *To Err Is Human: Building a Safer Health System* (Washington: National Academy Press, 2000).

- **Neglecting to advise** patients of potential side effects or interactions with other drugs.

- **Masking symptoms** via over-sedation from narcotics, barbiturates, and/ or tranquilizers. "Masking the symptoms or signs of a disease process creates a false sense of security, a sense that all is well when the disease may be progressing and getting worse, especially in patients with abdominal pain of unknown cause. Antibiotics are contraindicated in undiagnosed abdominal pain as they suppress the infection, mask symptoms, and delay the diagnosis. The rule is to stop the drugs; wait and re-evaluate."[18]

- **Not recognizing and treating drug interactions** in a timely fashion. Serious reactions, such as those that result between rifampin and warfarin or between linezolid and serotonin reuptake inhibitors like fluoxetine, should be considered and avoided if possible. Combining lithium with loop diuretics or ACE inhibitors can lead to slurred speech or seizures. Theophylline together with cimetidine can cause seizures and should be avoided if possible. Similarly, the possibility of propranolol counteracting the positive effects of albuterol should, of course, always be considered in the management of asthma. Also, ACE inhibitors with amiloride or triamterene for high blood pressure can cause high blood potassium levels.[19]

- **Failure to identify and attend drug allergies.** Penicillin and related antibiotics are the most common cause. Other drugs that often cause allergic reactions include sulfa, anticonvulsants, insulin preparations (especially animal sources of insulin), and iodinated x-ray contrast dyes.

- **Withholding needed medication,** e.g., thrombolytic therapy such as streptokinase, urokinase, or tissue plasminogen activators from a qualified patient with a developing MI or stroke. This encompasses failing to contact family members, poor documentation in patient charts regarding the start time, or withholding the drug against AHA guidelines and thereby depriving the patient of a better outcome.

- **Improperly maintaining a course** of medication/treatment when its discontinuance is indicated.

- **Illegible handwriting** which may cause the wrong medication to be given.

---

[18] Richard E. Kessler and Patrick Trese, 3, 6, 95.
[19] "Dealing with Infectious Disease," *American Medical Forensic Specialists* (Oct. 28, 2011).

- **Using inappropriate antibiotics** such as fluoroquinolones, i.e., ciprofloxacin, levofloxacin, nalidixic acid, or moxifloxacin during pregnancy, or inappropriate/ineffective antibiotics such as Kefzol/Ancef that will not cover anaerobic bacteria, i.e., the bacteroides species in an abdominal infection.

- **Failure to adequately anticoagulate.** This includes withholding or unnecessarily delaying anticoagulants and/or failing to adequately monitor INR (international normalized ratio is a way of standardizing the results of prothrombin time tests) to maintain a safe therapeutic range.

- **Off-label prescriptions.** Physicians hold an unlimited license to practice medicine. As such, they may prescribe any medication of their choosing for the benefit of their patients. The FDA cannot restrict a physician's judgment in the practice of medicine. That is true even when the medicine is prescribed for a different medical indication than that which the Food and Drug Administration (FDA) had originally approved for the drug, as listed in the *Physician's Desk Reference* (*PDR*). It remains lawful even if there is no evidence that the medication is of any proven value for the condition being treated, e.g., Paxil for weight loss, or gabapentin for migraine prophylaxis.

  For this reason, off-label prescriptions are completely legal. Furthermore, the FDA lacks the authority to regulate the practice of medicine,[20] and the Food, Drug, and Cosmetic Act of 1938 creates no physician liability for off-label prescriptions.[21] However, unapproved uses of drugs should be in accordance with the manufacturer's recommendations; otherwise, the physician's deviation from those recommendations is prima facie evidence of negligence.[22]

  Therefore, so-called off-label prescribing is not a significant malpractice liability issue unless warnings, contraindications, or dosage instructions were ignored or informed consent was not obtained.

---

[20]"Legal Status of Approved Labeling for Prescription Drugs; Prescribing for Uses Unapproved by the Food and Drug Administration," 37 Fed Reg. 16503, 16504, (July 30, 1972).

[21]J.B. Riley and P.A. Basilius, "Physicians' Liability for Off-Label Prescriptions," *Hematol Oncol News Issues* 24–27 (2007). http://www.mcguirewoods.com/news-resources/publications/health_care/Off_Label.pdf. Accessed April 10, 2012.

[22]*Mulder v. Parke Davis & Co.*, 288 Minn. 332. 181 N.W. 2d 882, 887 (1970).

Developing Defensible Monitoring Procedures

Patient monitoring is a major component in the management of both acute and chronic diseases. It is vital to patient care, assessment, and proper clinical decision making, including making appropriate referrals. Acute monitoring includes tracking by medical and nursing staff, as well as a variety of medical devices to measure physiologic variables in intensive care units, operating rooms, recovery rooms, and telemetry units. Chronic patient monitoring principles can help prevent increased damage from diseases such as diabetes, cardiovascular disease, arthritis, or depression.

MEDICOLEGAL RULES TO REDUCE MONITORING MALPRACTICE CLAIMS

Rule 1: No condition can be well-managed without being well-monitored at intervals based on a reasonable assessment of the acuity of the problem. Physicians are trained to quickly recognize changes, complications, and risks associated with the patient's condition, disease, medications, or procedures and, where reasonably necessary, should respond to those situations without delay.

Rule 2: Doctors must establish and implement a patient follow-up plan to obtain knowledge of the patient's current health status and medical needs and to perform appropriate screening tests. Screening tests ensure that patients receive reasonable protection from preventable or modifiable disease risks.

Rule 3: Some patients may be noncompliant. Doctors must recognize this and make an effort to improve compliance. This can be done by red-flagging medical records if the patient does not keep appointments or report for tests, examinations, or referrals and then by following up with a letter or e-mail or by involving family members or caretakers, if necessary.[23]

Rule 4: In complex cases or in cases that are non-responsive or inordinately slow to respond, physicians should make appropriate referral decisions based on the best interests of their patients.

The following scenarios may not be in keeping with good medical monitoring practices:

- **Neglecting to develop,** document, or implement an adequate and proper follow-up plan. An example would include the failure to admit a young post-tonsillectomy patient with a history of obstructive sleep apnea to monitor overnight for post-operative respiratory failure.

- **Failure to recognize** that current treatment is no longer beneficial, or that mounting evidence suggests taking a new clinical direction, e.g., indications for new diagnostics or a change in the course of treatment.

---

[23] R.A. Ulmer, *Legal Guide to Patient Compliance* (John Wiley & Sons, 1996), 39–40.

- **Non-action to prevent** known complications or conditions in the wake of known risk factors, e.g., DVT, developing stroke, or recurrent hypoglycemia from insulin or glipizide use, etc.
- **Not applying** accepted monitoring principles relating to a specific drug, e.g., chloramphenicol, coumadin/warfarin, nitroprusside, etc.
- In an intensive care unit, the **failure to properly monitor** the following practices are often sources of malpractice claims: feeding, analgesia (pain management), sedation, thromboembolic prophylaxis, head-of-bed elevation, pressure ulcer prevention, and/or glucose control.
- **Improperly or inadequately responding** to current, new, or changed complaints, symptoms, signs, risk factors, etc., e.g., pain that remains unusually strong or worsens despite narcotic pain meds, or a condition that worsens, e.g., abdominal pain that spreads from one quadrant to another.
- **Ignoring or not recognizing** and properly managing complications from a procedure, e.g., an ongoing infectious process following surgery, or not properly managing signs and symptoms of adverse side effects or known risks of medication use in a timely manner.
- **Not paying sufficient attention** to or dealing appropriately with the patient's status such as weight loss, metabolic or respiratory alkalosis/acidosis, changes in input and output (volume depletion or dehydration), nutritional status, etc.
- **Improper outpatient care** to properly manage and prevent complications and deterioration of a condition which results in the need for hospitalization or a specialist's care.
- **Failure to see the patient at optimal intervals, to** or perform timely re-evaluation of the patient's status, e.g., scheduling appointments too far into the future to properly monitor the condition.
- **No adequate follow-up** or an unreasonable delay in notifying a patient of abnormal lab results, pathology specimens, staging results, etc.
- **Omitting to contact the patient** or failing to pursue appropriate testing when indicated. The physician should not be liable for a patient who does not follow up on a scheduled lab test if the doctor has informed the patient of the consequences of delay or of not obtaining the test. The patient's duty is to comply, and if that patient has made an informed decision not to follow through with the testing procedures recommended and documented by their doctor, they must take responsibility for that choice.

- **Failing to advise patients** of a change in the doctor's opinion regarding the patient's current condition following review of the medical records.
- **Not following up** on missed or canceled subsequent appointments after the last visit. (See also "Abandonment," p. 77.)
- **Failure to properly supervise** and protect the patient, especially in a long-term care facility.
- **Failure to properly limit** any "watch and observe" time frame.
- **Accusations of referral mismanagement may be brought if there is:**
  - a failure to enlist the assistance of experts or to obtain a referral in a timely manner, or if there is unnecessary delay in obtaining a consultation or referral to a specialist
  - a referral to the wrong type of specialist, which puts the patient on a wrong path and wastes time in not considering viable alternatives
  - a negligent referral, i.e., referral to a practitioner who the doctor should have known was likely not competent or who has a history of problems in delivering the standard of care
  - a failure to track referrals, i.e., checking whether the patient made and kept the appointment
  - a failure to document that the consultant's report was received, read, and evaluated, as well as whether the recommendations were acted upon;
  - a failure to follow-up with necessary appointment(s)
  - a failure of the specialist to communicate with the referring physician in an appropriate way
- **Failure to provide continuity of care:** Being unavailable (without backup on call), not rendering or refusing needed care, not answering calls, and not examining or seeing the patient as often as necessary to adequately manage their problem are all a lack of due diligence in caring for the patient. (See also "Abandonment," p. 77.)

Preventing Employee Negligence

An employee's carelessness may be considered the doctor's carelessness as well. When an employee commits a careless act in the scope of their employment, the employer may be liable, even though the employer may have done nothing wrong. The rationale is that, in a sense, it is the employer who hires the employee, sets the employee into motion, and has the power to control that person's acts. Therefore, the employer is legally responsible for those acts.

If the employee's carelessness in their job is established, the employer is liable for that carelessness. For example, during an operation if a swab, sponge, or instrument is left in the patient's body due to a miscount by a circulating nurse, the surgeon in charge is responsible. This also often applies to an attending physician or to a fully-licensed monitoring physician when a surgical resident is negligent in the O.R.

These types of cases may also be based on improper and inadequate employee training or supervision or be a result of providing services beyond the recognized scope of expertise, e.g., an employee who plays doctor by giving advice on the phone or during a face-to-face with the patient.

Even when an employee is careless, the employer is not without recourse. The employer has every right to sue that negligent employee for reimbursement. As a practical matter, most employers do not choose to bring such an action because they have insurance coverage for employee negligence. Also, doing so may give plaintiff's lawyer more ammunition.

Res Ipsa Loquitur

When things inexplicably go horribly wrong, this is typically the result of improper management at some point. The manager who is in control of the circumstances at that time is assumed to be legally responsible under this principle. As such, the manager must show that he or she was *not* negligent in order to avoid losing this type of case.

The Latin phrase *res ipsa loquitur* means "the thing speaks for itself." Lawyers love flaunting their education as much as doctors, but readers should not allow the Latin phrase to mislead them into thinking it is a complicated legal concept. It simply means that it is obvious that something bad happened and that it couldn't have happened without someone committing an error. (See examples on the following page.)

When patients enter a hospital or other medical facility for treatment of a medical problem, they do not expect to leave with additional injuries, infections, or serious conditions that may occur during the course of their stay and that are unrelated to their initial condition. More often than not, the exact means by which such injuries happened is obscure and extremely difficult to prove.

Consequently, this rule of evidence allows special types of cases (see examples on the following page) to move forward without requiring injured patients to prove exactly how the negligence or malpractice occurred. This is deemed fair and just under certain circumstances because the law assumes that the harm would not have happened unless someone was careless. In any event, such cases are, however, decidedly rare.

The rule further assumes that the person responsible is the one who had control of the patient or mechanism that caused the injuries. Therefore, the patient does not have to prove negligence; instead, the person in charge must demonstrate that they were not careless or negligent in order to win the case.

Res ipsa loquitur is not only a rule of common law, but also a rule of common sense. The following *res ipsa*-type injuries are examples of implied negligence or carelessness:

- performance of surgery on the wrong side of the body, on the wrong body part, at the wrong spinal disk level, or on the wrong patient
- stage IV pressure ulcers and bed wounds—almost always the result of inadequate nursing care
- foreign objects retained in body cavities after surgery
- broken bones or dislocated joints that were not present when the patient entered the facility
- nerve injuries—often due to improper positioning during surgery
- the presence of burns following a medical procedure, especially in a body part unconnected to the area of treatment
- transfusion of the wrong blood type
- collapsed lung following a shoulder injection

Malpractice Through Nonclinical Negligence

Nonclinical negligence takes place when there is a violation of legal standards rather than medical standards.

Record-Keeping / Documentation

Both state and federal laws mandate the accurate, detailed, legible, and reasonably contemporaneous documentation of the doctor-patient encounter. Well-organized and well-written medical records form the factual basis for planning the patient's continuing care.

These records inform other health care providers of the course of the patient's evaluation and care, are utilized for malpractice defense and quality assurance, and support billing and reimbursement. They also result in higher care quality and improved continuity of care.

On the other hand, doctors are not stenographers. Good charting takes time and it is always possible to improve upon a chart, so there is always some reason for outside parties to express dissatisfaction.

As a matter of course, in a malpractice case the credibility of the medical record is weakened if the physician's progress notes are not consistent with the nurse's notes or other records, or if medically important information is missing from the record.

MEDICOLEGAL DOCUMENTATION RULES TO REDUCE THE RISK OF RECORD-KEEPING MALPRACTICE CLAIMS

Rule 1: The doctor has a duty to maintain charts that are reasonably complete and accurately reflect the evaluation and treatment of patients.

Rule 2: The golden rule of documentation is: "If it wasn't documented, it wasn't done." While not entirely true, jurors tend to believe that if it was important, it would have been documented.

Rule 3: A poorly-kept record is not proof of negligence by itself, but plaintiff's counsel can offer it to support a claim of substandard care.

The following examples would be considered below the standard of care:

- **Failure to chart or document** clinically significant data including referrals, results, or consultations. An example regarding peptic ulcer disease (PUD) might include the failure to document the eradication of H pylori with urea breath test (UBT), fecal stool antigen, or repeat upper endoscopy with biopsy in a patient with bleeding PUD. The persistence of *H. pylori* usually stems from a failure to use a multidrug regimen to eradicate the infection.[24]

- **Improper or negligent record-keeping**, e.g., unreasonably illegible, inaccurate, or incomplete records, or missing documents.

- **Falsifying the recorded chart** of evidence, for example, intentional alteration, falsification, or destruction of medical records to avoid liability. This includes intentionally reporting an incident inaccurately. (See also "Fraudulent record-keeping," p. 79.)

---

[24]"Peptic Ulcer Disease," *American Medical Forensic Specialists* (Dec. 3, 2008).

Failure to Obtain Consent

Informed consent originates from the legal and ethical right of patients to direct what happens to their bodies and from the noble duty of the physician to follow that fundamental principle through educating and by involving the patient in their own health care decisions. (See also "Chapter 6: Informed Consent.")

Consent may be implicit (the patient complies by doing as the doctor requests), or explicit (the patient literally grants permission either orally or by written agreement).

MEDICOLEGAL RULES TO REDUCE THE RISK OF INFORMED CONSENT CLAIMS

Rule 1: Good clinical practice and informed consent are inseparable.

Rule 2: The patient must consent to any nonemergency or nonroutine procedure. The failure to document the patient's actual agreement or consent to nonemergency/nonroutine care is negligence.

Rule 3: The failure to divulge adequate and accurate information to which the patient is ethically, morally and legally entitled may indicate negligence. It is generally not a good or accepted practice to fail to fully advise patients of the issues listed below:

- **their current condition** as well as any recommended procedures or treatments
- **the inherent** benefits, material risks, and dangers associated with the recommended procedure or treatment as well as the probability of success
- **any reasonably available and viable alternative procedures** along with their risks and benefits
- **the consequences of refusing** or failing to obtain the recommended test or procedure
- **the consequences of delaying or refusing** the treatment or procedure
- **a doctor's limited experience** in performing the procedure[25]

(See also "Chapter 9: Consents and Releases.")

The patient's consent can be negated by bad faith, misrepresentation, or fraud on the part of the doctor, and/or the patient's inability to understand

---

[25] See R.A. Dudley et al., "Selective Referral to High Volume Hospitals,: *JAMA* 283, no. 9 (2000): 1159 and J.D. Birkmeyer, "High Risk Surgery," *JAMA* 283, no. 9 (2000): 1191.

the consent due to incapacity or poor language skills. That is why in seeking the patient's signature on the consent document, it is usually a good idea to include a statement to the effect that prior to signing the patient had ample opportunity to read the document, to ask any questions, to understand, or to request clarification of the information and answers given.

Misrepresentation / False Advertising / Fraud

A doctor or doctor's group that misrepresents their credentials, experience, and/or skills, creates a cause of action for misrepresentation and false advertising. If the patient has relied on the misrepresentations and has received treatment or care for their condition, then the doctor or practice may be held liable. Charges for fraud may also be filed.

Breach of Contract

Breach of contract results from a failure to deliver on a warranty or promise of a specific result or cure. Such promises are often the result of:

a) Overly optimistic predictions.

b) The use of terms such as "permanent and irreversible" and other similar descriptions in sterilization procedures are often used to imply that the person can never again procreate. Since even a properly performed tubal ligation, for instance, may not render the patient permanently unable to conceive, an informed consent form is a good remedy here.

c) Phrases like "trust me" can create both a promise and a contract relationship in which specific results have been assured.

d) Misrepresentation of an existing fact.

e) Advertising, especially in the cosmetic surgical field which uses deceptive photographs or misleading claims such as "look as young as you feel" or "the look you've always wanted," can seem to minimize the risks and dangers of invasive procedures.

It is usually a good idea to document in some appropriate way that the patient was made aware of the possibility of an outcome that is less than what is desired.

Note that advertising itself is usually too general to comprise an offer to a contract. It is usually viewed merely as an invitation to make an offer; as with products for sale on eBay, everyone is invited to make an offer.

Breach of Confidentiality/Improper Disclosure

When an employee or the public accesses a patient's diagnosis, condition, or medical history, it is a breach of confidentiality. Every patient has the right to expect a reasonable effort to maintain confidentiality from the doctor or health care facility. Today this happens most frequently when there is improper access to patient databases via computerized record-keeping. Unfortunately, the nature of electronic communications is that they are inherently prone to interception and misuse.

Psychiatrists in particular must weigh the right of privacy against the public's right to know if the patient is a potential danger to someone or is plotting a crime. When confronted by this kind of dilemma, physicians should know that it is always wise to seek legal advice from their attorneys or malpractice insurance carriers.

Breach of Duty to the Patient

The following represent violations of legal duties:

- **Unauthorized release** of protected health information. A patient cannot file a lawsuit for violation of HIPAA. Some states, however, have established privacy rights that allow the filing of a civil lawsuit.

- **Breach of the doctor-patient contract.**

- Where there is a duty to test, the **failure to inform** a parent of the likelihood of fetal abnormality in a timely manner, e.g., elevated alpha fetoprotein.[26]

- **Failure to inform of diminished capabilities.** Several states now require doctors to inform and warn their patients of potential driving dangers when taking a drug or drugs with the propensity to cause drowsiness, dizziness, fainting, lightheadedness, sedation, or altered consciousness. In those states it may be wise to have such patients sign a paper acknowledging that they have received the compulsory warning. It may also be prudent to advise the patient to rely on their spouse or another person to handle driving chores for the likely duration of the anticipated impairment. Call your malpractice carrier for more specific guidance.

---

[26]*LeJeune Road Hosp. v. Watson*, 171 St.2d 202 (Fla., 1965), and Miselman v. Crown Heights Hosp., 34 N.E. 2d 367 (N.Y. 1941); Cf. Muse v. Charter Hospital of Winston-Salem, Inc. 452 S.E. 2d 589 (1995).

ABANDONMENT

Once a doctor-patient relationship has been established, the physician is legally and ethically bound to render medical services until the relationship is properly terminated. Abandonment occurs when a doctor withdraws from a case without proper notice or adequate time for the patient to secure another doctor. Abandonment also happens when the doctor is unavailable for an unreasonable amount of time when the patient needs care. In these situations, the doctor is essentially deserting the patient. Abandonment is a violation of the physician's commitment to provide continuity of care in the doctor-patient contract. There are two types of abandonment: (A) intentional and (B) inadvertent.

A. Intentional abandonment. When the doctor refuses to take or return calls or does not see the patient or render needed care, that is intentional abandonment. It is an improper termination of the doctor-patient relationship and is often related to:

- the patient's failure to pay the doctor's fee
- an insurance company's refusal to make payment
- personality or ethical conflicts
- a social event

Juries have little sympathy for physicians who deny necessary care to a patient because of an inability to pay the bill. Intentional abandonment can give rise to punitive damages or a claim of negligence and, where the law recognizes it, a separate cause of action for breaching the physician-patient contract.

B. Inadvertent or negligent abandonment. Here, due to a misunderstanding, the doctor fails to secure back-up coverage when he/she is unavailable, or unintentionally abandons the patient by failing to apply appropriate monitoring principles by:

- terminating care due to an error in judgment
- failing to see the patient as often as is indicated by the diagnosis and treatment plan
- not responding to an emergency call or urgent situation
- failing to perform adequate follow-up such as renewing needed prescriptions or providing periodic monitoring of the patient's condition or proper prescription dose
- failing to inform the patient about the need for continuing treatment
- refusing to let the patient talk to office or hospital medical personnel

Abandonment happens more often than you would think. In February 2018 a jury awarded over \$43 million in damages after a patient in an induced coma was abandoned without further treatment for over a month.[27]

As is often the case, the plaintiff entered into an agreement with the defendant's insurer guaranteeing a \$4 million payout to the plaintiff regardless of the verdict but would also limit the damages to \$9 million if the jury's verdict exceeded that amount.

Breach of Duty to the Public

In addition to their fiduciary duty to patients, doctors have the responsibility to protect and promote the health and well-being of the public. The following examples demonstrate a breach of public duty and, as such, could be negligence, but not malpractice:

- failure to abide by state licensure provisions and hospital accreditation guidelines[28]
- failure to report certain communicable diseases or specific injuries, e.g., gunshot or knife wounds, child abuse, substance abuse, etc.
- failure to warn or prevent exposure to communicable diseases
- failure to report a patient experiencing periodic loss of consciousness

Every state restricts drivers from having a license if they suffer from loss of consciousness, e.g., epilepsy. A seizure-free period of time is usually required before a driver's license can be issued. Whether a neurologist owes a duty to a third party for failing to report a patient for having a condition causing loss of consciousness is the primary legal question. This issue is unsettled with courts ruling in both directions. It would be prudent to err on the side of caution and report patients with epilepsy to the appropriate state agency.

To my knowledge, no liability has been imposed upon physicians to warn the public about any medical concerns regarding a patient's inability to drive safely due to drug addiction or alcoholism.

---

[27] *Billy Pierce v. East Texas Medical Center and Dr. Gary Boyd and the ETMC Digestive Disease*, 16-0853-C.

[28] *Thompson v. Sun City Community Hospital, Inc.* 688 2d 605 Ariz. 1984.

Intentional Acts

- **Battery.** This is a harmful or offensive contact that is both intentional and lacking consent. Whenever medical treatment exceeds the patient's consent, it is considered battery. For example, if a plastic surgeon operates on the right eye and while the patient is anesthetized and without consent, he operates on the left eye to improve its appearance as well. The result of such an unpermitted and unconsented performance of surgery is battery. This is true even in a case where the patient had no damages because the surgery was both successful and beneficial.

  Likewise, suppose a general surgeon does not indicate to his patient that an intern or resident will actually be performing part or all of the surgery. Without the patient's permission via consent, the surgeon may be liable for any and all potential injuries that result from the unpermitted performance of surgery.

- **Sexual misconduct** (also a form of battery). A sexual or romantic interaction between physician and patient is sexual misconduct since it is likely to exploit the vulnerability of the patient and may obscure the physician's medical judgment.[29]

- **Intentional misrepresentation.** This is a misrepresentation of fact by the doctor or staff member that the patient relies on and which results in further injury, e.g., the doctor promises a successful result from a cosmetic procedure like collagen injections, but the patient ends up deformed. Misrepresentation is usually very difficult to prove and most lawyers typically avoid these types of cases. Successful cases are more likely to involve advertisements or brochures that substantially exaggerate the expected medical outcome. For this reason, it is good practice to seek a lawyer's or a risk manager's review of any document you propose to display to the public.

- **Fraudulent record-keeping/intentional spoliation of evidence.** This involves intentionally altering, adding to, deleting from, substituting, fabricating, destroying or losing/omitting reports, radiographs, etc., from the medical record to misrepresent events in an attempt to avoid liability.

---

[29] *AMA Code of Medical Ethics* 8.14.

NOT RECOGNIZING RISKS: A CLINICAL BLIND SPOT

According to Daniel Levinson, Inspector General of the Department of Health and Human Services, it is reported that hospitals rarely change their policies or practices in order to prevent the repetition of certain harms or adverse events to patients. Similarly, hospital staff fail to report *most* events that harmed patients. How can this be? According to Mr. Levinson, the under-reporting problem is due to hospital employees not recognizing what events or occurrences could and did actually harm patients.

In addition, doctors do not always recognize that certain practices or behaviors lead to real problems and can harm their patients. The Harvard School of Public Health reported that physicians document less than 30% of their mistakes.[30] Is it any wonder that medical mistakes are reportedly the third leading cause of death in the U.S. or that 86% of physician errors in hospitals are never reported at all?[31] Physicians must recognize not only what is medically expedient for their patients, but also which other available courses of care may be safer in order to avoid needless harm to patients and to prevent lawsuits.

ASSESSING YOUR MALPRACTICE RISKS

Doctors are required to make choices every day. Some choices prevent further harm and put the patient on the road to recovery. Other choices may put the patient at risk for further harm and suffering. Each doctor chooses and directs the course of care. Why not make a safe choice on behalf of the patient, if circumstances allow? After all, that is what every doctor is trained to do and wants to do.

Consider the following example: A patient comes into the ER with severe chest pain and shortness of breath. The EKG is normal. The patient makes an earnest plea to be released in order to attend an anniversary celebration that evening. Should that patient be discharged and allowed to go home? Of course not! The risk to the patient is potentially catastrophic. The clinical benefit to the patient is virtually nonexistent. Overnight monitoring, with repeat electrocardiograms, cardiac enzymes, and/or a stress test may reveal an underlying problem and is a much safer course of care. If cardiac

---

[30]https://ethicalnag.org/2010/10/15/why-doctors-get-sued/. Last accessed June 19, 2016.

[31] Martin A. Makary and Michael Daniel, "Medical Error—The Third Leading Cause of Death in the U.S.," *BMJ* 353 (2016): i2139.

enzymes and the electrocardiogram are normal, but pain persists, a dissecting thoracic aortic aneurysm or PE, among other things, should be considered.[32]

In the preceding example, if a lawsuit resulted from sending the patient home before confirming the diagnosis, it is likely that the attorney in the closing argument would say, "This is a doctor who ignored obvious risks and harms, and plowed ahead with a clinical course that severely injured this patient." Although the correct choice sounds obvious, we read about cases just like this one much too frequently.

A brief risk assessment should be performed any time there is a significant shift in the direction of the patient's condition or care. Doctors should identify anything potentially problematic or unnecessarily risky in the recommended course of care that may increase the likelihood of a bad outcome for the patient. When risks are nearly equal to or outweigh the benefits, it is a red flag and may result in needless harm and a malpractice claim. At that point it would be wise to consider the availability of safer alternatives.

This is not an empty exercise. The analysis should be part and parcel of the legally mandated informed consent process required with any new or different course of care. (See also "Chapter 6: Informed Consent.") All too often, doctors fail to see that the course of care they have chosen is risky or potentially harmful. This blind spot may be a critical missing piece for improving both patient safety and malpractice prevention.

CONCLUSION

Knowing and understanding the causes of action for malpractice is to be forewarned and forearmed. Good and careful professional practice is the best preventative for malpractice litigation. Too many patients are injured as a result of medical negligence. Doctors should continue their quest to actively make care better and safer and will protect themselves in the process.

---

[32] Richard E. Anderson, *Medical Malpractice: A Physician's Sourcebook* (Totowa, NJ: Humana Press, 2005), 94.

BIBLIOGRAPHY

Kessler, Richard E., and Patrick Trese. *Bitter Medicine: What I've Learned and Teach about Malpractice Lawsuits and How to Avoid Them.* Create Space Independent Publishing Platform, 2012.

Medical Malpractice Law & Strategy Law Reporter.

National Medical Malpractice Review and Analysis. 2004–2012. www.juryverdictreview.com.

Reisman, Anna B., and Davis Stevens. *Telephone Medicine.* American College of Physicians, American Society of Internal Medicine, 2002.

CHAPTER 6

Informed Consent
– Medicine's Golden Rule –

"Every human being of adult years and sound mind has a right to determine what shall be done with his own body..."
— *Canterbury v. Spence,*
464 F.2d 772, 780; 150 U.S. App. DC. 263, 271 (1972)

LEGAL RATIONALE FOR INFORMED CONSENT

After a thorough examination, if the physician were the patient, he or she would want a full explanation of the risks, benefits, side effects, and known complications of any proposed procedure or treatment. This truism along with fundamentals of patient rights form the ethical framework for the legal doctrine of informed consent.

Informed consent is both a legal requirement and an ethical principle. All 50 states have enacted legislation requiring some level of informed consent. The concept of informed consent stems from an individual's fundamental right of self-determination. After all, every competent adult has a common-law right to accept or refuse any recommended medical treatment or procedure based on sufficient knowledge of the benefits, burdens, alternatives, limits, and risks involved; and it is the doctor's obligation to provide patients with that knowledge.

Informed consent necessitates that all patients be given appropriate, relevant, reasonably accurate, and unbiased information prior to making truly informed decisions regarding their own bodies.

The procedure of having to give informed consent generally does not apply to standard or routine medical practices but rather to risky, potentially harmful, or complex medical tests, treatments, or procedures, e.g., anesthesia or surgery, especially if an alternative treatment or method exists.

The legal doctrine of informed consent provides a remedy for patients with injuries that result from undisclosed risks, even if they consented to the treatment and are unable to show wrongdoing in the diagnosis or treatment. Any adverse result from a procedure that is within the realm of dangers and risks involved, and which was not revealed to the patient, may, depending on the jurisdiction, be compensable. This consequence of liability is intentional as an additional legal incentive for doctors to be fully forthcoming and honest with patients about any complicated or risky procedures/treatments the doctor recommends.

Therefore, all significant risks associated with the procedure or treatment need to be disclosed. (See "Material Risks in the Procedure or Treatment," p. 87.) After these disclosures have been made, the patient has the option of voluntarily accepting the inherent risks disclosed in the competent delivery of that procedure or treatment, or the patient may refuse care.

Informed consent should never be an attempt to deceive the patient into adopting a certain point of view. The law dictates that no adult should be forced to submit to unwanted treatment and that patients should never be manipulated into doing so based on false, inadequate, or inaccurate medical information. This is also a bedrock principle of medical ethics.

By giving patients all the relevant data and facts needed to decide whether to undergo any proposed medical test, treatment, or procedure that is potentially harmful, and by letting them make the choice, both the legal requirements and ethical principles are satisfied. In addition, this type of openness and honesty from the physician further solidifies the doctor-patient relationship.

To this extent, physicians must work in partnership with patients to ensure that consent is based on valid and adequate information.[1]

Clinical Example

Let's assume that a patient is at simultaneous risk for clotting, e.g., from atrial fibrillation or obesity, and also for bleeding while recovering from a recent surgery. Deciding whether to give heparin in such a scenario is complicated because both withholding and administering anticoagulation carry risks.

According to medical experts, the risk of stroke in patients with atrial fibrillation who do not receive anticoagulation is about 5%. Therefore, the risk of stroke for a patient who does not receive anticoagulation for a week is less than 1%. Some doctors may not appreciate this relatively small risk and may mistakenly insist on administering heparin to patients who are at higher risk for bleeding, e.g., due to hypertension, a history of previous

---

[1] Alan J. Williams, *Physician Protect Thyself* (Denver, CO: Margol Publishing, 2007).

GI bleeds, recent surgery, etc. This medical approach may be riskier than withholding anticoagulants and therefore can be inappropriate.[2]

If, under the circumstances described above, such a patient were to bleed out as a result of heparin administration, a lawsuit citing the lack of informed consent as well as malpractice might be brought. Risks of both receiving anticoagulation therapy as well as the risks of withholding the therapy need to be weighed and discussed with the patient and the immediate family. That process should also be thoroughly documented in the medical records.

Doctors who fail to have such conversations with the family and other treating physicians, or do not adequately document the discussion of the risks and benefits of anticoagulation administration in the medical record, are at increased risk for a lawsuit.[3]

TABLE 6.1: THE COMPLETE PROCESS OF INFORMED CONSENT

a) Explain the nature and purpose of the procedure and available alternatives in simple and straightforward terms.

b) Discuss the associated benefits, risks, and dangers. There is no obligation to discuss every possible risk, but the significant, severe, unpleasant, and otherwise negative aspects (also known as the material risks) associated with the procedure should be clear.

c) Discuss the probability of success and limitations associated with the procedure/treatment as well as the likely costs.

d) Explain reasonable alternative treatments, if any, that are available.

e) Describe potential consequences of doing nothing, of failing to obtain the procedure, or of delaying the procedure.

f) If asked, the doctor is obligated to disclose his particular experience and personal rate of success with any given procedure.

g) Have a discussion with and answer any questions the patient may have.

h) Conduct an assessment of the patient's competency that includes their actual comprehension of the risks, benefits, and limitations of the recommended procedure or treatment.

---

[2] Faiza Patten, experts@theexpertinstitute.com, "Hematologist Advises on Anticoagulation in Patients at Risk for Stroke" (June 2, 2014). http://www.theexpertinstitute.com/case-studies/hematology-expert-witness-advises-on-anticoagulation-in-patients-at-risk-for-stroke/.

[3] Ibid.

i) Obtain the patient's signature on a consent form that identifies and fully discloses the material risks, limitations, potential complications, and dangers of the medical procedure. The more thorough the form, the better. A thorough and signed informed consent form, indicating that the patient is fully aware of the potential problems and voluntarily accepts the risks, is a document that offers powerful protection should any of those risks or dangers materialize. The form should include clauses such as: "I have had the opportunity to raise questions and all my questions have been answered fully and to my satisfaction in terms that I understand before signing this document" and "At the time of my signature, all blanks on this document were filled in legibly except the signature itself and the date."

j) Further document this process in the SOAP notes or as a supplement to the EHR.

If a reasonable person/patient who was given the information as outlined above would consent to the procedure, then the informed consent process, i.e., that the doctor informed the patient and the patient consented, is valid and complete in most states.

BRIEF HISTORY OF INFORMED CONSENT

Consider the following early example of failure to give informed consent. In the late 1700s, the case of *Slater v. Baker and Stapleton*[4] involved a patient with a broken leg. When the leg had healed to the point that it would bear weight, the patient dragged himself over to the local physician. The physician looked at the leg, removed the bandages, and applied a "heavy steel thing that had teeth and would stretch or lengthen the leg."[5] The physician also re-broke the leg, without telling the patient first. This did not please the patient.

As a result, the patient's attorney made a unique and unprecedented argument. Instead of contending that the doctor should make restitution because the injuries were a result of the doctor's treatment, he called expert witnesses (other doctors) who testified they would not have re-broken the leg under the same circumstances and would have secured the patient's consent before proceeding. The courts subsequently found the doctor

---

[4] *Slater v Baker and Stapleton* [1767] 8 Geo 111 860–863.
[5] Ibid.

negligent. The other doctors said that the care provided was below the standard of the profession and added that, "It was reasonable that a patient should be told what was about to be done with him."[6]

This one case set a precedent for three important modern legal developments:

1. **Expert witnesses:** doctors who testified both for and against the defendant doctor
2. **Medical standards:** contemporary standards of care were utilized as a method of proving negligence
3. **Informed consent:** the importance of explaining to patients in advance of what was going to happen to them during medical treatment

VITAL INFORMATION THAT MUST BE DISCLOSED

Every physician has a duty to reveal a sufficient amount of information to enable patients to make a reasonably informed decision.

Why This Procedure Is Recommended

First, the physician must include information regarding the nature and purpose of the proposed procedure or treatment.

Material Risks in the Procedure or Treatment
FOR PROCEDURES

It clearly seems prohibitive and unrealistic to expect physicians to discuss every possible risk of a proposed procedure, no matter how small or remote. According to the law, not all risks must be disclosed. However, the law does insist that all *material risks* be revealed but does not specifically define the term. It should be noted that courts have fairly interpreted material risks to mean significant risks that a reasonable person would want to be made aware of before deciding to undergo or reject a recommended procedure.

Once again, the legal definition and court definitions offer very little meaningful guidance or advice to physicians about how to educate their patients. Therefore, it is a good protective strategy to disclose all risks that are likely to be severe or unpleasant, e.g., pain, numbness, scarring, in addition to those that may cause any potential loss of function. Any risk of a prolonged, difficult, or potentially incomplete recovery should also be acknowledged.

---

[6] Ibid.

FOR TREATMENTS

Again, all material risks must be divulged. With respect to medications, it has generally been accepted that a drug manufacturer has no duty to warn individual patients of associated risks and side effects of their medications. The manufacturer's duty is limited to properly informing the doctor of the inherent risks and dangers.

This theory further supports the view of the doctor as a "learned intermediary" who uses the information from the pharmaceutical companies to evaluate the risks and benefits of a particular course of care for a specific patient. With few exceptions, it is entirely the doctor's responsibility to inform patients of the hazards inherent in any prescribed medication.

Therefore, when physicians prescribe a medication that is associated with significant side effects or risks, or is experimental in nature, informed consent should be obtained from the patient.

SPECIAL CIRCUMSTANCES

There are some exceptions. According to most courts of law, certain risks are not required to be disclosed to patients under specific circumstances. These include:

- Risks in emergency treatment for serious injuries or as a result of a grave condition. Consent is implied by law in an emergency for public policy reasons. For example, in the case of a patient who presents to the ER with a traumatic aortic tear, no consent is needed for emergency surgery. However, once stabilized, it may be wise to advise the patient of the risks regarding postoperative infection and other complications.[7]

- Risks that are known to the patient or that are so obvious that they are presumed to be known.

- Risks that are commonly known to be a possibility but are relatively remote.

- Risks that are unknown to the physician or could not be ascertained through the exercise of ordinary caution.

Potential Benefits, Limits, Costs, and Chances for Success

In addition to discussing the risks inherent in a proposed procedure or treatment, the physician must also explain its reasonably foreseeable benefits and limits. Full disclosure should include the costs of the treatment or procedure and the likelihood of success.

---

[7] James E. Schutte, *Preventing Malpractice Suits. A Handbook for Doctors and Those Who Work with Them* (Seattle: Hogrefe & Huber Publishers, 1995), 88.

Alternative Reasonable Treatments/Procedures

A patient has a duty to disclose all information necessary for the doctor to make a diagnosis and determine a course of treatment. In return, the doctor has a duty to evaluate and disclose all courses of treatment that are medically reasonable under the circumstances (along with their risks and benefits).

In short, the patient should be informed not only of the procedure that the physician recommends, but also of other reasonable alternatives that the physician is not recommending. If the physician does not discuss these reasonable alternatives, the plaintiff's attorney can argue that the doctor effectively made the decision for the patient.

Risks of Noncompliance

Similarly, the risks or dangers inherent in doing nothing, not obtaining the procedure, or delaying the procedure must be explained to the patient. (See Table 6.1, p. 85.)

PATIENT MUST BE COMPETENT TO CONSENT

Upon disclosure of all the necessary information, the doctor should have a discussion with the patient to answer any questions the patient may still have. Thereafter, the physician must make an evaluation about whether the patient is rational and has a genuine understanding of the recommended procedure, its risks, benefits, and limitations prior to securing what should be knowledgeable consent.

THE PATIENT ACCEPTS THE PROCEDURE OR REJECTS IT

Finally, after a competent patient has been adequately educated and informed of the risks and alternatives to the procedure, in addition to any risks in refusing or delaying the procedure (even if it is to obtain a second opinion), the physician must secure the patient's actual consent or refusal to undergo that procedure/treatment.

OBTAIN CONSENT AT AN OPTIMAL PLACE AND TIME

The law finds it acceptable for the physician to give informed consent any time before the procedure starts and the process may take place at any location.

Nevertheless, the informed consent process should ideally be conducted during an office visit days or weeks before the scheduled procedure. When it is done in the hospital, or worse yet, in a pre-op area minutes before the procedure is performed, it appears to be rushed with undue pressure placed on the patient. Clearly, anyone who is in an embarrassing gown and lying atop a gurney in an uncomfortably cold hallway probably feels powerless and vulnerable. Furthermore, a patient in this situation is likely to be experiencing some degree of emotional distress induced by anxiety and fear, and may therefore understandably be unable to fully concentrate. The patient may even be partially sedated and/or feel coerced just to sign the form and get on with it.

Although a physician has a duty to inform the patient, no law currently exists that requires the physician to personally inform the patient. However, prudent policy dictates that the doctor should play a primary role in informing the patient and should be present when the patient signs the consent form. Delegating these duties would, at a minimum, appear to be bad form or, worse, give the doctor the appearance of being uninterested and uncaring.

Documenting the Informed Consent Process

True informed consent means the voluntary, knowledgeable assent from the individual to be treated/diagnosed after he or she has been given an adequate disclosure of information and an opportunity to engage in a question and answer session. The disclosure itself should be by way of oral discussion and in a written document.

The physician should verbally explain the purpose, benefits, and limits of the procedure, and give special attention to the associated risks and complications of the proposed procedure to the patient in words that the patient can understand. Next, this discussion should be documented in the SOAP notes (if used) or EHR.

In addition, the physician should have the patient read and review a written consent form and thereafter secure the patient's signature. Many states give substantial weight to signed consent forms in assessing whether informed consent was actually given. Although no single form can adequately replace a full and complete discussion of the procedures, a signed informed consent form can wield significant power as a legal defense under these circumstances. (See also "Chapter 9: Consents and Releases" and the Appendix.)

The informed consent form gives patients the truth and should not unreasonably withhold any information about all the material or serious risks and known complications of the procedure. This includes the limitations of a proposed treatment or procedure, as well as the possible benefits and the alternative treatments available. The unmitigated truth in an easy to read and understand form is the physician's best friend in preventing and defending claims where patients allege that risks were not explained to them. (See Table 6.1, p. 85, and "Chapter 9: Consents and Releases.")

The informed consent document is vital if a trial takes place years after the procedure, because a jury may be reluctant to take the doctor's word that the patient gave verbal consent. Without written documentation, the plaintiff's lawyer can argue that there is no hard evidence that any material risks were ever disclosed. Finally, informed consent forms themselves are not written in stone. They should be updated frequently and, in many instances, customized to the particular procedure planned.

WHICH OF THE PATIENT'S DOCTORS MUST OBTAIN INFORMED CONSENT?

Regarding surgery or a specialized procedure, there is some question about who is responsible for obtaining the consent of the patient. The basic rule is that responsibility lies with the doctor who is to perform the recommended diagnostic test or medical procedure. Thus, when a general practitioner refers a patient to a surgeon, the duty falls to the surgeon to explain the risks and dangers of the procedure to be performed and to obtain consent. No other health care provider is in a better position to disclose the benefits and burdens associated with that particular surgery than the specialist.

CONCLUSION

It is every physician's obligation to properly inform the patient of material or significant risks. The failure to do so may have serious consequences and the potential to result in a legitimate case for failure to give informed consent or even for claims of battery, fraud, or conspiracy.[8]

The patient assumes all the risks and complications of a competently performed procedure with a signed informed consent form. While it is true that the doctrine of "informed consent" can, under narrow circumstances,

---

[8] See, e.g., Cruzan v. Dir., Mo. Dept. of Health, 497 U.S. 261, 269 (1990), "Every human being of adult years and sound mind has a right to determine what shall be done with his own body; and a surgeon who performs an operation without his patient's consent commits an assault, for which he is liable in damages," *Id.* (quoting Schloendorff v. Soc'y of N.Y. Hosp., 105 N.E. 92, 93 (1914)).

create some legal bumps for doctors, it is also clear that a signed medical release form that acknowledges informed consent, resolves far more issues than it creates. (See also "Chapter 9: Consents and Releases" and "Chapter 13: The Physician's Defenses.")

TABLE 6.2: MEDICAL INTERVENTIONS THAT REQUIRE WRITTEN INFORMED CONSENT PER THE HARVARD MEDICAL INSTITUTIONS[9]

a) All surgical procedures performed under general or spinal anesthesia and selected procedures performed under local anesthesia.

b) Selected biopsies and excisions including bone marrow.

c) Cardiac catheterizations and angiography.

d) All major endoscopies.

e) Bronchograms, lymphangiograms, myelograms, pneumoencephalograms, splenograms, ventriculogram, and radiation therapy.

f) Extracorporeal and peritoneal dialysis.

g) Cancer chemotherapy.

h) Electroconvulsive therapy.

i) HIV testing.

j) Blood and blood product use, including blood donation and autologous and other blood transfusions.

k) Major radiologic and/or imaging procedures involving the use of contrast media.

l) Medications and/or other therapeutics with the potential for particularly severe side effects.

TABLE 6.3: MEDICAL BATTERY OR NEGLIGENT FAILURE TO OBTAIN INFORMED CONSENT

A medical battery claim or negligent failure to obtain informed consent is established when:

a) A physician-patient relationship exists giving the physician a duty to disclose risk information as well as possible available alternatives.

b) There is either a failure to provide material information regarding its purpose, risks, benefits, and/or alternatives, including noncompliance or delay in obtaining the procedure; or undue influence, coercion, or misinformation was used to obtain the consent.

---

[9] Risk Management Foundation of the Harvard Medical Institutions for the benefit of its affiliates (Mar. 1990).

c) With full disclosure, a reasonable patient would reject the procedure (objective standard) or, having had the information provided, this patient would not have consented to the procedure (subjective standard).

d) One or more of the undisclosed risks develop causing injury or damage to the patient, so that the failure to disclose this information was a foreseeable and direct cause of the injury and damages.

BIBLIOGRAPHY

Forum. Risk Management Foundation of the Harvard Medical Institutions, Inc. *Informed Consent Review* 11, no. 6.

Hospital Law Manual, Aspen Publications.

"Informed Consent Problems Become More Complicated." *Hospitals* (Mar. 20, 1991).

Medico-Legal Primer. 1st ed. American College of Legal Medicine Foundation, 1991.

Ophthalmologists Mutual Insurance Company (OMIC). www.omic.com.

Treatise on Health Care Law. Matthew Bender and Co., Inc.

Williams, Alan J. *Physician, Protect Thyself.* Denver, CO: Margol Publishing, 2007.

=

Maximum Malpractice Protection

CHAPTER 7

Practice Structure
– The Starting Point for Asset Preservation –

THE BIG PICTURE

One of the first decisions that any practicing doctor and business owner has to make is how the business should be structured. This is the first essential step toward protection of personal possessions and business assets. Regrettably, most doctors fail to address this need until it is too late. DO NOT hesitate. See "Bonus tips" in Chapter 16 and follow through.

Every business must adopt some legal configuration. That choice, once made, will have ramifications for many years to come. The goal of this chapter is to have those ramifications be mostly positive ones.

All businesses are formed under state law and are governed by the Uniform Commercial Code (UCC) and/or other uniform codes in every state except Louisiana.

Key Considerations

Seven core issues must be considered and carefully weighed before determining which business form to adopt. The business organizations that a health care practice can take deal with each separate issue differently. Before embarking on establishing a sole proprietorship, a form of partnership or corporation, or a limited liability company, the unique positive and negative qualities for each issue must be evaluated in the context of the prioritized goals to be achieved and the specific type of business to be formed in order to determine which business structure would be best to accomplish the sought-after goals. Those specific issues are:

- taxation
- liability
- risk and control
- expense and formality
- transferability
- degree of protection for personal assets
- continuity of existence

The doctor's business structure can and should allow for legal separation of personal property and resources from business assets. Mixing of personal assets with business assets, as in a solo practice or sole proprietorship, is counterproductive and places personal finances and possessions unnecessarily at risk. The right practice structure can be a safe-harbor for many assets.

Additionally, the doctor's practice form should ideally possess considerable business and legal advantages under the circumstances with few disadvantages, such as paying a higher corporate tax rate, having a complicated set-up, time-consuming regulatory compliance issues, dual accounting fees, or expensive ongoing or regular attorney involvement. (See "Types of Business Organizations" on the following page.)

Biggest Perils Facing Your Practice

The greatest threat to any doctor's savings and assets is from taxes. Do not take this section lightly. Taxes will negatively affect physicians in every year of their work lives and possibly beyond. Limiting taxation and minimizing risks should be major goals for every doctor.

Liability, or legal responsibility, e.g., court ordered monetary obligation from a malpractice verdict, is a feared risk in clinical practice. Therefore, limited liability is a valued feature for professionals that wish to protect personal assets and businesses (non-manufacturing) that have more than a few employees. With limited liability, the owner(s) are not personally responsible for business debts and obligations. Furthermore, owners are better shielded from employee negligence liabilities.

I'm Already in Practice

If a doctor is already in private practice or is employed by a large corporation, the table is pretty well set regarding their liability exposure, taxes, and the degree of asset protection available. However, there may be wiggle room. If in private practice, the type of business can be changed to a more advantageous structure. If not self-employed, the doctor should speak to someone in the corporate law office to see if the corporation can hire the physician's business structure instead of the doctor personally. There may be some distinct advantages to doing so. Confer with an experienced business attorney on the matter to optimize results.

TABLE 7.1: GOALS IN DECIDING ON A BUSINESS STRUCTURE

- Relative ease of establishing the business structure.
- Avoiding burdensome regulations. This minimizes expensive ongoing or frequent attorney involvement to be in full compliance.
- Dodging overly complex business structures and minimizing accounting and attorney expenses.
- Decreasing tax consequences from earned income.
- Limiting liability (decrease risk) and increasing protection of personal assets.

Caveat: Unfortunately, some attorneys may recommend relatively complex business structures that may require attorney services on a regular basis for compliance and administration. Such arrangements can be a better continuing source of revenue for the lawyer than an advantage for the doctor.

TYPES OF BUSINESS ORGANIZATIONS

The following outline should highlight and clarify important points to consider. It should further serve as a general guide to aid the doctor or other health care professional in helping to determine the most appropriate business form for them.

Sole Proprietorship
OVERVIEW

- The doctor is in business for himself or herself.
- One person or a married couple (sole proprietor) owns all the assets of the business, assumes all its debts, and bears responsibility for most acts of employee conduct as well.
- The law makes no distinction between the owner and the owner's business—therefore, liability is unlimited and personal as well as business assets are at risk.
- No special legal formalities are required to set up a sole proprietorship.
- The doctor is his or her own boss, having total control and total responsibility over business operations and goals.
- No separate legal entity.
- No separate income tax return. The individual files a personal tax return. In other words, profits are taxed as personal income.

- Two or more sole proprietors may "office together" to share expenses. The doctors must avoid sharing profits, pooling funds, or "acting as partners." If the public *perceives* the doctors as partners, then a *de facto* partnership can be formed. Therefore, a conspicuous sign is needed in the reception area saying that "Dr. A and Dr. B are separate practitioners."

ADVANTAGES
- The owner/doctor is in complete control.
- Extremely fast and easy to set up—just open the office and start doing business.
- Reduced startup expenses.
- Sole recipient of profits.
- Losses offset profits, including the spouse's income.

DISADVANTAGES
- Sole responsibility for initial capital investment.
- Business risk is unlimited and falls entirely on the owner.
- The owner is personally liable for all business debts.
- Exposure to personal liability. Assets, e.g., income, bank accounts, house, cars, and/or real estate, are not protected.
- Difficulty taking time off.
- Debtors can reach the owner's personal assets in addition to the business assets.
- Limited ability to raise capital or borrow at lower preferred interest rates may lead to difficulties with capital and financing.
- Sharing office space with one or more other doctors can impose unwanted liability if it reasonably appears to be a partnership to the public.

General Partnership
OVERVIEW
- The Uniform Partnership Act regulates business partnerships.
- A partnership means that two or more persons own the business.
- Each person contributes money, property, labor, and/or skill, and share in the profits and losses of the business.
- Each partner is personally liable for the legal actions, taxes, debts, and obligations the partnership may face even though under the law a part-

nership is a legal entity separate from the individual owners (Revised Uniform Partnership Act of 1997).

- Partnerships are easily formed and simple to organize via "Articles of Partnership." A DBA or "fictitious name" registration must also be filed with local and state agencies as well as put on record with the IRS.
- If the doctor was previously in a sole proprietorship, that doctor will need a new Employer Identification Number (EIN) from the IRS.
- There is no significant cost to form a partnership.
- The partners jointly manage day-to-day business operations and each has an equal voice in management.
- Each partner contributes financially to the company and shares in its profits or losses in proportion to his/her ownership interest. Unless stated otherwise in the agreement, profits and losses are divided equally among the partners.
- Partnerships do not pay a separate tax but do have to file a Form 1065 tax return that shows the partnership's gains or losses for the year.
- A written partnership agreement is recommended and should be prepared, setting out the rights and duties of each partner. The agreement should also cover the duration of the partnership, the initial investment(s), salaries, splitting of profits and losses, how the partnership can be dissolved, and any agreement to compensate a partner who withdraws or compensation to his or her family in case of a partner's death. In the absence of any such agreement, state law determines the rights and duties of each partner.
- Buy-sell agreements, trusts, insurance, and other legal tools can be used to prepare for the death or disability of a partner.
- There is minimal government regulation, so there are fewer regulations and less supervision than with a corporation.
- A partnership can operate in more than one state without needing a separate state business license to do so. Of course, a license to practice by every doctor is necessary in each state of operation.
- Partners can own property or equipment as tenants in partnership.
- A partner's right to possess and control partnership property cannot be transferred to a third party outside the partnership.
- There is no such thing as an income tax on a partnership.

- A partnership is usually dissolved due to death, disability, bankruptcy, or dislike of a partner.
- When separate practitioners share an office, if it reasonably appears to be a partnership to the public, it will be treated as a partnership under the law.

ADVANTAGES

- Built in help in operating the business.
- Easier to take time off for illness or personal matters or to get back-up coverage for patients.
- Joint capital available to set up the business.
- Relatively stable business life, i.e., a partnership, is more stable than a sole proprietorship.
- Flexibility—can often respond more rapidly to changing conditions of business.

DISADVANTAGES

- Conflicts over management and division of profits and losses may arise.
- Ownership is difficult to transfer.
- Unlimited liability—Partners are personally liable for debts of the partnership business, including contract claims such as payroll, tax payables, and bank debts, as well as negligence settlements. This means that if the partnership does not have enough money to pay a creditor, the creditor can go after any partner he chooses to collect the debt. Thus, a creditor may hold any partner for the entire debt of the partnership.
- One partner can, through his actions, bind all other partners to liability if the actions were made with the apparent authority of the partnership— a serious disadvantage!
- Assume one partner buys a yacht, telling the salesman that it's for entertaining potential clients and that it will benefit the partnership. Depending on the law of the state, even if the purchasing partner is flat broke, the partnership may be liable for the purchase since the purchasing partner had apparent or implied authority as an agent to make such a purchase. The good news is, if a reasonable third party, which is the boat's seller, should realize or suspect that the agent/partner did not have actual express authority to make this purchase, the partnership will not be held to the contract.

- Partners are taxed on their representative share of the profits. This is so whether the profits are distributed or not. Therefore, partners often pay income tax on money they do not receive.
- If one partner is sued for malpractice, the lawsuit will likely name the partnership and each individual partner as co-defendants since partners share in the "debt" of a case settlement or verdict.
- A judgment against a partnership is collectible either out of partnership property or out of the private property of the owners.
- Partners are responsible for their own negligent acts, their partner's acts, and employees' acts (personal, partner's, and personnel's acts).
- Difficulty disposing of partnership interests.
- Unlimited liability of equal partners.

TABLE 7.2: SAMPLE MEDICAL PARTNERSHIP AGREEMENT ISSUES AND FORMAT

1. Intent to create a partnership for the practice of_____
2. Name of the enterprise.
3. The laws of [state] will be used to interpret the provisions of the agreement.
4. Nature and location of the business.
5. Date the partnership commences and its duration.
6. Contribution amounts in money and/or property by each partner.
7. Time frame in which the contributions are to be made.
8. Distribution of profits and losses—Each partner's proportionate share of profits and losses while the business operates and upon dissolution. Unless otherwise stated in the partnership agreement, profits and losses are divided equally among the partners.
9. Salaries and drawing accounts, if desired.
10. Division of work and duties and the function of each partner in the business. This should include the amount of time each partner is to devote to the partnership practice.
11. Vacation and sick leave.
12. Office hours.
13. Professional fees and expenses.
14. Management, e.g., equal or majority vote, etc.

15. New partners—admission requirements for any possible new partners.

16. Disability or prolonged illness of a partner—how salaries will be handled, e.g., full pay for the first month, 75 percent for the second month, 50 percent for the third and fourth months and 25 percent for the balance of the year.

17. The procedures to follow in the event of death, disability, divorce, mental incompetence, or bankruptcy. Any of these circumstances can impact all the partners.

18. Any restrictions on a partner's power to bind the enterprise and other partners into contracts, equipment, real property, etc.

19. Delineation of partnership assets from each individual partner's assets.

20. Bookkeeping, audits, and accounting methods to be used.

21. Life insurance and other insurances, e.g., malpractice, premises, umbrella coverage, etc.

22. Withdrawal, expulsion, or exclusion of a partner to include a covenant not to compete and the buyout formula, e.g., for an equal share two-person partnership, one-half the replacement value of the equipment plus 40% of the previous year's income plus 40% of the accounts payable to be made in regular installments.

23. Indicate whether withdrawal or exclusion terminates the partnership.

24. How to determine the value of a withdrawing or excluded partner's interest.

25. Dissolution—Procedures to notify partners and creditors in case of a partnership dissolution.

26. Which partners will be in charge of winding up the business?

27. Procedures for settling disputes between parties, e.g., arbitration or mediation.

Limited Partnership
OVERVIEW

- Regulated, in chief, by the Revised Uniform Limited Partnership Act (RULPA) although some states still use all or part of the older Uniform Limited Partnership Act (ULPA).
- Created by agreement in the certificate of limited partnership.
- A limited partnership certificate must be recorded in the county of the principle place of business or with a designated state official.

- A copy of the certificate must be filed in every county where the partnership has offices or conducts business.
- A limited partnership has both general partners and limited partners. The general partner invests in the partnership and is totally responsible for its management.
- Typically, limited partners invest cash or property, but not services, and have no authority in management decisions. Therefore, they have limited liability.
- There must, at a minimum, be one general partner and one limited partner.
- General partners are personally liable for partnership debts. A limited partner's potential liability does not exceed his investment.
- Legally complex.
- Families often form limited partnerships with parents as general partners and children as limited partners to reduce estate tax and protect family assets.

ADVANTAGES
- A limited partnership is a hybrid that contains many elements of a corporation with the advantages of operating as a partnership but with limited liability.
- Limited partnerships in succession planning can offer valuation discounts for estate and gift tax purposes as well as gifting of equity interests without transferring control.

DISADVANTAGES
- At least one partner has unlimited liability.
- Limited partners lose their limited liability if they participate in control of the business.
- The 1986 Tax Reform Act knocked most of the guts out of limited partnerships as a tax advantage and safe haven for assets.

Professional Associations (PAs)
a.k.a. Limited Liability Partnerships (LLPs)
OVERVIEW
- A limited liability partnership is a group of individuals called by a common name and bound together by a contractual relationship. These business set-ups are most popular in real estate and/or investment ventures

but have also found favor with groups of doctors and attorneys to limit their liability.

- The professional association is a legal entity.
- An association may sue on behalf of its members or be sued. Formerly, in some states, an unincorporated professional association was considered a partnership. Under the Uniform Partnership Law an association is no longer a partnership. Nonetheless, most LLPs are treated as general partnerships.
- Membership is a privilege, not a right. Therefore, courts cannot compel admission into an association.
- Offers the pass-through taxation of a partnership and the limited liability of a corporation.

ADVANTAGES
- A money judgment against the association is not enforceable against any individual member, which is a nice benefit.
- Partners are not liable for debts and obligations resulting from the negligence of other partners, another nice advantage.

DISADVANTAGES
- Not all states recognize LLPs and the IRS is not fully settled on how it can or will treat these business forms.
- If considering an LLP, it is best to contact a local business attorney to explore the pluses and minuses of this business entity.

Corporate Structures
OVERVIEW
- Corporations, under the law, are considered to be "persons" existing on paper only. This little legal fiction allows a group of persons to be treated under the law as a single individual. Like a natural person, the corporation must have a place of residence and pay taxes. That's why corporations can open a bank account, have a phone line, own property, inherit property, conduct sales, manufacture goods, and provide services as if its members were one person.
- A corporation is made up of a group of persons who obtain a charter giving them certain rights and privileges and is formed by a state when it issues the charter or certificate.

- The application for a charter is termed the "Articles of Incorporation." It is a legal document that should be prepared by an attorney.
- A corporation is owned by its shareholders. Shareholders have no direct say in managing the corporation. That responsibility rests with the board of directors, which the stockholders elect. The board, in turn, delegates most day-to-day operations to the corporate officers, i.e., president, vice-president, secretary, treasurer, etc. Thus, the top dog in a corporation is the chairman of the board of directors, not the president.
- A corporation is a legal entity with rights and liabilities separate from those of its individual shareholders.
- Corporations must pay taxes on their earnings. If they distribute dividends to their owners (shareholders), those persons must pay tax on such payments, effectively subjecting profits to double taxation.
- Corporate tax rates can be lower than individual rates.
- Shareholders are not liable for the debts of the business.
- Corporations have limited liability.
- Shareholders have ultimate control because they are the owners of the company and elect the directors.
- The power to make most decisions rests with the board of directors.
- A corporation needs to obtain a certificate of authority in each state it plans to do business.
- For most small and medium-sized businesses, particularly those that derive their income from one state, it makes sense to incorporate in that home state for the following reasons:
  - one filing fee
  - one state to file a report in
  - no multi-state income tax forms
  - convenience
  - attorney's knowledge of home state laws

The S Corporation
OVERVIEW

- S corporations are corporations that elect to pass corporate income, losses, deductions, and credit through to their shareholders for federal tax purposes.

- For all practical purposes, S corporations are treated by the IRS like partnerships. The corporate designation acts as a liability shield. That means that the company's income (and corresponding expenses, write-offs, and deductions) will actually flow through to its shareholders and be split among them according to each shareholder's ownership percentage. As in a partnership, income tax is paid on profits or earnings whether distributed or not.

- An S corporation is structurally the same as a C corporation, i.e., it has officers, directors, and not more than 100 shareholders, but with one key difference. An S corporation files an election with the IRS, called a Form 2553, that provides it with a flow-through tax structure as found in entities such as partnerships and limited liability companies.

- The S corporation's taxes will actually be paid by its shareholders, at their individual tax rates and in proportion to their individual ownership percentages. No tax is assessed on the corporate income. For all other purposes, it is a corporation.

- The law traditionally requires at least three directors, but most states require one or two directors in corporations where there are only a few shareholders.

- A close corporation is an S corporation where the stock is held by a few people, often members of the same business group or family. A close corporation is also one in which, as a general rule, all or most of the shareholders are actively involved in managing the business. Stocks are not to be sold outside the family or group.

Most privately held or closely held corporations:

a) Pay salaries to corporate officers to minimize the double tax.

b) Are managed as if they were partnerships.

c) Are restricted by law as to the number of stockholders and the transfer of stock.

d) Are formed in the same manner as all other private corporations.

e) Are permitted in several states to allow shareholders of smaller closely held corporations to enter into written agreements setting forth how the business will be run. Among the various subjects generally covered by a partnership agreement or shareholder control agreement are how much time each owner will be required to devote to the business, the amount of capital to be contributed by each partner or shareholder, which partners or owners are in charge of which aspects of the business, compensation and payment terms to the partners or shareholders, employment of family members, staff salaries, the right to have the business dissolved, and the manner in which disputes are to be resolved. In addition, if there are two or more owners of the business, there should be an agreement as to what will happen if one of the owners dies, retires, becomes disabled, or wants out of the business.

f) Do not offer shares of stock for sale to the public.

ADVANTAGES

- An S corporation may be a good way to structure a business that provides a service, not a product.
- Limited liability for its owners, officers, and directors.
- No federal corporate tax. Avoids double taxation.
- A separate legal entity.
- Perpetual existence, e.g., not terminated by the death of its owner or owners.
- Avoids the accumulated earnings tax (AET).
- Can offset business losses against personal income.
- Allows shareholders/stockholders a 100% deduction for health insurance.

DISADVANTAGES

- Burdensome formation, maintenance requirements, and increased (banking, accounting, legal, and regulatory) costs. Required to follow the same internal and external corporate formalities and obligations as a C corporation, such as adopting bylaws, issuing stock, holding shareholder and director meetings, filing annual reports, and paying annual fees.
- Profits are taxed on the owner's tax return.
- Estate, gift, and generation-skipping transfer taxes still apply.
- Forced liquidation of the business in the event of the owner/operator's incapacity or death may be required.
- Many significant tax advantages were removed years ago.

The C Corporation—
Also Known as a Regular, or Business, Corporation

OVERVIEW

C corporations, such as IBM, Coca-Cola, and General Motors, are good entities for beginning businesses that:

- Want to retain earnings, rather than disbursing them each year.
- May have large start-up costs and expect to have losses in the first few years.
- Want to look for outside investors and may plan to go public.
- Want to have multiple classes of stock and to sell stock to anyone, anywhere in the world.
- Want the option of providing their owners with tax-free benefits, as well as its employees.
- Have high-income owners.

ADVANTAGES

- Ease of securing capital.
- Permanence of existence for the business enterprise.
- Protection for personal assets.
- Protection against personal liability of individual shareholders with respect to claims against the business.
- Corporate benefits—the chief benefit to the small business owner is the ability to take deductions for legitimate business expenses such as pension plans, profit sharing plans, health insurance, business transportation, etc. These benefits must be offered to all corporate employees.

DISADVANTAGES

- Expensive to set up, organize, and maintain, and with high organizational and administrative costs.
- Annual meetings and recorded minutes required.
- Extensive governmental regulation.
- Tremendous amount of paperwork that will likely require regular legal expertise.
- The profit of a corporation is taxed to the corporation when earned, and then is taxed to the shareholders when distributed as dividends. This

creates a double tax. The corporation does not get a tax deduction when it distributes dividends to shareholders.

- Inability to take losses as deductions to offset personal income.
- Double accounting—an accountant for both the corporate books and taxes and again for personal tax returns will be needed.
- If stock that's been owned for more than six months is sold at a profit, capital gains taxes must be paid. If money is lost on a stock sale, only a portion of the loss may be written off as a loss of income, except in Subchapter S corporations.
- Although the "corporate shield" protects shareholders from individual liability, this advantage is not as great as it initially appears for two reasons. First, most banks and suppliers will require the shareholders to personally guarantee the corporation's debts. Second, most businesses, including larger shareholders, obtain or should obtain insurance to protect themselves against claims.
- Many tax advantages for corporations were removed several years ago.

The Professional Corporation (PC)
OVERVIEW
- Similar to a typical business corporation except that its directors and stockholders must be licensed to practice the profession(s) for which the corporation has been created.
- Formerly, a professional corporation could be organized only for the purpose of rendering one specific type of professional service and services ancillary thereto.
- More states are enacting laws that allow a doctor of medicine, a chiropractor, a nurse practitioner, an optometrist, a psychologist, a registered nurse, a licensed practical nurse, a pharmacist, a physical therapist, an osteopath, or a podiatrist to engage in a combination practice through a professional corporation, limited liability company, partnership, or professional association.
- The corporation formed cannot control the professional clinical judgment of those professionals rendering treatment. This eliminates fee splitting as a cause of discipline in this type of group practice.
- In many states, the corporate name of any professional corporation shall not be used to imply superiority and shall end with the word "chartered"

or the word "limited" or the abbreviations "Ltd." or "Inc." or the words "professional association" or the abbreviation "PA."

- A professional corporation must file its articles of incorporation with the board that has jurisdiction over its professional activities.

- A professional corporation may issue its stock only to and admit as a member only natural persons licensed to render the kinds of professional services that the corporation is authorized to render. Transfers of such stock may be made only to other members of the corporation or to individuals qualified to practice in the service of said corporation. No proxy to vote any share in the professional corporation may be given to a person who is not licensed.

- A professional corporation must report the death of any of its shareholders or members to the board with jurisdiction over the professional services rendered within thirty (30) days of such death. Within ninety (90) days following the death, all shares of stock owned by such shareholder shall be transferred to and acquired by the professional corporation or persons qualified to own such shares.

- Every officer and director of the corporation shall be a professional who is licensed to render the services of the type the corporation is authorized to render.

- Any board, or any employee designated by such board, shall have the right at all reasonable times of free access to all books and records of any professional corporation and may summon and examine under oath the officers, directors, and employees in all matters concerning the operation of the corporation.

- Tax advantages are marginal.

ADVANTAGES

- Insurance (life, health and accident and/or disability), meals, lodging, and qualified transportation costs are available as tax write-offs for eligible corporate employees if they can be characterized as ordinary and necessary expenses.

- Protection from malpractice on the part of shareholders remains an important motive for incorporation. Some states, however, do not protect shareholders from personal liability.

DISADVANTAGES

- Stockholders and employees may be individually liable for negligence relating to professional activities, meaning that a professional corporation is responsible for the wrongful acts of its officers, agents, or employees acting within the scope of their employment.
- Personal liability may still apply.
- See also Corporations.

Nonprofit Corporations
OVERVIEW

A nonprofit corporation is recognized as tax exempt by the IRS and is organized for a public or charitable purpose. The American Cancer Society and the Muscular Dystrophy Association are two such organizations, but so is the NFL. For private purposes, this type of corporation has severe limitations and should not be considered as a viable business organization for a doctor's practice.

Limited Liability Company ("LLC")
OVERVIEW

- An LLC is an unincorporated business organization with the limited liability features of a corporation and the tax efficiencies and operational flexibility of a partnership.
- An LLC is created like a corporation by filing "articles of organization" with a state official, usually the Secretary of State. There are no shareholders, only members. Individuals or another business entity may own the LLC. Thus, one LLC may own another LLC in part or in whole. Members/owners are not personally liable to third parties.
- In an LLC, the owners are called members instead of stockholders. They receive membership interests based on the value of assets or services contributed by each member. LLCs can either be governed collectively, by all of their members, or by one or more managers who are voted in by the members and who carry out the day-to-day functions and business of the LLC. Managers can also be members, or they can have no ownership rights in the LLC at all. Managers may be individuals or entities. An LLC governed by a manager or managers is, not surprisingly, known as a "manager-managed" LLC, while a collectively governed LLC is called a "member-managed" LLC. The rules by which the LLC is governed are set out in its operating agreement, which is signed by all of the members.

- LLCs provide both the limited liability protection found with corporations, as well as the flow-through taxation of a partnership. They allow the LLC to divide up profit and loss allocations among the owners in varying ways, not based strictly on ownership percentages as is required in C and S corporations. Individuals, corporations, or trusts may hold ownership interests and there are no restrictions on where the owners live. Annual meetings are not required but are strongly recommended, both as a good method of communication between the managers and the members, and as a means to establish that the LLC is a legally distinct, stand-alone entity. That last point is important since, if corporate formalities are not followed, creditors may find it easier to reach through the LLC to the managers and members personally. This is known as piercing the corporate veil.
- Most states allow a single owner/member to establish the LLC. Massachusetts requires at least two members.
- Since an owner has limited liability, his or her business debts are satisfied out of business assets, not out of personal assets.
- Properties held in an LLC are easy to transfer and incur less tax on a subsequent sale than would be assessed if that same property were held in a C or S corporation. LLCs work well for family asset-based entities where the goal is to increase the family wealth, plan for the future, and maximize tax savings. Many different items can be placed into an LLC, such as property, day-trading accounts, stocks and bonds, insurance policies, and annuities, etc.

ADVANTAGES

- An LLC provides the same organizational and management flexibility as a general partnership, while also providing more accounting flexibility than either C or S corporations.
- An LLC protects assets from creditors. Instead of unlimited liability in a sole proprietorship or partnership, there will be limits on liability.
- LLCs further provide limited liability protection for their owners/members, like that provided to the shareholders of a corporation.
- LLCs have the benefit of pass-through taxation, like a partnership, while not forcing the complexities of a limited partnership on its members.
- An LLC is less rigid and formal than an S corporation.

- Members can divide up the profits and losses in ratios other than strict ownership percentages.
- The LLC can hold interests in the names of other entities or trusts.
- LLCs are often good estate-planning vehicles to transfer wealth to the next generation.
- The LLC protects its members from the liabilities of the company.
- Control of the LLC cannot be transferred to the judgment creditors of any member.
- The combination of flexibility, limited liability, and avoidance of the two-tiered tax on C corporations, as well as having estate planning advantages, makes an LLC very attractive.

DISADVANTAGES
- Corporate fringe benefits such as life insurance, medical coverage, disability insurance, accident and health plans, etc., are not available to employees. However, LLC members are entitled to the current 60% deduction for self-employed health insurance premiums.
- An LLC generally needs to file more paperwork than does a sole proprietorship or a partnership, resulting in some increased fees and expenses.
- Very few disadvantages with an LLC.

ATTORNEY INVOLVEMENT
At the very least, a business should regularly consult a lawyer about loans, major transactions, and compliance problems. The legal documents of a limited partnership, an LLC, or a corporation should be reviewed on a regular basis, preferably at least once a year.

This annual legal audit can uncover omissions, such as the absence of corporate minutes and/or necessary changes in contracts, releases, policy and procedure manuals, or other documents necessitated by changes in statutes and regulations. As part of this process, an attorney may uncover potentially serious legal problems at a time when they can be resolved in an efficient and cost-effective manner.

CONCLUSION

A dizzying array of business structures is available, each with its pluses and minuses. A review of this section, however, should provide an insightful guide as to which genre of business may be the best organizational form to pursue as a matter of practicality and convenience. It is usually best not to complicate business life too much, while still providing asset protection and an easily manageable entrepreneurial scheme.

Before choosing a business entity for your specific situation, consult a business attorney who can check federal, state, and local statutes for compliance, and to maximize the business and personal advantages of the chosen practice structure.

BIBLIOGRAPHY

Beatty, J.F. *Business and the Legal Environment*.

Cheeseman, H.R. *Business Law*. 5th ed.

Eisenberg, Melvin Aron. *Corporations and Other Business Organizations: Statutes, Rules, Materials and Forms*. 2007.

Goldman, A.J., and W.D. Sigismond. *Business Law Principles and Practices*. NY: Houghton Mifflin Co.

Hamilton, Robert W. *Business Organizations: Unincorporated Businesses & Closely Held Corporations: Essential Terms & Concepts*. 1997.

Klein, William A., and John Coffee, Jr. *Business Organization and Finance, Legal and Economic Principles*. 2007.

Mann, R.A., B.S. Roberts, and Smith and Robertson's Business Law.

CHAPTER 8

The Medical Record
– Three Walls of Defense –

Excellent records are the best defense a physician can provide.

MEDICAL RECORDS

Keeping good medical records is a daunting task for every professional. Under current requirements, the medical record must contain valuable and necessary information that simultaneously meets the needs of the patient, the health care industry, insurance companies, governmental and accreditation agencies, and the legal system.

The medical chart is the lifeblood of a patient's care and the cornerstone for effective continuity of care. Basically, the process in which medical records are maintained is required for the patient's safety and welfare and to improve the quality of care. Therefore, the medical file is kept in the patient's best interests. It is always important for the patient's sake that the current provider review the records made by other past and present health care providers.

Regarding the ownership interests of the file contents, it is the medical facility or practitioner that owns the patient's physical records, whereas the patient owns the information contained therein. Additionally, patients have the legal right to access their own records in a timely fashion and to receive copies of those records. Each state has its own laws on the acceptable methodology and copying charges.

FUNCTIONS OF THE MEDICAL RECORD

Every medicolegal inquiry begins with the medical record. Insurance audits, peer reviews, state board investigations, government agency inquiries, personal injuries, workers' compensation, and malpractice litigation all begin with the record.

The medical record is recorded in the normal course of business at or near the time that care is given, with no incentive to fabricate or embellish what occurred. Thus, in court or other proceedings, it is considered to be credible and trustworthy.

The health care record is a source of information that is dedicated to the patient and one that all other health care providers use. Its core purpose is to accurately document prior medical care and the reasons for the course of care taken or recommendations made. The medical record exists to refresh the current physician's memory of the care rendered and why, and to ensure seamless future quality of care and coordination of care by the physician-led care team. Coordination of care is facilitated by communicating this medical information between providers who contribute to the patient's care when necessary.

Every doctor receives extensive training on the importance of documentation. The record not only documents what the health provider has observed and done, but also serves as a patient profile for other doctors and nurses. All health care professionals rely on the accuracy of the chart. If important information is omitted, terrible and even fatal mistakes can be made.

Nothing prevents a doctor from recording his or her observations in the chart or submitting a correction or late entry if necessary. While there is no excuse for a bad record, even a good record is never a substitute for good care. To put it another way, the documentation in a patient's chart or medical record should clearly reflect the quality, nature, and clinical rationale behind any care that has been provided.

In addition to communicating important information to other health care providers, the record serves as a database and legal record of what has happened to any patient. The medical record is also valuable for demonstrating regulatory compliance, in addition to medical necessity for billing and reimbursement purposes.

TABLE 8.1: LEGAL USES OF THE MEDICAL RECORD

The following are a few of the legal uses of the medical record:

- malpractice actions
- administrative proceedings
- reimbursement decisions
- Medicare/Medicaid determinations
- regulatory compliance assessments
- peer review

- teaching
- credentialing (for managed care organizations, hospital privileges, etc.)
- product liability matters because of injury to the patient as a result of equipment-related accidents
- workers' compensation determinations
- risk management

LEGAL OBLIGATION(S) TO CREATE A MEDICAL RECORD

The doctor and health facility rendering care are under a legal duty to create and maintain an accurate medical record. That duty is mandatory whether it comes from statutory, regulatory, and/or professional sources.

The first source of legal duty to create a medical record, and in some ways the most important, is the custom of the medical profession. Physicians have created and maintained charts long before any bureaucrat or agency required them to do so. Additionally, the federal government and many states have statutes and regulations governing the content, confidentiality, and other related responsibilities concerning the medical record.

Federal Sources[1]

a) Medicare, including the Health Care Finance Administration
b) The Omnibus Budget Reconciliation Act
c) The Health Care Quality Improvement Initiative
d) The Health Care Quality Improvement Act (1988)
e) The Drug Enforcement Administration
f) The National Board of Medical Examiners
g) Medicaid 42 U.S.C.A. S1392 r-2
h) The Medicare statute
i) The Joint Commission—independent statutory authority for granting hospital accreditation has been supplanted by making the TJC subject to the Centers for Medicare and Medicaid Services (CMS) regarding accreditation requirements.

Insurance personnel as well as Medicare and Medicaid carrier auditors are all trained to review medical documentation and to look for certain deficiencies. As a consequence of this heightened scrutiny, complete and accurate documentation has never been more important.

---

[1] Elliot B. Oppenheim, *The Medical Record as Evidence* (Lexis Law Publishing, 1998), 315, 410, 412.

State Sources[2]

a) State medical licensure laws and licensing boards

b) State medical disciplinary acts

c) State Medicaid statutes

d) State statutes and/or administrative codes—many states have specific regulations regarding medical records, the length of time for retention, and patient access. Several states, including Georgia, maintain that inadequate record-keeping is considered to be unprofessional conduct.[3]

Professional Sources[4]

Many professional organizations have published guidelines or policies that are commonly regarded as a customary standard for documentation. Although these standards are not laws, they are often treated with similar importance and have a comparable impact.

a) Medical staff rules and regulations

b) AMA/AOA/ADA/etc.

c) Specialty and subspecialty associations

d) State professional organizations

Hospital Standards

The Joint Commission (TJC) is an independent, not-for-profit organization that provides detailed requirements for accreditation of hospitals and health care facilities including standards for generating and maintaining medical records. Although the format and forms will vary, the standards for organizing the contents and the types of information to be included in the records are set. These standards apply to both paper and electronic health records.[5] The Joint Commission is the largest, but not the only, entity that establishes standards for medical records toward hospital accreditation.

Physician Standards

While every doctor is under a professional duty to create and maintain medical records, compared with TJC no laws or regulations exist to set standards for the contents of private physician office records. Consequently, there can be significant variation in the quality of doctors' office records.

---

[2] Ibid., 421, 428.

[3] https://medicalboard.georgia.gov/what-unprofessional-conduct.

[4] Oppenheim, 373, 400–401, 403.

[5] Comprehensive Accreditation Manual for Hospitals, 2018, by The Joint Commission.

This is in part due to the fact that private office record-keeping styles evolved during a period that demanded less comprehensive record-keeping than is necessary today.

Originally, office records were typically kept by a single physician who treated a group of long-term patients. The record served to remind the physician of each patient's medical history and to record the patient's treatment. Owing to the high probability that patients today will be cared for by more than one doctor over time or by multiple doctors at the same time, in addition to the increase in multiple physician clinics, and the number of available therapies, there is heightened pressure to document ever-increasing amounts of information on each visit.

GOALS OF THE MEDICAL RECORD

Obviously, the best medical record is one that is reasonably accurate, timely, and complete in order to facilitate good care. Each patient chart must contain enough information for a physician who is unfamiliar with that patient to provide appropriate care. The medical record should furnish the patient's health care providers with a reasonably concise and accurately written picture of the patient's actual and potential medical problems including risk factors, the planned care, and the actual care given, as well as the patient's response to that care.

The medical record, in addition to documenting the patient's clinical course, should be organized in a sequential and logical format. In simple terms, the chart should reflect what the doctor did and why. To accomplish this, the chart must explain the physician's reasoning and actions in the course of the medical decision-making process so that another physician who has never seen the patient could understand the attending physician's assessment, rationale, and plan. For example, the record should explain why treatment proceeded in a particular manner even if a diagnosis was still provisional. It should also depict the complexity of any difficult clinical problem, as well as any consideration of alternate courses of care.

In case of a complication, there should be an explanation, if known. All complications in the record should be documented as to how and why they occurred. It is important to remember, however, that an unavoidable complication is not malpractice.

It is critically important to document all important conversations, including recommendations and instructions to the patient or care giver, as well as discussions with other health professionals involved in the patient's care.

DOCUMENT TELEPHONE COMMUNICATIONS

Phone calls that relate to and focus on health care should also be documented in the medical record, preferably using the caller's own words, and physicians should note whether they were received at work, home, or on the go. Records of telephone conversations may offer additional insights into the doctor's reasonable rationale for the course taken. These notations also help the physician demonstrate that proper professional attention has been given to the patient's problem which can be a very important point in the defense a lawsuit.

Telephone records should include documentation of the advice given and whether a qualified staff member, e.g., LPN, RN, NP, PA, or the doctor gave that advice. It should be self-evident that only relatively minor problems should be managed over the telephone. More complicated problems may require an office or emergency room visit. (See also "Chapter 16: Achieve Maximum Malpractice Protection.") Appropriate documentation can usually be accomplished with standard phone log forms except for more complex calls.

Any prescription given via telephone or e-mail communication should generally be for the lowest possible dose and number of pills, should be made part of the permanent record, and should include the instruction that an office visit is imperative prior to any further prescriptions. Should the practice utilize e-mail instead of telephone calls, a standard disclaimer is warranted, e.g., "Electronic mail is not secure and should not be used for urgent or sensitive issues." If adequate and accurate information is not forthcoming from the patient in the electronic format, or if a sensitive or emotionally charged issue is involved, the doctor may want to switch to the telephone or to an in-person evaluation.

USE ELECTRONIC HEALTH RECORDS

Many hospitals and doctors' offices have switched to Electronic Health Records (EHRs). Ambulatory surgery centers will be required to implement EHR systems within the next few years and participation in Medicare/Medicaid will depend on it. The Centers for Medicare & Medicaid Services currently provide incentives for practitioners to use EHRs. If eligible providers have not already acquired, implemented, and demonstrated meaningful EHR use, their Medicare payouts will likely be reduced.

The government's position is that the EHRs can improve patient care by:

- reducing the incidence of medical error by improving the accuracy and clarity of medical records
- making the health information available, reducing duplication of tests, reducing delays in treatment, and making patients well-informed so as to be able to make better decisions
- reducing medical error by improving the accuracy and clarity of medical records

One feature that purportedly improves patient safety in the EHR is "clinical decision support" which includes potential adverse drug/drug interactions and drug allergy alerts. If these alerts are bypassed or ignored, plaintiffs can argue that physicians have an obligation to consider and respond to standard drug/drug and drug allergy alerts on EHRs.

It's best to become familiar with and use EHRs. The standard is quickly changing to require them. Don't get left behind.

POTENTIAL EHR PROBLEMS

The pace of medical malpractice claims in which electronic health care records (EHRs) contributed to patient injury has more than tripled since 2010.[6]

If the EHR is customizable, the doctor may be using the product in a non-standard way so that the system cannot generate critical clinical prompts and alerts. During any investigation the doctor will be asked, "Were you using the system as intended?" If not, then certain care items may have been ignored.[7]

Every physician must also know that the Health Insurance Portability and Accountability Act (HIPAA) dictates that it is the health care provider's responsibility to maintain the integrity and confidentiality of the patient's medical record. This applies to EHRs because physicians will have had EHR training and signed an end-user license agreement (EULA) that confirms that they understood how the EHR works. This is intended to take blaming the software or its seller for poor office records out of the equation. If there is a legitimate software problem, the physician is still ultimately responsible because software vendors do not practice medicine.[8]

---

[6] "A Slow Death by Charting," newsletter@kevinmd.com (Sept. 12, 2019).
[7] "8 Malpractice Dangers in Your EHR," *Medscape Business of Medicine* (Aug. 21, 2014).
[8] Ibid.

Thus, physicians are likely bound by the EULA agreement. As discussed in Chapter 2, "The Doctor-Patient Contract," doctors must take this legal document seriously. Attorneys for the EHR company wrote the EULA agreement in that company's best interests, not in the physician's. All health care practitioners should consider having an attorney, experienced in both HIPAA and technology contracts, review the document in order to remove or modify unfair provisions before the document is signed.

If a software glitch is encountered, physicians should contact their vendor immediately to insist that it be fixed right away; they should also document that contact, as well as the date the problem was discovered. If the doctor was aware of a flaw in the product and made no attempt to have it fixed, it could be argued that he or she knowingly jeopardized the patient.

To save time, some doctors copy and paste information from one electronic document into another. The problem with this practice is that old symptoms, vital signs, or test results can appear to be current, which can potentially threaten a patient's safety. Similarly, an erroneous entry may become accepted as fact, either by the providers, or by the jury, or both. Therefore, cutting and pasting is rarely a good idea.

Furthermore, if large blocks of text are repeatedly copied in the EHR, this is easily revealed in the legal discovery process and can make the doctor appear haphazard and careless in patient care methods.[9]

In general terms, EHRs are a bureaucratic solution to ensure the completeness of the medical history. However, EHRs cannot provide the focus and direction that medical histories were always supposed to have under the skilled guidance of an experienced physician. EHRs have made friendly doctor-patient interactions less personal. Also, EHR notes typically do not reflect the doctor's thinking or plan, which can be a significant failing.

Another existing problem with EHRs is the "monster note, a creation of autofilled blanks with vital signs and test results that tell you very little about what's really going on and confers an overall lack of a good impression."[10]

Unfortunately, once a bureaucratic standard is established, meaningful changes, i.e., improvements, are nearly impossible to implement. If the bureaucratic burden is too cumbersome or time consuming, most doctors will likely seek ways around what they perceive as EHR shortcomings.

---

[9] Ibid.

[10] Allen M. Block, MD, "Now Missing in EHR Charts: A Good Impression," *Family Practice News* (Oct. 4, 2017).

HOW NOT TO DOCUMENT

The poorest medical records are those that have been improperly altered. Such faulty modifications may include erasures, skipped lines, or blank spaces, may contain words that have been blacked out or crossed out, may appear to have extra words inserted, or are incomplete.

Important information missing from the medical record may inspire suspicion and doubt. The credibility of medical records is usually attacked by demonstrating that significant portions of necessary data are absent. A sizable percentage of medical malpractice suits are rendered indefensible because of poor medical records. Altered records may further allow the insurance company to deny coverage and can result in additional charges and increased damages.

Physicians would be wise to remember that generally in a malpractice case, poor records mean a poor defense; no records mean no defense; and altered records mean alarmingly bad results including the possible loss of the case.

THE MEDICAL RECORD IN A MALPRACTICE ACTION

The most important "non-testimonial" evidence in a legal proceeding is the medical record itself. The record is the first wall of malpractice defense because a good medical record can prevent a case from ever being filed.

If a case is filed, the second line of defense is that a well-kept record will significantly lessen the chance of that case ever going to trial. In some cases, the records may be somewhat misleading in that they do not initially provide an explanation for a problem, complication, or a poor outcome.[11] A number of these cases are litigated for some time until the plaintiff understands the medical cause of the outcome and dismisses them.

And if the case goes to trial, the record itself will, as a last stand, likely attest to the good care rendered and is very unlikely to support accusations of carelessness. A good medical record is absolutely essential for the doctor's defense; indeed, it can be the strongest defense available.

---

[11] David R. Barry as quoted in "Physicians Shouldn't Rely on 'Code of Silence,'" *Physician Risk Management* (Nov. 2012), AHC Media: Continuing Medical Education Publishing. https://www.reliasmedia.com/articles/77235-want-to-prevent-lawsuit-chart-decision-making.

CONCLUSION

As explained above, the starting point for all medicolegal inquiries is the medical record. The medical record is considered to be credible and trustworthy because it is compiled in the course of business with no incentive to reshape or misstate what occurred.

In the event of litigation, that record is the central and most crucial piece of evidence in the matter. The preservation of that original well-documented record without alterations is absolutely critical and invaluable in the defense of malpractice.

BIBLIOGRAPHY

Battista, M.E. "Malpractice Risks of Documentation." *Physician's Management* (Feb. 1985): 232–258.

Campion, Francis X., MD. The Risk Management Foundation of the Harvard Medical Institutions Incorporated. *Grand Rounds on Medical Malpractice.* Chicago, IL: American Medical Association, 1990.

"Good Medical Records Can Be Strongest Malpractice Defense." *Michigan Med* (Jan. 1983): 6–8.

http://plague.law.umke.edu/xfiles/x186-201.htm.

Oppenheim, Elliot. *The Medical Record as Evidence.* Lexis Law Publishing, 1998.

CHAPTER 9

Consents and Releases
– An Added Layer of Security –

There are two types of consents. The first involves granting permission for the doctor to do standard tests or procedures. This is a general consent fully indicating that the patient approves and permits routine office or hospital procedures like an examination, laboratory tests, or x-rays, if needed. This consent may be acquired verbally, in writing, or by implied assent from the patient's conduct, i.e., the patient complies with the doctor's directions or requested actions.

The second type of consent is informed consent where the patient is told of the inherent material risks, complications, and side effects of complex medical tests or procedures including surgery, chemotherapy, endoscopy, etc. This specific subject matter is dealt with in more detail in Chapter 6.

It is wise to use a general release and consent for office practices that patients routinely expect. Utilizing a general consent form for regular procedures can sidestep many potential problems. Consider using such a consent as part of your standard office intake forms after obtaining specific advice from an attorney familiar with your state's laws.

Obtaining the patient's general consent for routine office procedures and their informed consent for more complicated ones is consistent both with the physician's ethical duties and the physician-patient contract. Office forms can be an invaluable aid in meeting a doctor's obligations and deflecting a number of negligence suits that allege lack of consent.

Below appears an example of a typical general consent form for routine office procedures and tests.

GENERAL CONSENT AND AUTHORIZATIONS

HEALTH CARE DECISIONS/PATIENT RIGHTS: I acknowledge receiving information regarding my rights as a patient, and my rights to be a participant in and make decisions regarding my health care, including the right to accept or refuse testing and/or treatment.

PATIENT'S STATEMENT: I understand that I am seeking professional services, care, and/or treatment and do hereby consent to such. I agree to the performance of diagnostic and treatment services, including routine invasive or minor surgical procedures as in the opinion of my doctor are deemed necessary for the diagnosis or improvement of my condition. This authorization does not cover any type of major surgery or other complicated procedures. As with any professional care and treatment, I fully realize that medicine is not an exact science and that there are potential risks involved, including known consequences of care and the possibility of complications. I also acknowledge that no guarantee or assurance has been given by anyone as to the results that may be obtained. Unless revoked in writing, this authorization and permission will remain in effect while I am under the care of this doctor or facility.

CONSENT TO ROUTINE DIAGNOSTIC
AND TREATMENT PROCEDURES

The undersigned freely and voluntarily consents to and authorizes the doctor to perform relevant diagnostic examination procedures as well as laboratory procedures, imaging studies, or other related routine diagnostic service(s) rendered or ordered under the general and/or specific instructions of the doctor or doctor's assistants. I also consent to routine treatment procedures.

I acknowledge that a referral to another physician or facility may be necessary to help diagnose or treat my problem and further authorize the doctor to make such a referral if deemed necessary.

_____   _____
Patient's Signature   Date

CONSENT FOR RELEASE OF
PROTECTED HEALTH INFORMATION

I authorize the doctor and this office to release and/or send to any insurance company or payor, its agents, servants, or employees, and attorneys, all medical information compiled by the doctor and this office received from another health care facility/agency or physician. I understand this authorization is executed to better enable the doctor(s) and this facility to obtain, or attempt to obtain, proceeds, benefits, or amounts due to me or members of my family from insurance companies relating to my treatment and care. In consideration of the doctor and this facility's cooperation in securing, or attempting to secure, said amounts for me, I release this doctor and this facility, its agents, servants, and employees from all responsibilities and/or liabilities incident to their release of my records or other appropriate information. I authorize the doctor and this facility to release and/or send copies of pertinent portions of my medical record to my referring doctor and to subsequent requesting physician(s) and doctors who may be involved in my current and/or future care.

BY AFFIXING MY SIGNATURE BELOW, I hereby consent to this facility and its personnel both using and disclosing my Protected Health Information for the purpose of rendering treatment and care to me and/or payment of professional services rendered to me as well as for this practice's general health care operations purposes. A Notice of Privacy Practices for this health care facility has been offered to me and/or physically given to me and I have reviewed and had all my questions answered prior to my signing this document. I also understand that I have the right to revoke this consent in writing, at any time, except to the extent that the Practice has acted in reliance on the consent.

I confirm that I have read and fully understand the above and that all my questions and concerns have been answered to my satisfaction prior to my signing this form.

_____

Patient, Guardian, or Representative's Signature

_____

Witness

Date: _____ Time: _____ am/pm

HIPAA COMPLIANCE

Congress passed the Health Insurance Portability and Accountability Act in 1996. To fully comply with HIPAA's national minimum standard for the privacy of medical records each doctor must:

1. Give notice of his or her policies or the medical organization's privacy policies.

2. Have a form for patients to request a restriction on your organization's use and disclosure of their health information. The organization does not have to grant the request. The request can be denied for any reason. If the request is granted, compliance with the request must be fully documented.

3. Allow requests for alternative means to communicate health information, e.g., the patient may request e-mail reminders of appointments, test result reports, or billing information. If the request is reasonable and not an undue burden, the health facility must agree to it.

4. Permit each patient to inspect and obtain a copy of their records within 30 days of the request. Limited exceptions to this rule include access to psychiatric or psychological records. Reasonable copying, postage, or preparation charges can be billed to the patient.

5. Further allow patient to request amendments to their records to correct any errors. Requests may be denied if the doctor feels the record would be inaccurate. If the request is denied, the facility must give the patient a written explanation for the denial and inform the patient that he or she may submit a statement disagreeing with the denial. The patient may further request that his or her disagreement statement be attached to all future disclosures. The health care organization should also explain how to complain to your own organization or to Health and Human Services about the denial.

6. Grant each patient the right to a full accounting of all disclosures of the health information when requested. Fortunately, this does not include disclosures made to obtain payment, to carry out treatment, or for health care operations.

Disclosures by any billing company, accountants, and/or business associates must be made along with the date and reason for disclosure. The patient cannot be charged for the first accounting.

SAMPLE PRIVACY PRACTICES FORM FOR HIPAA COMPLIANCE

NOTICE OF PRIVACY PRACTICES
FOR PROTECTED HEALTH INFORMATION

THIS NOTICE DESCRIBES HOW HEALTH INFORMATION ABOUT YOU MAY BE USED AND DISCLOSED AND HOW YOU CAN GET ACCESS TO THIS INFORMATION. PLEASE REVIEW IT CAREFULLY.

This notice of privacy practice sets out how we may use and disclose your protected health information to carry out treatment, payment, health care operations, or for other purposes that are permitted or required by law. Our practice is dedicated, and we are required by applicable federal and state laws, to make reasonable efforts to maintain the privacy of your health information. These laws also require us to inform you of your rights to access and control your protected health care information as well as our obligations concerning your health information. Protected health information is information about you, including demographic information, that may identify you and that relates to your past, present, or future physical or mental health or condition and related health care services. We are required to follow the privacy practices described below while this notice is in effect. We may change the terms of this notice at any time. Upon your request, we will provide you with any revised notice of privacy practices by asking for one at the time of your next appointment or by telephoning the office and requesting one.

1. USES AND DISCLOSURES OF PROTECTED HEALTH INFORMATION

TREATMENT, PAYMENT, HEALTH CARE OPERATIONS: You should be aware that protected health care information may be used and disclosed by the doctor, office staff, and others outside our office who are involved in your care and treatment for the purpose of providing health care services to you. Your health care information may also be used use to obtain payment for your health care bills and for health care operations. Although not meant to be exhaustive, the following are descriptive examples of the types of uses and disclosures that may be carried out by this office.

Treatment: We may use or disclose your health information to provide, manage, or coordinate your health care and any related services. This includes disclosure to a third party that may need access to your protected health information. This can include, for example, a home health agency, laboratory, and/or another doctor who may be treating you or involved in your care to ensure that the necessary information to diagnose and treat you is available to them.

Payment: We may use and disclose your health information, as needed, to obtain payments and/or to allow you to seek applicable reimbursement for your health care services. This may include certain activities that your health care plan may undertake before it approves or pays for health care services such as determining eligibility or coverage for insurance benefits, reviewing services provided to you for medical necessity, and undertaking utilization review activities.

Health Care Operations: We may use and disclose your health information, as needed, in connection with our health care operations. Health care operations include quality assessment and improvement activities, reviewing the competence or qualifications of health care professionals, evaluating practitioner and provider performance, business management, and conducting or arranging other business activities. For example, we may use a sign-in sheet at the registration desk where you will be asked to sign your name and/or indicate your treating doctor. We may also call you by name in the waiting room or contact you to remind you of your appointment.

Your protected health information may be shared with business associates that may perform various functions, e.g., billing or transcription services for the practice. We may use the information to provide you with information about alternatives or other health related benefits or services. Health information may also be used for in-house marketing activities such as sending you a newsletter about our practice, products, and services we offer. Other uses and disclosures of protected health information will be made only with your written authorization, unless otherwise permitted by law as described below.

USES OR DISCLOSURES REQUIRED BY LAW: We may use or disclose your health information when we are required to do so by law, including for public health reasons, e.g., disease reporting. In some instances, and in accordance with applicable law, we may be required to disclose your health information to appropriate authorities if we reasonably believe that you have certain communicable diseases or are a possible victim of abuse, neglect, domestic violence, or other crimes. We may also disclose your health information to the extent necessary to avert a serious threat to your health or safety or the health or safety of others. We may disclose health information in response to judicial or legal proceedings, law enforcement inquiries including coroner's or funeral director's inquiries as permitted by law, and to authorized federal or state officials as required for performance of their lawful activities including but not limited to any health oversight agency, public health, department of corrections, workers' compensation, research, organ donation, Food and Drug Administration, military and national security activities.

YOUR AUTHORIZATION: You may specifically authorize us to use your health information for any purpose, or to disclose your health information to anyone, by submitting such an authorization in writing. Upon receiving an authorization from you in writing, we may use or disclose your health information in accordance with that authorization. You may revoke an authorization at any time by notifying us in writing. Your revocation will not affect any use or disclosures permitted by your authorization while it was in effect. Unless you give us a written authorization, we cannot use or disclose your health information for any reason except those permitted by this notice.

DISCLOSURES TO FAMILY AND PERSONAL REPRESENTATIVES: We may disclose your health information to you, as described in the "patient rights" section of this notice. Such disclosures will be made to any of your personal representatives appropriately authorized to have access and control of your health information. Unless you object, we may disclose your health information to a family member, relative, close friend, or any other person you identify as authorized to have access and control of your health information. In the event of your incapacity or in emergency circumstances, we will disclose health information based on a determination using our professional judgment, disclosing only health information that is directly relevant to that person's involvement in your health care.

2. YOUR RIGHTS

The following is a summary of your rights with respect to your protected health information and a brief description of how you may exercise these rights.

You have the right to inspect and copy your protected health information that is contained in a "designated record set" for as long as we maintain that protected information with limited exceptions. A "designated record set" contains medical and billing records and any other records used by your doctor to make decisions about you. You may obtain a form to request access by using the contact information listed at the end of this notice.

Under federal law you may not inspect or copy the following records: psychotherapy notes, information compiled in reasonable anticipation of, or use in, a civil, criminal, or administrative action or proceeding, and protected health information that is subject to law that prohibits access to protected information.

You have the right to request a restriction of your protected health information. You may ask us not to use or disclose any part of your protected health information for the purpose of treatment, payment, or health care operations. You may also request that any part of your protected health care information not be disclosed to family members or friends who may be involved in your care. A written request must be submitted to our Privacy Contact stating the specific restriction requested and to whom you want the restriction to apply. The doctor is not required to agree to a restriction that you may request. If the doctor believes that the use and disclosure of the protected information is in your best interests, your information will not be restricted. If a restriction is granted, your protected information will not be disclosed except as needed to provide emergency treatment.

You have the right to request that we provide copies in a format other than photocopies. We will accommodate reasonable requests. We may condition the accommodation by asking you for information as to how the payment for costs directly relating to providing this accommodation will be handled. If you prefer, we will prepare a summary or an explanation of your health information for a fee. Contact us using the information listed at the end of this notice if you are interested in receiving your health care information in an alternative format or a summary of your information instead of copies.

You have the right to request the doctor to amend your protected information. This means that you may request an amendment to your protected health information that is in a designated record set as long as the information in that set is being maintained. If your request is denied, you have the right to file a statement of disagreement with us; we may prepare a rebuttal to your statement and, if so, will provide you with a copy of such rebuttal. Please use the services of our Privacy Contact to make such a request.

You have the right to receive an accounting of certain disclosures we have made, if any, of your protected health information. This right applies to disclosures for purposes other than treatment, payment, or health care operations and valid authorizations or incidental disclosures as described in this Notice of Privacy Practices. It excludes disclosures we may have shared with you, or a facility, or to family members or friends involved in your care, or for notification purposes. The right to receive this information is subject to certain exceptions, restrictions, and limitations.

You have the right to receive a paper copy of the Notice of Privacy Practices from us upon request, even if you have agreed to accept this notice electronically.

You have the right to revoke this consent in writing, at any time, except to the extent that the doctor, the practice, or the facility has acted in reliance on this consent.

3. QUESTIONS AND COMPLAINTS

If you want more information about our privacy practices or have questions or concerns, please contact us.

If you are concerned that we may have violated your privacy rights or if you disagree with a decision we have made or any decisions we may make regarding the use, disclosure, or access to your health information, you may complain to us using the contact information listed below. You may also submit a complaint to the U.S. Department of Health and Human Services. Regional office locations are listed at www.hhs.gov/ocr/regmail.html. We can also provide you with the address to file such a complaint upon request.

We support your right to the privacy of your health information. We will not retaliate in any way if you choose to file a complaint with us or with the U.S. Department of Health and Human Services.

Please direct any or your questions, concerns, or written complaints to:

Contact: _____

Telephone: _____ FAX: _____

E-mail: _____

Address: _____

This Notice was published and became effective on this _____ day of _____, 2_____.

CONSENT FOR PURPOSES OF TREATMENT, PAYMENT, AND HEALTH CARE OPERATIONS

I, _____, consent to the Doctor's or the Practice's use and disclosure of my Protected Health Information for the purpose of providing treatment to me, for purposes relating to treatment, for the payment of services rendered to me, and for the Practice's general health care operations purposes. I understand that the Doctor's or the Practice's diagnosis or treatment of me may be conditioned upon my consent as evidenced by my signature on this document.

_____   _____
Signature of patient or representative   Date

_____   _____
Print name of patient or representative   Describe personal representative's authority

ACKNOWLEDGMENT OF RECEIPT OF NOTICE OF PRIVACY PRACTICES

I, _____, acknowledge that I have received, reviewed, understand, and agree to the Notice of Privacy Practices of _____, which describes the Practice's policies and procedures regarding the use and disclosure of any of my Protected Health Information created, received or maintained by the Practice.

_____   _____
Date   Signature

          _____
          Print name

FOR OFFICE USE ONLY IF NOTICE OF PRIVACY PRACTICES COULD NOT BE PROVIDED TO THE PATIENT

The Practice has made a good-faith effort to obtain an acknowledgment of _____ [patient's name] receipt of our Notice of Privacy Practices. Despite these efforts, the Practice has been unable to obtain a signed acknowledgment of receipt for the following reasons (check all that apply):

☐ Patient unavailable
☐ Patient physically unable
☐ Patient unwilling

In an effort to obtain the patient's acknowledgment, the Practice has attempted to provide this patient with a Notice of Privacy Practices in the following manner (check all that apply):

☐ In Person   ☐ Mail   ☐ Phone   ☐ Other: _____

_____   _____
Date   Signature

_____
(Name of Practice and/or Doctor)

INFORMED CONSENT FORM

Failing to give relevant information to the patient concerning a proposed medical procedure nullifies any consent, whereupon the physician may be liable for any injuries and damages sustained by the patient as a result of the procedure. This is true even though the doctor exercises the highest degree of medical care in performing the procedure. The following is a sample informed consent form. Please be aware that the requirements for disclosure may vary with the state. You are advised to read this for educational purposes and, if you wish, to use it as a basis for crafting a document more narrowly tailored to the requirements of the relevant jurisdiction. You are also advised, however, not to rely on the exact wording in this form without conferring with counsel, your carrier, or a knowledgeable risk manager.

DISCLOSURE AND INFORMED CONSENT FORM FOR MEDICAL, SURGICAL, AND DIAGNOSTIC PROCEDURES

Patient Name: _____

Date of Birth: _____   Age: _____

TO THE PATIENT: You have the right, as a patient, to be given information about your health condition, and the medical, surgical, or diagnostic procedures recommended, as well as the risks and hazards involved. This should allow you to make an informed decision whether or not to undergo the procedure(s) scheduled to be performed. This disclosure is not intended to scare or alarm you; it is simply an effort to make you better informed, so you may give or withhold your consent to the procedure(s).

1. VOLUNTARY REQUEST FOR TREATMENT: I hereby request that Dr. _____, as my physician, and such associates, technical assistants, and other health care providers as the physician may deem necessary, treat my condition via the proposed procedures which have been presented to me as outlined below.

I **(do)/(do not)** grant permission for other physicians, including physicians in post-graduate medical education training, personnel/students of medical, nursing, and other clinical training programs affiliated with this facility, to participate in the procedure(s) described below.

2. PLANNED PROCEDURES: I understand that the following diagnostic, surgical, medical, and/or treatment procedure(s) are planned for me and I voluntarily consent to and authorize these procedures:

A. _____

B. _____

3. DISCOVERY OF OTHER CONDITIONS: I understand that my physician may discover other or different conditions which require additional or different procedures than those planned. I authorize my physician and such associates, technical assistants, and other health care providers to perform such other procedures that are advisable in their professional judgment.

4. BLOOD TRANSFUSIONS: I **(do)/(do not)** consent to the use of blood and blood products as deemed necessary for these procedures. I understand that the following risks and hazards may occur in connection with transfusion of blood and blood products and that the risks of transfusion may be immediate or delayed: (i) bruising or swelling at the site where the needle is inserted into the vein; (ii) fever; (iii) allergic reaction; (iv) transfusion reaction which may include kidney failure or anemia or even death; (v) heart failure; (vi) hepatitis; (vii) AIDS (acquired immune deficiency syndrome) or HIV transmission; (viii) other infections; and death.

5. RISKS AND HAZARDS: I understand that there are risks and hazards related to any medical or surgical procedures. Just as there may be risks and hazards in continuing my present condition without treatment, I realize and accept that there are also risks and hazards related to the surgical, medical, and/or diagnostic procedure(s) planned for me. I realize that common to surgical, medical, and/or diagnostic procedures is the potential for infection, blood clots in veins and lungs, excessive bleeding, hemorrhage, allergic reactions, and even death, with or without anesthesia. I further understand that, in addition to the risks and hazards generally disclosed, those listed below may occur in connection with this particular procedure:

_____

_____

I also have full knowledge that there is the possibility that the procedure may not have the benefits or results intended and that there are risks and dangers to life and health associated with medical procedures and treatments which can cause adverse consequences not ordinarily anticipated in advance.

6. NO WARRANTY, GUARANTEE OF RESULT, OR CURE: I hereby acknowledge that no warranty or guarantee has been made to me as to result or cure. My physician has explained the possible use, availability, risks, and benefits of alternative treatments, if applicable, and the risks of doing nothing.

7. SPECIFIC POINTS OF DISCUSSION WITH MY PHYSICIAN:
The following subjects have been explained to me by the physician.

A. The nature of the proposed care, treatment, services, medications, interventions, or procedures, along with approximate costs.

B. Potential benefits, risks, or side effects, including potential problems related to recuperation.

C. The limitations of the procedure and the likelihood of achieving care, treatment, and service goals.

D. Reasonable alternatives to the proposed care, treatment, and service and the material risks, benefits, and side effects related to those alternatives, including the possible results of not receiving care, treatment, and services.

E. When indicated, any limitations on the confidentiality of information learned from or about me as the patient.

F. Assistants needed in the procedure to perform delegated tasks under my physician's supervision.

8. DISPOSAL OF REMOVED TISSUE: I authorize the Hospital to use its discretion to retain or dispose of any tissue(s) removed during any operation or procedure.

9. OBSERVATION OF PROCEDURE: I **(do)/(do not)** consent to the admittance of observers during the operation or procedure for the purpose of medical health education.

10. PHOTOGRAPHING OR VIDEOTAPING OF PROCEDURE:
I **(do)/(do not)** consent to the photographing or videotaping of the surgery or procedure(s) to be performed, including appropriate portions of my body, and the inclusion of such pictures in my medical record. In addition, I **(do)/(do not)** consent to the use of such pictures for medical, scientific, or educational purposes, providing my identity is not revealed by the pictures or descriptive texts accompanying the pictures.

11. ANESTHESIA: I understand that anesthesia involves additional risks and hazards, but I **request/refuse** the use of anesthetics for the relief and protection from pain during the planned and/or additional procedures. By requesting anesthesia, I voluntarily consent to the use of anesthetic agents. I further realize the type or delivery method of anesthesia may have to be changed possibly without explanation to me.

12. ANESTHESIA COMPLICATIONS: I understand and accept that certain complications may result from the use of any anesthetic, including cardiac or respiratory problems, aspiration, decreased blood pressure, nausea and vomiting, drug reactions, awareness, paralysis, nerve or brain damage, or even death. Other risks and hazards which may result from the use of general anesthetics range from minor discomfort to injury to vocal cords, lips, teeth, or eyes. I understand that other risks and hazards resulting from spinal or epidural anesthetics include headache, hematoma or blood clot formation, spinal cord injury, seizures, infection at the site of placement, meningitis, neck or back discomfort, chronic pain, and death. For pregnant women, additional risks and hazards include prolonged labor, decreased fetal heart rate, fetal distress, and fetal death. Alternative types of anesthesia, if applicable, have been explained to me by my doctor.

I acknowledge and understand that moderate or conscious sedation may progress to deep sedation or general anesthesia. I further understand that anesthesia may include placement of invasive monitors with risks and hazards such as bleeding, infection, lung collapse, irregular heartbeat, artery or major vessel injuries, decreased blood flow, perforation of the heart or esophagus and the need for additional procedures. If I am a female of childbearing age, due to the risks to an unborn child, by consenting to this procedure I also consent to pregnancy testing as deemed appropriate by my physician.

13. OPPORTUNITY TO ASK QUESTIONS: I have been given an opportunity to ask questions about my condition, alternative forms of anesthesia, treatment, risks of non-treatment, the procedures to be used, and the risks and hazards involved; I believe that I have sufficient information to give this informed consent.

14. CERTIFICATION—UNDERSTANDING OF CONSENT FORM:
I certify this form has been fully explained to me, that I have read it or have had it read to me, and that any and all blank spaces have been filled in prior to my signing. I further understand the contents of this form and voluntarily accept the risks and hazards. I fully recognize and realize that additional risks and hazards may be involved.

_____

Patient's Signature/Date/Time

_____

Other Legally Responsible Person's Signature

_____

Printed Name of Legally Responsible Person and Relationship to Patient

_____

Reason Why Patient Cannot Sign

_____

Witness Signature

I certify that the patient/parent/guardian/or other legally responsible person has been provided information on the risks, hazards, benefits, and alternatives to the treatment as outlined above. I've answered any medical questions in my area of expertise and verify that the patient has given consent to the proposed procedure(s).

_____   _____

Signature of Physician Performing Procedure   Date and Time

_____   _____

Signature of Anesthesiologist/Anesthetist   Date and Time

In an attempt to negate the consent form, a lawyer may argue that you waited until the last possible minute prior to the procedure to flood the patient with a tidal wave of information and that the patient was nervous, anxious, under stress, and no doubt felt pressure to undergo the procedure in order to have a chance of getting better. All this last-minute information was an elaborate formality, like initialing the volumes of papers in a mortgage just prior to buying a house but had no idea what they said or meant. This patient was already sick with a medical condition limiting the ability to concentrate, let alone to understand this amount of technical material.

To counter this tactic, consent should be obtained a few days or weeks prior to the procedure. A short assessment regarding the patient's status during the process is vital. The evaluation needs to be documented in the medical record.

The following is a sample form for a patient refusing diagnostic or treatment interventions.

REFUSAL OF RECOMMENDED TESTS, MEDICAL, OR SURGICAL INTERVENTION

Patient: _____ DOB: _____

The following has been explained to me by my doctor:

That I have the following actual or potential condition(s):

_____

_____

_____

1. That the following tests, procedures, and/or interventions have been
   recommended:

   _____

2. The nature of the recommended procedure or treatment is as follows:

   _____

3. The purpose of and need for the recommended tests or treatment are:

_____

4. The possible alternative(s) to the recommended procedure or intervention for which I refuse and withhold consent include:

_____

5. The nature and likelihood of the consequences of not proceeding with the recommended procedure/intervention or the above described alternative(s) have been fully explained to me and include _____

_____. I have no further questions and do not desire more information on the subject.

6. I understand that my failure to accept the recommended procedure/ intervention may endanger my life or health; I have been given all the information I need and want to have in order to make an informed decision and I nonetheless refuse to give my consent to it.

7. My reason for refusal is: _____

_____

_____

_____

_____   _____
Patient (or person authorized to sign for patient)   Date

_____   _____
Witness   Date

OFF-LABEL PRESCRIBING

Off-label prescribing, per se, poses no increase in malpractice liability. Consent for off-label prescribing is not necessary. Informed consent, however, to document the patient's understanding of the off-label drug's risks is advisable. The sample form below should be modified to fit the specific drug and purpose of that medication for any individual patient.

A form is recommended especially if the prescribed drug is experimental or if significant side effects may occur, e.g., psychotropic drugs such as Risperdal, clonazepam, lithium, etc. The following sample consent is for meclizine.

SAMPLE CONSENT AND RELEASE
FOR OFF-LABEL DRUG USE

I have been advised that when the Food and Drug Administration (FDA) approves a drug or device for medical use, the manufacturer produces a "label" to explain its uses. Once a medication is approved by the FDA, physicians may use any medication "off-label" for other purposes if in their judgment that is a prudent course for their patient.

The drug known as Antivert, or meclizine hydrochloride, is classified as an antihistamine. It was approved to treat dizziness, nausea, and vomiting related to motion sickness. This medication has been selected to aid me in the management and prevention of travel-induced migraines by reducing the tendency of prolonged travel and passive motion to induce a migraine attack.

Alternatives, such as attempts to avoid circumstances that can minimize the effects of passive motion during travel like sitting in the front seat of a moving vehicle or avoiding traveling by train or plane have been explained to me. Also, I have been advised to avoid prolonged travel altogether or, if possible, to break up a trip with frequent stops.

I know that symptoms of drowsiness or blurred vision have occasionally been reported with Antivert. For this reason, as a safety precaution, a single trial dose of 25 milligrams will be prescribed for use on a weekend or weeknight when I will not be driving, using machinery, or engaging in activities that require alertness and so, therefore, will not be a risk to others or to myself. Any side effects will be reported to the doctor prior to continuing the medication.

If side effects are relatively minor or nonexistent, the doctor may prescribe Antivert to be used prior to travel that would be expected to last longer than 45 minutes. I will report any suspected side effects experienced during the prescribed use of the medication to the doctor.

I will advise my doctor immediately if I experience mental or mood changes including confusion, fast or irregular heartbeat, shaking, difficulty urinating, or other significant changes.

I understand that Antivert, also known as meclizine, was approved by the FDA for prevention and treatment of motion sickness. Nevertheless, I wish to have Antivert to use in helping to prevent and treat migraine symptoms likely induced by travel and I am willing to accept the potential risks that my physician has discussed with me. I readily acknowledge that there may be other unknown risks which cannot be anticipated in advance and that the long-term effects and risks of regular Antivert usage are not known.

I freely consent to the "off-label" prescription for this medication and fully accept any and all risks associated with its use.

_____   _____
Patient's name   Patient's signature

_____   _____
Witness   Date

DOB: _____   Date: _____ / _____ /20

CONCLUSION

A medical consent form can be a physician's best friend and best defense against charges that informed consent was lacking. A signed form means that the patient assumed all the risks and complications of a properly performed procedure. (See also "Chapter 6: Informed Consent.")

Inform your patients of the risks, dangers, alternative procedures or treatments available, and the risks of not undergoing the recommended procedure or treatment or of doing nothing. Have a thorough and signed informed consent form along with your own well-documented notes on the subject and patient encounter.

BIBLIOGRAPHY

Forum. Risk Management Foundation of the Harvard Medical Institutions, Inc. *Informed Consent Review* 11, no. 6.

"Give Six New Privacy Rights to Patients." *Health Information Compliance Insider*. Brownstone Publishers, 2001.

Hospital Law Manual. Aspen Publications.

Hudson, T. "Informed Consent Problems Become More Complicated." *Hospitals* 65, no. 6 (Mar. 20, 1991): 38–40.

Medico-Legal Primer. 1st ed. American College of Legal Medicine Foundation, 1991.

Treatise on Health Care Law. Matthew Bender and Co., Inc.

Walker, M. *Starting in Medical Practice*. Oradell, NJ: Medical Economics Books, 1987.

CHAPTER 10

Malpractice Insurance
– Special Forces for the Doctor's Defense –

"Insurance companies have a proclivity for hiring lawyers with beguiling smiles and attractive personalities. They seem quite unimposing, quite humble, quite kind, quite gentle, quite to-the-toenails right. People inevitably look to them and listen to them, and because they tend to believe nice people, they usually win." —Unknown

THE MASTER PLAN

The primary function of the insurance business as a whole is risk management. Like all insurance companies, malpractice liability carriers collect premiums from policyholders, invest the money (typically in low-risk investments), and then once the policyholder has a claim, those funds are used to defend the claim and to pay any judgment amount up to the policy limit.

Many significant changes have occurred in the U.S. insurance industry since its inception in the late 1600's. Today, the insurance industry collects about one trillion dollars in premium payments per year and is legally exempt from federal antitrust laws, including price fixing.

The insurance industry is, at its core, designed for the purpose of helping the consumer. Even so, insurance companies are often viewed with suspicion and even hostility. Few industries are despised as much as insurance.

To outsiders it can seem that insurance companies are like a strong-arm syndicate demanding protection money. Most of us are intimidated by the costly negative turns life can take, and we reluctantly fork over the dollars to protect ourselves against these potential calamities. Despite the prevailing attitudes about insurance companies as a sort of necessary evil, these companies comprise an incredibly powerful, unique, and necessary industry that can help medical professionals when they most need it.

THE CHOICES

Doctors have two primary choices regarding professional liability insurance:

1. They can obtain a reasonable malpractice policy. At least 11 states require physicians to obtain minimal professional liability coverage.

2. They can decline to purchase liability insurance, i.e., go bare, if their state allows it.

Securing Malpractice Protection

Though most people believe that they are great drivers and will never have an accident, just about everyone carries some form of automobile insurance. The reason is that we all know mistakes happen, and we need to be protected.

Just as having automobile insurance does not prevent car accidents from happening, malpractice insurance does not prevent doctors from suffering moments of inattention, uninterest, forgetfulness, or other oversights, and thus making mistakes.

Everyone makes mistakes. Insurance does, however, prevent the loss of personal property and hard-earned savings in the event of a mistake or lapse in judgment that results in a lawsuit, a settlement, or a negative verdict.

In virtually every state, physicians must have minimal levels of liability insurance coverage in order to obtain and maintain hospital staff privileges and to participate in insurance provider panels or plans. Malpractice insurance coverage is almost always a must for any physician offering full, i.e., admitting and inpatient, services. Therefore, as a practical matter, most physicians need insurance coverage in order to function and practice in the real world.

Malpractice insurance is absolutely essential for doctors who desire to protect their assets, their practices, their professional standing, and their valuable time. Malpractice insurance provides real protection on many levels. It is an indispensable comfort and an invaluable wellspring of resources that can be mustered on the doctor's behalf when necessary.

Going Bare

Some physicians are under the mistaken assumption that if they do not carry medical malpractice insurance, so there is no insurance money for a plaintiff to go after, that they will not be sued or are less likely to be sued. This is an erroneous and potentially devastating misconception.

Some states, such as Ohio, do not mandate malpractice insurance coverage, but require doctors who lack malpractice coverage to give written notice directly to their patients and obtain a consent form from them before administering nonemergency care. This notice and consent must be maintained in the patient's file.

Going bare will likely preclude the physician from participating in an HMO/MCO or acquiring hospital privileges. The reason is that most HMOs/MCOs and hospitals require physicians to have a liability coverage agreement before granting privileges.

Therefore, those physicians without coverage are restricted to performing medical procedures in outpatient centers or medical offices.

In the event of a lawsuit, not having malpractice insurance coverage forces the doctor to pay out of pocket for all discovery and trial expenses. This may include filing fees, record service fees, subpoenas, court costs, medical records, investigative fees and expenses, consultant fees, specialized non-testimonial nurse and medical expert fees, court reporter fees, transcription fees, telephone calls, photocopying, postage/shipping costs, obtaining transcripts, fax transmissions and receipts, messengers, preparation of exhibits and photographs, witness fees and mileage, travel time, lodging expenses, car rentals, parking, meals, expert witness fees for evaluation, reports, testimony time along with commercial and private transportation, and other costs and expenses.

By the way, attorney fees will also need to be added to the above list. Anyone in the business knows that defense attorneys are not easy on the wallet. Many malpractice defense firms charge between $300–$600 per hour or more for preparation, research, writing briefs, memos, and court documents, taking and making telephone calls, sending and reading e-mails, analyzing medical records, reviewing court documents, as well as finding, interviewing, and hiring experts/consultants, etc.

After paying all those out of pocket expenses, you still must tack on the additional amount of any jury verdict should you not come out victorious in your defense. In case you are still not convinced, call a malpractice insurance carrier and inquire about the average costs of going to court to gain additional insight and an object lesson on this topic. If a doctor lacks sufficient assets to pay the cost of the judgment, the court has the ability to garnish the physician's future wages.

On analysis, the concept of "going bare" is not an option that any physician should seriously consider—there is simply too much at stake.

THREE TYPES OF MALPRACTICE POLICIES
Occurrence Policy
The older traditional malpractice insurance policy was an occurrence policy. This type of insurance provided coverage for an injury or act that took place during the policy period, regardless of when the claim was reported. Even if a claim was not presented until after the expiration of the policy, the claim would still be paid.

Some claims might not be filed for some time after these types of policies expired. Insurance companies call coverage purchased separately for these claims "tail coverage." Tails can take several years to be filed and resolved, which made it difficult for the carriers to do loss projections. As a result, malpractice insurance companies began to abandon occurrence policies several years ago, and most now offer only claims-made policies.

Claims-Made Policy
Today, insurance companies write almost exclusively claims-made policies. These liability policies cover only those claims that are presented or filed during the time the policy is in effect. If a patient is injured while the policy is in force, a resulting claim is covered only if it is filed before the expiration date of the policy. Once the policy lapses, there is no longer any protection for any claim brought after that date unless you purchased tail coverage.

On first entering practice, physicians have no history of potentially injured patients who may make a claim against their insurance. Over the years, the number of potential claimants begins to increase until it reaches a plateau. In part, that's because under the statute of limitations, older potential claims become time-barred. The risk plateau is typically reached within a few years of beginning practice.

Claims-made policies were introduced in order to lower premium rates by reducing the uncertainty of future payouts. Nowadays, the vast majority of policies offered are only claims-made policies which are significantly less expensive than occurrence policies.

Tail Coverage
Tail coverage is needed for a claims-made policy, but not for an occurrence policy. This is why physicians must be very careful, because when a claims-made policy expires, the physician is no longer insured against claims that may have happened during the term of the policy but have not yet been filed.

They are still on the hook. To cover these claims, the physician must invest in tail coverage insurance, also known as extended reporting coverage. Tail coverage protects against claims that are brought against a doctor after cancellation of a claims-made malpractice policy. Physicians must usually purchase the tail coverage within 30 days of canceling the current policy.

When acquiring a position with a new employer or if doctors during their careers want to switch and purchase coverage from a different professional liability carrier, they should consider purchasing "prior acts coverage," also known as "nose coverage," from the new carrier as an alternative because it is usually less expensive than tail coverage.

When doctors retire or otherwise no longer practice medicine, they still must purchase tail coverage to protect themselves from risks related to past events.

Tail coverage can cost one and a half to three times the annual premium of a claims-made policy. This increased cost of tail coverage is a major determinant of a doctor's ability or inability to change employers, move to another state (where the current carrier does not write policies), leave the current practice, or simply switch malpractice insurance companies.

The terms of availability for tail coverage are an important consideration when evaluating the cost of a malpractice insurance policy. The cost of the tail should be predictable and its availability guaranteed.

Underwriting Standards

From a doctor's point of view, the most contentious issue in malpractice insurance is rate setting. Doctors want affordable insurance and insurance companies want maximum income. There are three underlying reasons why premiums remain high, despite recent tort reforms.

First, rates and competition are inextricably linked. The insurance business in general is less competitive than other comparable businesses. As mentioned previously, that is attributable in part to the fact that the industry is exempt from federal antitrust laws. This insulation from market forces allows insurance companies to charge higher rates than those that would exist in a free market.

Minimal competition among insurance companies allows them to manipulate markets in ways that would not be tolerated by the customers of other businesses. For example, a typical business strategy is to enter a market with low rates and attractive terms. Once a group of doctors is insured with the company, the rates are quickly raised. The cost of tail coverage is then set quite high, essentially trapping physicians who switched companies because of discounted rates so they must ultimately pay more for insurance for several years to come.

Second, the National Bureau of Economic Research (NBER) found little correlation between malpractice payouts from lawsuits and malpractice premiums charged to doctors. Researchers at NBER concluded that "increases in malpractice payments made on behalf of physicians do not seem to be the driving force behind increases in premiums."[1]

Third, malpractice insurance premiums are not experience rated. Unlike automobile insurers, malpractice insurers do not necessarily charge differential rates based on individual physician lawsuit histories or risk factors, which means that physicians with an increased number of claims may not pay higher rates. This lack of individual ratings puts responsible doctors at a financial disadvantage because they essentially subsidize the high-risk individuals in their specialty.

INSURANCE PREMIUMS

Unfairly high insurance rates for malpractice are unsettling and a true concern for many physicians. As stated previously, insurance coverage is part of the cost of doing business in most industries, whether it's the construction industry, moving freight, or practicing medicine. An overwhelming number of practitioners have malpractice insurance. Although it is expensive, especially in certain states and for some specialties, it is necessary.

Insurance premiums generally rise and fall in concert with the state of the economy. "When the economy is booming and investment returns are high, companies tend to maintain premiums at modestly high levels; however, when the economy falters and interest rates fall, companies tend to further increase premiums in response."[2]

Unlike other industries, the insurance industry has never faced any kind of sustained governmental investigation or scrutiny. This includes their practices and rationale for setting medical malpractice policy rates. To ensure that doctors pay a fair premium and are not being gouged for

---

[1] http://www.nber.org/papers/w10709.
[2] J. Robert Hunter, "Medical Malpractice Insurance: Stable Losses/Unstable Rates," *Americans for Insurance Reform* (Oct. 10, 2002).

needed coverage, the insurance industry, including their policies concerning malpractice liability premiums, should be more closely inspected. (See also "Chapter 10: Malpractice Insurance.")

THE INSURANCE COMPANY'S DUTIES

The malpractice insurance company has only two obligations. The first is to defend their client, the doctor. The second is to pay any judgment rendered up to the policy limits. The doctor will be defended, but a judgment will be paid only to the extent of the coverage amount.

If there is a coverage question, e.g., the amount of coverage or whether there is any coverage at all, the doctor may receive a "reservation of rights" letter. By sending this letter, the company is informing its client that it is investigating and defending the claim, but that they may deny coverage for some or all of the claim.

Similarly, the doctor may be asked to sign a "non-waiver agreement." This means that the insurance company will agree to defend the policy-holder, but the question of their obligation to pay any judgment will be deferred until the coverage question is resolved. Typically, the policyholder does not have to sign that agreement, but is on notice that part or all of the claim may not be paid by the company.

COVERAGE "UNTOUCHABLES"

Insurers have no obligation to cover the consequences of intentional behavior such as battery, criminal behavior, or sexual misconduct. Such acts are clearly not considered to be part of medical practice and the policy will either have an exclusion or simply not include such conduct under acts they will cover.

Intentional harmful conduct can also tack on a demand for punitive damages which would not be covered by the insurance carrier. In these cases, an "asset-ectomy" may be performed without anesthesia on the defendant doctor.

However, let's assume a plaintiff alleges lack of informed consent to a procedure. That could technically be a claim of battery for intentional unconsented contact or touching which would not normally be covered. Even such an assertion involving intentional action may not necessarily create a bar preventing coverage under the policy since the same claim could have been brought in a negligence or malpractice action which would be covered.

A New Dawn of Coverage?

Fortunately, some carriers are beginning to offer coverage for the defense of actions taken by a medical board, such as a hearing to consider revocation or suspension of a license or to take other disciplinary actions against a doctor. This is an indication that some insurance companies will venture into types of coverage where other companies have refused to go.

Other recent policies can provide limited payments to the doctor for expenses in his/her own defense, for example, compensation for time away from the office if done at the insurance company's request.

Defense cost coverage for allegations of sexual misconduct are also being written into some policies, provided the misconduct is part of a malpractice allegation.

Purchasing Malpractice Insurance

The following are three critical considerations when purchasing malpractice insurance.

First, policies must be evaluated on their potential long-term costs. It is foolish to change carriers because of a slightly lower rate that may evaporate at renewal time. Doctors should attempt to determine the company's timing for anticipated rate increases and the potential amount of any such increase.

Second, there are policies that allow the defendant to influence the conduct of the litigation. In particular, some policies offer a "consent to settle clause," providing that the matter may not be settled on any terms unless the physician (insured) agrees. These clauses are attractive because they diminish the tendency of some carriers to settle too easily to save defense costs, and because they give the doctor a measure of control over whether his name is added to the National Practitioner Data Bank. Such clauses can increase the carrier's costs, however. A company's offering of a consent-to-settle clause undermines that consent it by imposing a so-called "hammer clause" under the policy. This type of clause allows the company to estimate how much it will cost to settle the suit. If the doctor refuses to settle at that point, the company can then explain that the decision is up to the doctor, but that the company will only contribute the estimated settlement cost toward the judgment. Physicians must also realize that every dollar the company spends in the defense of individual claims ultimately comes out of their own pockets.

Third, and most importantly, when buying insurance, doctors must determine the cost and terms of availability for the tail coverage.

Another point of consideration involves the question of the company's financial stability; insurance is useless if the insurer is bankrupt. The carrier's rating for financial strength is graded by A.M. Best, Inc., and other rating organizations. A.M. Best can be accessed by telephoning 1-908-439-2200 or through their website at http://www.ambest.com/homepage.asp.

Although it can be difficult to determine if a company is honest in its projections, it is useful to investigate the company's behavior both historically and in other states. Physicians must do their homework on an insurance company's business reputation.

POINTS TO CONSIDER WHEN BUYING MALPRACTICE INSURANCE

- The type of coverage and the limits.
- Cost of premiums and whether rate increases are automatically due, and in what specific amounts?
- Cost and availability of tail coverage and/or umbrella policy?
- Do defense costs come out of the face value of the policy or are they accounted for separately?
- What is the definition of a claim and how must the doctor report the claim?
- Policy exclusions.
- Does the policy require the doctor's consent to any settlement? Is there a "hammer clause."
- Can the covered physician choose the defense attorney/firm?
- Are any consulting activities, including telemedicine services, covered?
- Is there coverage if "there is a failure to use telemedicine where its use is alleged to be required under the applicable standard of care?"[3]
- Is there coverage for any disciplinary matters?
- Are advertising activities included?
- Are an employee's inadvertent and intentional acts included or excluded?
- What is the grace period for late premium payments?
- On what grounds, if any, can the company cancel the policy?

---

[3] Joe McMenamin, MD, JD, "Questions to Ask Your Telemedicine Malpractice Carrier," *CTeL News Update* (Aug. 28, 2015). https://utn.org/resources/downloads/questionsasktelemedicinemalpracticecarrier.pdf.

- If a doctor should lose his or her license, or is stuck with a temporary suspension for any reason, does he or she still have coverage?
- Will the rate be increased in the event of a set number of claims or payouts?
- Is there a policy that is renewable and cannot be canceled by the company?
- How can the policyholder cancel the policy?
- If immediate coverage is necessary, doctors should ask for a binder to protect themselves while the application is being evaluated.
- Doctors should also consider dealing with a mutual insurance company. Mutual companies have no stockholders or shareholders to satisfy, which helps lower rates.

CONCLUSION

You don't have to cause a severe injury to face a serious lawsuit. Simply failing to return a phone call can result in charges of abandonment if damages result. Oversights and mishaps happen all the time. Thus, acquiring malpractice insurance is simply part of the cost of doing business, just like leasing office space, buying equipment, or hiring staff. Failing to secure an appropriate level of insurance coverage opens the door to serious financial risk and is not recommended in most circumstances.

BIBLIOGRAPHY

American Medical Association Advocacy Resource Center. Feb. 2008.

Anderson, R.E., ed. *Medical Malpractice: A Physician's Sourcebook.* Totowa, NJ: Humana Press, Inc.

Campion, Francis X., MD. The Risk Management Foundation of the Harvard Medical Institutions Incorporated. *Grand Rounds on Medical Malpractice.* Chicago, IL: American Medical Association, 1990.

Ohio Revised Code. 4731.143.

Ohio Revised Code. 4731.22(B)(30).

Richard, Edward P. University of Missouri, Kansas City School of Law.

CHAPTER 11

Plaintiff Attorney's Deposition Outline for Defendant Doctor
– Questions to Consider –

FUNDAMENTALS

In depositions, doctors can be questioned on matters that will be inadmissible at trial. Inquiries regarding issues may be asked in ways that will never be asked at trial such as "Why?" This is designed to uncover valuable information such as the doctor's reasoning for his/her actions and possible defenses to the charges.

No deposition outline can be entirely complete since the facts of each case are unique and different. Also, attorneys have different personalities and approaches such that all potential questions cannot be anticipated. However, the following is a good variety pack of questions to help the doctor prepare for the ordeal of deposition and avoid undue surprises.

INTRODUCTORY MATERIALS

"Good morning, Doctor, I'm Charlie Theisler and I have the honor and responsibility of representing the Simmons Family in this matter."

Q: Ever had your deposition taken before?

Q: I'm sure your attorneys have described the process to you, but I want to make sure you understand how we will proceed today, okay?

Q: If you do not understand any question, please ask me for clarification so I can be sure that we are communicating—is that satisfactory?

Q: If you don't tell me otherwise, I will assume that you both heard and understood my entire question—is that fair?

Q: Try not to shake your head yes or no in response to my questions, but speak clearly so the court reporter can accurately take down your answer, okay?

GROUND RULES

Q: Now, Doctor, I am going to be asking you a series of questions today and I would like to establish some guidelines with you, alright?

Q: Will you try not to answer or interject until I have completed my entire question?

Q: And will you agree that if I ask for your opinion, I am asking for an opinion to a reasonable degree of medical probability or medical certainty?

Q: I have tried very hard to phrase my questions so that they can honestly be answered yes or no. Will you do your best to answer my questions that way and if you can't, tell me so before you answer the question?

Q: Okay, let's begin.

PRELIMINARY QUESTIONS

Q: Do you understand that you are under oath during this deposition?

Q: Do you understand what it means to be under oath?

Q: Do you understand that being under oath means you that have an obligation to tell the truth during this deposition and to respond truthfully to each question asked of you here today?

Q: If I ask you a question and you don't know the answer to that question, would you please tell me that you don't know the answer and that you won't speculate? Can you assure me of that?

Q: State your full given name, please, and spell your last name for the court reporter.

Q: You are a physician?

Q: And you are the defendant in this case?

Q: Where are you employed?

Q: Do you drink alcohol or take illegal drugs?

Q: Are you taking medication of any kind not prescribed by your doctor.

DISCOVERY MATERIALS

Q: You recall receiving some requests for information from me?

Q: Do you have those requests and materials with you today as instructed?

Q: To the best of your knowledge are all your responses to those requests true and accurate?

Q: Did you bring original hospital and office medical records as instructed in the subpoena?

Q: And are those records accurate, detailed, and complete?

Q: Do you have any materials, including correspondence, that discuss this case in any way?

PREPARATION FOR DEPOSITION

Q: Tell me everything you did to get ready for this deposition.

Q: Read any witness statements?

Q: Perform a literature search regarding any issues in this case?

Q: What medical literature have you reviewed to prepare for this deposition?

Q: Will you provide me with copies of what you reviewed?

Q: What books do you have regarding the subject of this case in your own personal library?

Q: Do you have any independent recollection of this patient or their care (without looking at records or notes) outside of the records?

Q: What materials, records, or documents did you use to recall the events and prepare to testify today?

Q: Make any notes on the records as you reviewed them or make any notes or memoranda of any kind about the records you reviewed?

Q: After your review of the records, did it refresh your memory or revive any independent recollections outside of those records?

Q: Do you have a copy of the medical records with you?

Q: And are those records complete and accurate to the best of your knowledge?

Q: Have you or anyone else deleted or taken anything from this file?

Q: Modified, altered, or added anything to the file or chart?

Q: I'll need a complete copy of those records and the notes you made.

Q: Utilize any other resources to prepare to testify?

Q: Did you read all or part of anyone else's deposition in this matter?

Q: Are there records you have not reviewed?

Q: Are there any records that relate to this patient in any way that are kept elsewhere?

Q: Other than your own lawyer, whom have you talked to regarding this case?

Q: What was the purpose of the conversation?

Q: When was the last time you talked to your lawyer about this case?

Q: Was anyone else present when you met with your lawyer?
(If yes, witness may have waived attorney-client privilege.)

DEFINITIONS

Q: What is an acute abdomen?

Q: What is your hospital's definition of an emergency?

Q: At any time during the course of care was this patient's case an emergency?

Q: Are these definitions commonly accepted in the medical community or are there other schools of accepted definitions for the terms we have just discussed?

GETTING THE STORY—WHO, WHAT, WHERE, WHEN, AND WHY

Q: Ever have occasion to examine and treat Plaintiff?

Q: When was that?

Q: Where was that?

Q: At that time did you take a history?

Q: Okay. You were working in the course and scope of your employment at the emergency room in August of last year, taking care of Mrs. Simmons, correct?

Q: What were this patient's presenting symptoms?

Q: Take me through the rest of the history.

Q: Was there anything else?

Q: What happened next?

Q: And after that?

Q: What was your plan at that point?

Q: And then what?

Q: After completing the history, did you do a physical exam?

Q: What tests did you perform and what were the patient's responses?

Q: The tests listed on this form were the only procedures performed that day, correct?

Q: Was your physical exam helpful in diagnosing the problem?

Q: What were the significant physical findings?

Q: Doctor, after taking her history, listening to her complaints and doing a physical examination, did you have some early thought on what her problems were?

Q: What were they?

Q: What was your list of conditions to rule out?

Q: Order any diagnostic tests?

Q: When you look at this EKG, what do you see?

Q: How can you tell if that is reassuring?

Q: What would you see if it was non-reassuring?

Q: At any time did you alter your differential diagnosis or working diagnosis and give the reasons for any such revision?

Q: What was your diagnosis before you began treatment?

Q: What was your prognosis when you first examined the patient?

Q: What did the patient need?

Q: Do you consider this patient to have been generally compliant?

Q: What did you rely on most to make your diagnosis?

Q: Did you consult others about the diagnosis?

Q: Tell us all recommendations, instructions, consultations, and orders that you made or obtained regarding the Plaintiff.

Q: Could you list all the classic signs and symptoms of the diagnosis?

Q: What did you do to confirm the diagnosis?

Q: What were your orders regarding the monitoring of your patient and the condition?

Q: Alright, when did you realize that Mrs. Simmons was not getting better and may be getting worse?

Q: What was that based on?

Q: Did you change your diagnosis and treatment plan?

Q: How were the patient's needs different from before?

Q: Who else was present during the procedure?

Q: What was your rationale for implementing that procedure?

WHY

Q: Why did you choose that surgical technique to attempt?

Q: Why did you choose this medication for this particular patient?

Q: Why did you take a different course of care and not follow the expert's advice?

Q: Why didn't you order...?

Q: Why didn't you follow your own hospital's policies?

Q: Why didn't you consult the medical literature on this subject?

Q: Why...?

COMPLICATIONS

Q: What measures or procedures did you undertake to manage the post-operative care?

Q: As to each procedure, when was it performed?

Q: As to each procedure, did any person except you render any post-op care?

Q: Was each procedure documented?

Q: Where in the record?

Q: Did any complications affect the recovery?

Q: And a complication is another way of saying that the patient's course took an unexpected turn—that's fair, isn't it?

Q: Have you heard or were you taught that when a disease or condition takes an unexpected turn to reconsider the diagnosis?

Q: Just common sense, isn't it?

Q: And this condition took such a turn, did it not?

Q: Did you reconsider the diagnosis?

Q: Tell me how you did that?

Q: Please describe each complication for this patient.

Q: Was each complication documented?

Q: Please describe every precipitating event that led to each complication.

Q: Was each precipitating event documented?

Q: What steps and actions did you take in response to each complication?

Q: Was each step or response documented?

Q: Where in the record?

Q: What is your take or theory on what happened to Mrs. Simmons that day?

RULES OF THE ROAD—SECURE AGREEMENTS ABOUT THE RULES OF PRACTICING MEDICINE

Medical History

Q: Now, the patient's history is very important, isn't it sir?

Q: In fact, the history and physical are the first steps in the sequential analysis of a patient's problems, correct?

Q: Now, the history is the portion of the evaluation where the information regarding the patient is obtained and the initial clinical impression is developed, correct?

Q: And doctors should listen to everything a patient says is wrong with them, true?

Q: This is important for the doctor's ability to reliably diagnose and effectively treat a condition?

Q: The process employed in history-taking and the depth to which the doctor elicits a health history is a critical factor in the doctor's ability to professionally and effectively provide good health care, true?

Q: So, is it good practice to be thorough in your patient procedures?

Q: And it's important to record the history accurately and completely, true?

Q: You've been taught the importance of taking an accurate patient history, have you not?

Q: You've been instructed and trained to fully note the patient's medical history, and to write up that history in the chart, true?

Q: It was explained to you in your education and training that these notes must include all the relevant data, right?

Q: The bottom line, very simply, is that the medical chart must reflect your rationale and what you have done, correct?

Q: After all, if the history is wrong, then the rest of the evaluation based on that clinical foundation can be on shaky ground, true?

Q: So, to the extent that a physician failed to take an adequate history, that would be unacceptable, right?

Q: And to the extent that a doctor omitted crucial facts from the chart, that also would be unacceptable, true?

Q: The goal is continuity of care is for the patient's sake, correct?

Q: The goal, after all, is properly caring for the patient, true?

Q: The end goal is to allow others reviewing the chart to see firsthand what was done regarding the patient, correct?

Q: Would you agree with me that a reasonable doctor would never make a diagnostic or treatment decision without obtaining a careful, detailed history and recording it?

Q: So, you would agree that obtaining the chief complaint, history of the present illness, family history, past health history, review of systems, and other risk factors are very important for the effective treatment of any patient, including your patient?

Q: Bottom line—obtaining a complete history is very important, yes?

Q: And, therefore, you would agree, as a general proposition, that the more you know about the patient, the better position you are in to properly evaluate and advise the patient, true?

Q: And a failure to obtain such a complete history and to document that history would be a danger to the patient?

Q: And you agree, do you not, that a doctor's failure to take an appropriate and complete history could cause serious jeopardy to a patient's receiving effective treatment?

Q: And this failure could be a matter of serious consequence, isn't that true?

Q: Another physician or health care worker providing care for a particular patient should be able to rely on the records for that patient that were made by you and your office, true?

Q: If important information was missing, that could change a doctor's opinion, couldn't it?

Q: Now, the chief complaint or symptom is also very important, correct?

Q: In other words, a competent doctor asks appropriate questions about the symptom bothering the patient the most? (Description of quality, character, intensity, frequency, location, radiation, duration of symptoms, date of onset, course, and what makes symptoms better or worse.)

Q: And you asked and recorded all those questions about the chief complaint, right?

Q: A thorough history also includes a review of systems, past health history, family history, and psychosocial (occupation, activities, exercise, recreational activities history, correct?

Q: You agree that it's important to have pertinent information about the patient so that you, as the physician, can select and organize the most relevant information leading to the development of a differential diagnosis list?

Q: That failure to have that pertinent information could also be a matter of life and death in some circumstances, true?

Q: Any doctor or physician providing future care would understandably want to rely on your history and documentation for an accurate historical record of the patient, right?

Q: Can you think of any reason that you, as a practitioner of a healing art, would not want all of that information in a complete history?

Q: And if the patient's data that you wanted in the file were incomplete, that sort of calls into question any physician's whole evaluation, treatment, recommendations, and opinions, doesn't it?

Q: And, once again, it is essential that the information elicited be accurately recorded in a narrative fashion and that an initial problem list be developed, true?

Q: Many times you base your clinical decisions and reasoning on the history you obtain from the patient, isn't that correct?

Q: And if the history is wrong or incorrect, certainly that could throw the whole evaluation—or at least open it up—to some type of questioning, couldn't it?

Q: Part of that history is assessing how the medical problems are developing, including the speed of development, true?

Differential Diagnosis

Q: Now, a symptom may be common to a number of diseases, correct?

Q: Another way of saying the same thing is that a patient's history of pain or other symptoms may be consistent with one or more causes?

Q: And that is a prime reason that doctors must accomplish what is called a differential diagnosis. You agree with that statement, don't you?

Q: Do you agree that a differential diagnosis is the process of determining which of several diseases is actually causing the patient's symptoms?

Q: And any opinion about the cause, without a differential diagnosis, would be unreliable, isn't that a fact?

Q: So, the differential diagnosis is the "determination of which of two or more diseases or conditions a patient is suffering from…," right? (*Dorland's Illustrated Medical Dictionary*)

Q: And the doctor must perform a sufficient differential diagnosis to safely care for the patient, correct?

Q: So, any competent physician must understand and identify those potential causes of the patient's symptoms and differentiate among them?

Q: And there are rules in following a system, or a logical order for doctors to follow, when trying to rule out conditions, isn't that true?

Q: And you agree that the possible causes of illness must be ruled out in order of severity and the need for timely attention?

Q: So, first you look at life threatening conditions?

Q: And then you look at other serious conditions?
  or

Q: So, you agree then that physicians, especially ER physicians, must rank or prioritize diseases that require the earliest treatment in terms of both underlying severity and risk of morbidity and mortality?

Q: In other words, rule out the "worst first?"

Q: That is the primary rule, is it not, in differential diagnosis?
  or

Q: Alright, to sum it up, what we're saying is that the most serious potential diseases, I mean the ones more likely to cause disability and death, must be ruled out first?

Q: Do you agree that to the extent you cannot diagnose with certainty among all potential causes, you must maintain a sufficiently detailed history, perform an adequate physical examination, and accomplish the necessary studies that will permit you to rule out serious causes of the symptoms?

Q: And identify or rule in the actual cause?

Q: So, if a doctor was evaluating someone, for example, with abdominal pain, you would want to first rule out surgical or life-threatening causes of abdominal pain, right?

Q: You're trained in how to accomplish a differential diagnosis? (See *Dorland's* definition.)

Q: In fact, failing to perform an adequate differential is bad medicine, true? Below the standard of care?

Q: It's unreasonable for a trained physician to fail to complete a differential diagnosis?

Q: And unsafe?

Q: Do you also agree that the very reason for a differential diagnosis is not only to challenge the obvious diagnosis for the purpose of confirming it, but better still, to rule out other serious causes for the patient's safety?

Q: After all, a patient can have more than one condition causing their symptoms, true? (For chest pain—HTN, high cholesterol, CAD, COPD, MI, angina, etc.)

Q: Differential diagnosis is not simply a speculative exercise or guessing game, is it?

Q: Do you agree with the principle of doctors that "if you can't rule it out, you'd better check it out"?

Q: Do you agree that when doctors are uncertain of the diagnosis, they should obtain an emergency consultation with someone with more training or experience who can better decide what needs to be done next?

Q: Do you agree with the statement that limiting the differential diagnosis just because of the location of the pain can lead to errors in diagnosis?

Q: You would not want to limit your differential diagnosis until all the serious causes have been ruled out, would you, doctor?

Q: What follow-through should a competent doctor perform to rule out each condition for severe chest pain, head pain, or non-traumatic abdominal pain?

Q: I assume you agree that the early detection of all surgically amenable causes of abdominal pain is extremely important?

Q: Do you agree that, as a general proposition, the earlier you detect a surgical cause of abdominal pain, the more you can do about it?

Q: Do you agree in that context that "later is never better than sooner"?

Q: The very reason that doctors have an obligation to make as prompt a diagnosis as possible is to give the patient every chance for a better outcome, right?

Q: Do you agree that if any patient had an early diagnosis of, say, bowel obstruction, acute abdomen, or appendicitis, that the prognosis in general terms would be improved?

Q: You have heard the medical saying "never let the sun set on a bowel obstruction"?

Q: And that medical aphorism means that a bowel obstruction is a dangerous and deadly diagnosis if untreated, correct?

Physical Examination

Q: Now, as to the examination of a patient, I want to go over that concept a little bit.

Q: Isn't it true that the physical examination gives key information as to the patient's clinical status?

Q: Doctors attempt to use observation, testing, etc., and to be as objective as possible in the physical examination, true?

Q: You were trained to correlate information obtained in the examination with the history, true?

Q: And you must have the ability to recognize and differentiate normal findings from abnormal findings, correct?

Q: And a reasonable doctor knows and recognizes, because of education and training, variants of normal findings from variants of abnormal, true?

Q: After all, not everything is a textbook case, can we agree on that?

Q: And you are aware of that before you see any of your patients, correct?

Q: Physicians are expected to be able to interpret and assess the clinical importance of significant physical examination findings. You agree with that statement?

Q: Moreover, the standard of care requires doctors to develop objective data through the physical examination process which is appropriate to the health status, history, and chief complaints of your patient. You would agree with that, wouldn't you?

Q: The examination process, among other things, helps determine if the patient is truly sick?

Q: And the nature of the condition?

Q: How serious the condition is?

Q: And how quickly the doctor must act?

Q: Now, one of the main objectives of the physical exam is to localize the area of disease, correct?

Q: And the standard of care requires you to obtain and record vital signs of a patient and examination findings in an organized manner, correct?

Q: And you would also agree that one set of vital signs cannot indicate hemodynamic stability?

Q: It's a single sample, not a verified trend, correct?

Q: And for that matter, even a dead person's vital signs are stable, true?

Q: What are the clinical hallmarks or signs of…?

Q: Did you conduct a complete and thorough examination of this patient?

Q: Were there other tests available to you in the physical examination that you did not perform on the patient?

Q: Any other tests available to you?

Q: And the standard of care also requires that you be able to recognize and record significant non-verbal signs and behaviors exhibited by the patient?

Q: What were those?

Q: Isn't it true that an undone or incomplete physical assessment can get both the doctor and the patient into more clinical trouble?

Q: Would you agree that more is missed from not looking than from not knowing?

Q: And there are other assessment procedures that you did not use that could have presented more information?

Q: Is it true that a doctor should pay attention to what is different about a patient, rather than only to things that are similar to other patients?

Diagnostic Tests

Q: Would a core principle in medicine be that a doctor should "test and not guess" what's wrong with the patient?

Q: When considering a diagnostic test, would a competent doctor consider:
The expense to a patient? (No)
The risk to the patient?
Whether the test could accurately predict the diagnosis?

Q: Is there a name for tests with hardly any error rate for predicting a particular diagnosis? (gold standard)

Q: Did you order any gold standard tests for this patient?

Q: Is it also a prime directive that doctors should get all the test results before deciding what to do next?

Diagnosis

Q: You have heard that early diagnosis is the road to early treatment or cure?

Q: You would agree that a correct diagnosis is the essential preliminary to correct treatment?

Q: You understand that it is negligence for a doctor to deprive the patient of a chance for a cure by failing to respond quickly and correctly to the patient's complaint?

Q: Part of a doctor's job is to gather clinical data carefully in order to make an accurate diagnosis?

Q: Do you agree with the statement that it is a doctor's responsibility to generate and confirm a diagnosis or a clinical impression that explains each complaint?

Q: And every doctor must have facts and reasons to support the diagnosis?

Q: And there are certain rules about diagnosing medical conditions, aren't there?

Q: And the first rule you have to remember is that medical problems don't always appear in one textbook fashion, do they?

Q: And in general terms, the same condition can cause different symptoms or have different locations of symptoms for different patients, true?

Q: And do you also agree that the diagnoses must be based on clinical findings and therefore consistent with the history and examination findings?

Q: Is it true that prior to initiating care, a diagnosis or clinical impression must be generated?

Q: What is the purpose of the clinical impression?

Q: Would you agree that a patient should not be managed clinically without a diagnosis?

Q: Right, because you're more likely to hit something you're aiming at rather than if you're shooting randomly, correct? What I mean is that action without thought or rationale is rarely helpful, is it?

Q: And the way you develop the clinical impression or diagnosis is by recognizing and correlating significant information about the patient, right?

Q: What information from your initial contact with this patient did you recognize as being significant?

Q: Putting that another way, what information and/or data from this patient led you to the formulation of your diagnostic or clinical impression?

Q: And did you organize and develop a problem list with respect to this patient on the first visit?

Q: What was your working diagnosis?

Q: How did you determine what the problem was? What I am asking is, how did you reach that diagnosis?

Q: Did that diagnosis account for all the symptoms that this patient was experiencing?

Q: (If not), which symptoms were not accounted for?

Q: Did you consider any other diagnoses?

Q: And you took all the necessary steps to properly confirm that final diagnosis?

Q: What is the natural history of acute low back pain?

Q: Did you consult and rely on any texts, protocols, or guides in diagnosing this patient's condition?

Q: I am going to ask you some questions about the diagnosis for cauda equina syndrome, and I think they can be answered yes or no.

Q: One hallmark is severe low back pain?

Q: Leg pain is something we can see with cauda equina syndrome?

Q: That is a yes, we can see it?

Q: Leg weakness is also something we can see with cauda equina syndrome?

Q: That's also a yes?

Q: Radiating pain is something we can see with cauda equina syndrome?

Q: And that is still a yes?

Q: And numbness?

Q: And despite this patient having all those symptoms, the diagnosis of cauda equina was never seriously considered?

Treatment

Q: Why did you select the treatment given?

Q: Can we agree that patient safety is important?

Q: Is it fair to say as a principle of medical care that "patient safety comes first?"

Q: And that is the thought underlying medicine's first rule of "do no harm," is it not?

Q: Each medical procedure or treatment has its own set of potential adverse reactions and side effects, correct?

Q: Because of those side effects and adverse reactions associated with medical treatment, you would agree with the medical aphorism that "no treatment is better than misdirected treatment"?

Q: And a doctor should always choose the safest course of care available, right?

Q: Do you also believe that, once having undertaken a case, a physician should not neglect the patient?

Q: Is it true that any treatment given should be clearly indicated?

Q: And any known risks associated with that treatment should be addressed before the treatment is given?

Q: That guidelines for care are considered to be safe, effective, and current (if published in the last 5 years)? (That's how they get to be guidelines.)

Q: That treatment guidelines and patient protocols exist to decrease morbidity and mortality?

Q: That the goal of all good doctors is to reduce the degree of sickness and death?

Q: And that is the reason that health care providers and especially physicians need to be familiar with and follow treatment guidelines and recommendations?

Q: And a physician's approach to health care should be based on the best scientific evidence available, true?

Q: When prescribing medicines, it's a good idea to start low and go slow. That's true isn't it?

Q: Physicians should not deny their patients access to appropriate medical tests or services?

Q: In medicine, a primary care doctor should be attentive to each of the patient's needs, true?

Q: And it's important that those needs be recorded and tracked as well?

Q: And that's usually done with a cover sheet, true?

Q: A simple form with check boxes, for example, to indicate immunizations, drug allergies, family problems, risk factors, diagnoses, etc.?

Q: That this is a must for the patient's safety and the doctor's ability to rapidly obtain an overview of this patient's status?

Q: You agree that physicians must avoid as much as possible the routine practice of phoning in instructions or treating the patient by phone?

Q: Do you agree that a hospital should help, not hurt a patient?

Records

Q: Is it true that no condition can be well-managed if it is not well-monitored?

Q: And an important monitoring tool is the medical record, correct?

Q: Doctor, would you agree that it is good medical practice to ask a patient what problems they have on each and every visit?

Q: Is it good medical practice to record that information in your medical chart?

Q: The reason why it is good medical practice is so that you and other health care providers in your office will know what specific problems and complaints the patient had on a specific date?

Q: You agree that it's good medical practice to take accurate notes?

Q: You agree that it's good medical practice to take thorough notes?

Q: Would you also agree that it is good medical practice to keep complete records?

Q: If a physician fails to ask the patient about what problems or complaints they have when they first come into the office, would you agree that would be a violation from the basic standard of medical care?

Q: If the doctor does ask a patient about problems and complaints, but fails to record that information in the patient's chart, that would be sloppy record-keeping, correct?

Duty

Q: Was Mrs. _____ a patient of yours?

Q: Do you recall when she first presented to you?

Q: You examined her?

Q: Diagnosed her?

Q: Treated her?

The Standard of Care

Q: We're going to hear a bit about the standard of care, so I want to talk to you briefly about that subject, alright?

Q: You are familiar with the term "standard of care," correct?

Q: You agree that every specialty in medicine has standards of care?

Q: Do you also agree that it is the obligation of every physician to be familiar with the applicable standards of care in his or her specialty?

Q: Now I want to ask you about your job.

Q: Agree that one of the duties of your job is patient protection?

Q: Also one of the purposes of the standard of care?

Q: That the standard of care exists for the patient's benefit, not the doctor's?

Q: And part of your job is to follow safe and accepted practice guidelines?

Q: Agree that in some cases noncompliance with the standard of care can cause an otherwise preventable injury?

Q: You are also familiar with clinical or practice guidelines?

Q: And you understand how guidelines came into being, correct?

Q: One reason is that there was and is wide variation in physicians' diagnostic and treatment methods?

Q: And there was concern over the weakness of scientific underpinnings regarding many customary medical practices, correct?

Q: And still there was and is overuse of many medical and surgical procedures?

Q: In other words, there were genuine concerns about the quality of medical care?

Q: And those are just some reasons why guidelines were developed?

Q: And clinical or evidence-based guidelines represent both acceptable and good practice?

Q: Do you recognize that practice guidelines generally help doctors obtain better results for patients?

Q: What written medical guidelines or standards are you aware of that apply to your medical specialty or area of medicine?

Q: Any customs or practices apply to your field?

Q: Did you comply with any written professional standards?

Q: Which ones?

Q: One standard is that physicians are not allowed to needlessly endanger patient?

Q: That's a standard of care?

Q: No one should be allowed to needlessly endanger anyone else, right?

Q: And when diagnosing or treating, doctors make choices, correct?

Q: Sometimes some of those choices are more dangerous than others?

Q: So doctors have to avoid selecting one of the more dangerous ones?

Q: Because that is what a prudent doctor would do?

Q: Because when the benefit is the same, the extra danger is not allowed?

Q: The standard of care does not allow extra danger unless it might work better or increase the odds of success?

Q: So needless extra danger violates the standard of care?

Q: And there's no such thing as a standard of care that allows you to needlessly endanger a patient?[1]

Q: Is it your opinion that you did everything up to accepted medical standards within your specialty?

Q: Wouldn't you agree that it was your obligation under the standard of care to look at this patient's signs, symptoms, imaging studies, and laboratory findings as a whole and not in isolation?

Q: Would you agree that, given the signs and symptoms as coupled with the history and risk factors here, standard practice was to consider the presence of a myocardial infarction or a heart attack?

Q: Wouldn't you agree that it was your further obligation under the standard of care to recognize which signs, symptoms, imaging studies, and laboratory findings, if any, were consistent with a myocardial infarction or a heart attack?

---

[1] Alex Craigie, "Preparing Your Witness for a 'Reptile' Deposition," May 22, 2013. https://atcounseltable.wordpress.com/2013/05/22/preparing-your-witness-for-a-reptile-deposition/.

Q: With a family history of cardiac disease, a history of high cholesterol, and chest pain on presentation, a careful doctor would have to at least consider a myocardial infarction, true?

Q: Wouldn't you agree that under certain circumstances any doctor like yourself needs to have a high index of suspicion that his patient is having a myocardial infarction or a heart attack?

Q: Are you saying that it was impossible to see this looming disaster or likely bad outcome?

Q: Having a patient with persistent severe pain, shortness of breath, and a history of risk factors, do you agree that the standard of care requires you to 1) obtain an immediate cardiac or surgical consult or 2) continue to monitor this patient to gauge the progress of the condition in safety?

Q: Is it fair to say that a patient with these symptoms should be referred to a cardiologist?

Authoritative Literature

Q: Would you agree that there is a long-established tradition in medicine of recognizing that some physicians achieve superior levels of skill, knowledge, or understanding compared to their peers in the same specialty?

Q: One way for doctors to convey their superior knowledge to other doctors is to publish in peer-reviewed articles or textbooks?

Q: What texts were used in your training?

Q: You are familiar with the medical literature in your specialty?

Q: Do you consider and weigh the medical literature with respect to your medical decisions?

Q: When in doubt, do you rely on medical articles, textbooks, or clinical studies in helping to make a careful decision for your patient's safety?

Q: Is it fair to say that you wouldn't prescribe a medication you are unfamiliar with without first consulting reputable reference materials for possible serious side effects?

Q: Does the word "authoritative" in terms of the medical literature mean anything to you?

Q: Do you consider any source of medical literature to be helpful and authoritative?

Q: Why not?

Q: Do you consider any medical writings as reasonably reliable regarding any of the medical issues in this case?

Q: With respect to your specialty, which we are talking about today, can you name two or three of the leading texts in your field?

Q: Do you or your colleagues find any texts to be fairly reliable or trustworthy, not perfect mind you, or generally accepted as a reasonable source of medical information?

Q: Doctor, I'm not asking whether there are books that are reliable in all respects. I'm simply asking if, as a general proposition, any of these medical books or journals is considered to be a reasonable source of medical information?

Q: Any that are helpful from time to time?

Q: What books do you have in your personal library on this subject?

Q: Do you also subscribe to or receive any journals regarding your field?

Q: Isn't it true that many standard textbooks state that…?

Policies and Procedures/Rules and Regulations/Guidelines

Q: What hospital rules or regulations applied to this patient, their work-up, or their treatment? (medical staff, surgery department, hospital bylaws, or policies)

Q: What hospital or professional policies and procedures might apply to this patient, their work-up, or treatment and monitoring?

Q: How long have those policies been in effect?

Q: Might any subsequent policies apply?

Q: What hospital or professional guidelines, clinical flow sheets, or algorithms would potentially apply to a patient in similar circumstances as this patient?

Q: How long have those guidelines been in effect?

Q: Were this patient's circumstances considered an emergency?

Causation

Q: Isn't it true that infections can worsen without the proper antibiotics.

Q: What are the signs and symptoms of a worsening infection?

Q: Isn't it true that this patient had several of those signs a few days after the first antibiotic was prescribed?

Ethics

Q: It is a historical fact that years ago, clergy, lawyers, and doctors set themselves apart from other occupations because they considered themselves to be bound by special ethical duties. You recognize that, do you not?

Q: And, in fact, the very word "profession" means "bound by oath" in Latin, true?

Q: Did you take an oath as a medical doctor?

Q: That is what we've all heard to be the Hippocratic Oath, correct?

Q: Additionally, in medicine many years ago, the oath was abandoned and replaced by a code of ethics?

Q: Do physicians have any special ethical duties?

Q: Are you bound by one or more codes of ethics?

Q: What ethical code are you bound by?

Q: What are the specific requirements of that code?
   (See also "Chapter 2: The Doctor-Patient Contract.")

Q: Like the American Medical Association's Code, does yours require you to put the patient's interests first?

Q: And that is just doing the right thing by the patient, is it not?

Q: And like the American Medical Association's Code, does yours also require you to give timely attention to the patient's medical needs?

Q: It seems that that shouldn't need to be written down because that's just common sense applied to medical practice, isn't it?

Q: And to provide continuing care as long as necessary?

Q: What are some other requirement of your ethical code?

Risk-Benefit Analysis

Q: Now I have to ask you for some help in understanding a concept, alright?

Q: What is a risk-benefit analysis?

Q: So, basically, the upside is weighed against the downside, correct?

Q: And why is that important in medicine?

Q: Okay, at some point in the course of your care with this patient, you decided on a new or different course of treatment or to discontinue care or monitoring, is that true?

Q: At that time, you performed a risk-benefit analysis for your course of action?

Q: Would you show me that in your records?

Q: What factors did you consider?

Q: Did you consider that the results could be hazardous or catastrophic to your patient?

Q: Or could cause severe injury or critical harm?

Q: That was acceptable to you?

Q: You advised the patient of all the risks involved?

Q: You obtained informed consent?

Q: Where is that in your records?

Q: You claim to have done anything to lessen the risks, harms, or injuries you were exposing this patient to?

Hypotheticals

Q: I want you to assume that a myocardial infarction was in the differential under the standard of care. Assuming that, wouldn't you agree with me that a safe practice would have been to order follow-up cardiac enzymes? And electrocardiograms? And continue to monitor the patient?

Q: I want you to assume that this patient was in fact suffering from acute coronary syndrome when he entered the emergency department. If that is true, wouldn't you agree with me that this patient was at risk for sudden death if he were to be discharged from the hospital without an angiogram?

Concessions

Obtain admissions: "Was it foreseeable that…?" "You would agree that the standard of care requires…?" "Did you ever make a determination that…?" "Would it have been good and acceptable medical practice to…? "You told us a few moments ago that…, yet that's not what the records indicate, is it?"

Undermine the Doctor's Defenses

PATIENT CONTACTS

Q: Do you claim to have personal contacts with this patient, other than office and/or hospital visits, that are not documented in the medical records or hospital chart?

INDEPENDENT MEMORY

Q: Do you claim to have any independent memories or recollections of the plaintiff outside of these records?

If yes:

– How many patients did you see that day?

– What were the names of some of the other people you saw that day?

– Remember a particular event for any other patient seen that day?

– Remember the specifics of any other procedures or examinations you did that day?

Q: Have any independent recollection of any conversations between the two of you?

Q: You need these records, then, to refresh your memory as to what happened and did not happen, correct?

CUSTOM AND HABIT

Q: Is it your custom to note or record telephone conversations with your patients in their medical records?

Q: Doctor, would you agree that the practice of medicine is an art and not an exact science?

Q: As such, every surgical procedure is subjective and unique because no two conditions and no two patients are precisely alike or identical; is that correct? For example, the conditions you find in performing surgery following a ruptured appendix will be somewhat different in each patient?

Q: Although you might follow a general protocol or procedure in performing the surgery, the amount of material you remove and the damage you repair will vary from patient to patient; is that correct? Accordingly, Doctor, you cannot describe the details of a specific surgical procedure based on custom and habit because what you do in each procedure will depend upon the circumstances and will vary from patient to patient; is that correct?

Q: Furthermore, Doctor, in later dictating your summary of the surgical procedure, you generally use the same format for similar procedures and only dictate a general summary as you did in this case; is that correct? Sir, your custom and habit do not assist us in determining precisely what exactly you found, what you did as a result, or what went wrong in this procedure, do they?

DOCTOR DENIES FAULT

Q: Do you contend that the damages and injuries suffered by plaintiff were caused by someone other than yourself?

If yes:

– What facts support your contention?

– Are those facts documented?

– Where is that in the record?

– Is anyone else aware of the facts on which you base your contention?

Q: Is it your belief that the actions or inactions of any physician, nurse, or other health care provider who is not named as a defendant in this lawsuit may have contributed to the plaintiff's injuries?

Q: Do you contend that the plaintiff was negligent?

If yes:

– What facts support your contention?

– Are those facts documented?

– Where is that in the record?

– Is anyone else aware of the facts on which you base your contention?

– How did plaintiff's negligence cause or contribute to the injuries or damages?

Q: Do you contend that plaintiff's injuries are the result of a pre-existing condition?

If yes:

– What pre-existing condition?

– How did you make that determination?

– What facts support your contention?

– Are those facts documented?

– Where is that in the record?

– Is anyone else aware of the facts on which you base your contention?

Q: Do you contend that plaintiff's injuries or damages were caused by any acts or omissions of anyone other than yourself?

Q: Do you contend that your actions fall into the recommended approach for the diagnosis or chief complaint by a majority of doctors in your field?

Q: Do you contend that your actions follow a respected minority opinion?

Q: Are you aware of any medical literature supporting your actions or decisions as reasonable or recommended?

Q: Can you name a number of experts in the field, other than your paid testifying expert, who consider your actions or decisions to be viable options in the reasonable care of the condition or diagnosis or chief complaint that this patient had?

OPINIONS

Q: Isn't it true that medicine is an inexact science?

Q: And it's also true that in forming a medical opinion some speculation is necessarily involved?

Q: You understand that if I ask for your opinion, I am asking for an opinion to a reasonable degree of medical probability?

Q: Do you believe that you have the obligation to render only objective opinions in this case?

Q: Looking back on it now, is there any aspect of the care rendered in this case that you would have done differently?

Q: What is your opinion about each claim of negligence and your explanation for the same?

Q: Are your opinions based on reasonable medical certainty?

Q: What does the term "reasonable medical certainty" mean to you?

Q: Identify all books, articles, papers, or other materials on which you base your opinion(s)?

Q: Do you agree that no doctors' opinions are better than the facts or information that can be obtained from the patient?

Q: Have you at any time changed your opinions in this case? If yes:
  – When?
  – What information came to light that prompted you to change your opinion?

Q: What other explanations for this patient's condition did you consider?

Q: What other explanations for this patient's condition did you reject although they were possibilities?

Q: Before the occurrence, was everything fine or under control with the patient?

Q: Was this patient unreliable?

Q: Do you believe there was a failure by you or anyone else to exercise reasonable medical judgment in this case?

Q: Do you think there was a failure by you or anyone else to exercise reasonable prudence in this case?

Q: Do you believe anyone in the case was not careful or cautious in avoiding injury to the patient?

Q: How do you explain this patient's injuries or worsening condition?

Q: Are you aware of approaches different from your own that other competent physicians use under circumstances similar to those in this case?

Q: Have you discussed this case or your findings, opinions, or conclusions with any other physicians?

Q: Have you discussed the facts of case with any colleagues or others for their take?

Q: Are you aware of any physicians who may have reviewed any facts or records from this case for any reason?
    – Names
    – Reasons for review

Q: Are you aware of any special investigation, incident report, or other inquiry that hospital staff made about this patient that is not in the hospital records?

Q: Were any departmental case analysis reports generated?

Q: Are you aware of any personal notes or diary entries that were not found in the medical records but that were authored by a nurse or a doctor who was involved in the care and treatment of this patient?

Q: You have given us opinions today?

Q: And your opinions have been statements of fact and scientific data?

Q: And you would never misrepresent any statement of fact to a jury while you are under oath?

Q: You would never misrepresent scientific data?

Q: That would be a violation of the standard of care?

Q: That would be a violation of your own personal integrity?

Q: That would be unethical, true?

Q: Would the chance for recovery be greater if the procedure had been performed in a hospital or if the incident had not occurred?

Q: Wouldn't it have been a proper course of care to…?

Q: Is it not proper to do…when a patient has this problem?

Q: Don't you think that these injuries could have been avoided if…?

Q: Would the chances for survival or recovery have been better if…?

Q: Do you accept any legal responsibility for…?

OTHER DOCTORS' OPINIONS[2]

Q: Do you know Dr. Jones?

Q: Familiar with his work?

Q: You're aware that he has expressed an opinion different from yours?

Q: Did he get it wrong?

Q: What did he miss?

Q: Where was he mistaken?

Q: Why do you think Dr. Jones said you were wrong?

Q: Is he qualified to offer these criticisms?

NEGLIGENT REFERRAL

Q: How did you become acquainted with the physician you made a referral to?

Q: And what were this doctor's qualifications?

Q: You took his word for it?

Q: You weren't aware that this doctor had failed his specialty boards?

Q: That he had restricted hospital privileges?

Q: Lost his medical license in another state?

Q: Had multiple malpractice suits in the past?

Q: Has outstanding malpractice claims against him now?

---

[2] http://www.thejuryexpert.com/wp-content/uploads/KeeneCrossExamNov08TJE.pdf.

Q: Did you contact the hospital credentialing committee or peer review committee about this doctor's credentials?

Q: Contact your county medical society?

Q: The American College/Board of _____?

Q: Contact any professional organization?

Q: Did you ever ask this doctor if he had been sued for medical malpractice?

Q: So what you're saying is that it was okay to entrust the very life of your patient to this doctor, a doctor about whom you knew nothing?

Q: And you were comfortable with not bothering to obtain any credentials or meaningful background information?[3]

BACKGROUND

Q: Ever been arrested?

Q: (If yes) Ever been convicted?

Q: Do you drink alcohol or take illegal substances?

Q: Do you take medications not prescribed by your doctor?

Q: Are you, at this time, under the influence of any medications or substances?

Q: Have you ever gone by any other names?

Q: Earlier you told me that you have had your deposition taken before, correct?

Q: How many times?

Q: What is your current home address?

Q: How long have you lived there?

Q: Who lives with you?

Q: Ever been divorced?

Q: Previous addresses?

Q: What is your date of birth?

Q: Where were you born?

Q: What is your social security number?

---

[3] James E. Schutte, *Preventing Malpractice Suits. A Handbook for Doctors and Those Who Work with Them* (Seattle: Hogrefe & Huber Publishers, 1995), 115–116 (for all questions in this section).

Q: And what is your driver's license number?

Q: How long have you been a doctor?

Q: What is your specialty?

Q: Do you have a current CV?

Q: May I have a copy?

Q: Where did you go to medical school?

Q: What year did you graduate?

Q: Fail any examinations or classes while in school?

Q: What courses did you perform the poorest in?

Q: What was your standing in the class?

Q: What residencies have you entered?

Q: Complete each one?

Q: Done any fellowships?

Q: You claim any medical specialties?

Q: How many patients with the same problems as this patient did you deal with during your training?

Q: Are there people more knowledgeable than you on the subject of this action?

Q: What is your state license number?

Q: Have a DEA number?

Q: Have you applied for licensure in any other states?

Q: Licensed in any other states?

Q: Pass each part of the ECFMG on your first try?

Q: Did you serve in the military?
  – Branch?
  – Type of discharge?

Q: Are you board certified?

Q: Ever failed a board certification exam or recertification exam?

Q: What hospitals are you affiliated with?

Q: Have any teaching responsibilities?

Q: Associated with any universities?

Q: Could you list any professional associations you belong to?

Q: Tell me, have you done any research or have you published?

Q: Have there been other claims or lawsuits filed against you or a health care facility where you were employed at the time of the alleged misconduct?

Q: I'll need a list of all complaints filed against you. Will you send me that list in the next 30 days?

Q: Have you ever testified under oath regarding your practice of medicine?
   – Date
   – Place
   – Nature of proceeding

Q: Are there other reports about you in the National Practitioner Data Base?

Q: Any negative actions taken by a state medical board against you at any time or in any state?

Q: Have there been any grievances or complaints filed against you regarding your practice of medicine?

Q: How many times have you been accused of malpractice, misfeasance, or malfeasance?

Q: Have you ever been the subject of professional discipline?

Q: By what disciplinary authority?

Q: Please explain any disciplinary action against you.

Q: Other than this case, are you a party or witness to any other litigation?

Q: Has your license to practice ever been suspended or revoked?

Q: Has a hospital ever modified or restricted your clinical staff privileges?

Q: Ever been discharged from employment or asked to resign?

Q: Ever been investigated by any government agency or organization?

Q: Any history of financial difficulties, for example, filing for bankruptcy?

Q: Any history of addictions? Drug abuse? Alcohol? Gambling? Obsessive-compulsive behavior?

Q: Any history of a psychological or psychiatric disorder?

Q: Ever receive counseling for any problems?

Q: What is your experience with the medical condition and treatment at issue?

BIBLIOGRAPHY

Personal notes and papers.

Simonson, Paul. Sr. Partner, Simonson, Hess, Leibowitz & Goodman, P.C.
Chapter 10 of *New York Medical Malpractice*. New York State Bar Association.

CHAPTER 12

Cross-Examination of Physician Defendant

CASE BACKGROUND

A generally healthy 39-year-old woman with a history of smoking saw her PCP in September with complaints of some coughing with phlegm, chest pain, and congestion. Her chest pains were reported as non-exertional and made worse by coughing. The P.E. was unremarkable, and she was diagnosed with bronchitis and given antibiotics.

In November of the same year, she presented to the ER. She stated that she woke from a sound sleep with pain between her shoulder blades that radiated into her right arm along with chest pain or midsternal pressure. Afterwards, she had coughed so hard she had vomited. She rated her pain at an eight out of ten. On P.E. there was some wheezing in both bases of the chest, but her lungs were otherwise clear. Chest x-ray did not reveal any abnormalities. She was given an albuterol aerosol. She felt better and was released.

At approximately 5:15 that evening she collapsed from a heart attack. EMS took her to same hospital. She was pronounced dead at 6:09 PM. Cause of death on the autopsy report was "coronary sclerotic heart disease with acute coronary thrombosis, and remote organizing and acute myocardial infarcts." There was no evidence of acute or chronic bronchitis.

Plaintiff calls the Defendant ER doctor on cross-examination:

"Good afternoon, Doctor. It's good to see you again."

Q: Please state your full name and address.

Q: Where are you employed?

A: St. Mary's Hospital Emergency Room.

Q: You are a physician?

A: I am.

Q: You are the defendant in this case?

A: I am.

Q: Okay. And were you working in the course and scope of your employment in the emergency room on November 6, two years ago, taking care of a female patient named Mrs. Simmons?

A: Yes, I was.

Q: Same patient who was brought in dead on arrival also on November 6th on the same day, right?

Q: Now, you have been at St. Mary's since 1997, correct?

A: That's right.

Q: Are you still working in emergency medicine?

A: I am.

Q: And are you still working at St. Mary's?

A: Yes, I am.

Q: By the way, is St. Mary's a part of a clinic health system?

A: Yes, it is.

Q: And St. Mary's didn't have the capability to do catheterizations, did it?

A: That's correct.

Q: So, if you had to have a patient undergo a catheterization or bypass surgery or any other kind of intervention that patient would be sent from St. Mary's over to the clinic main campus; is that right?

A: Yes.

Q: Now, would you agree with me that potential cardiac symptoms include back pain, chest pain, vomiting and arm pain?

A: Correct.

Q: Now, when you are interested in trying to determine or diagnose whether a patient has myocardial ischemia, what kind of things do you do?

A: Initially I would talk to the patient, try and elicit a history. I would look at notes or vital signs that the nursing staff had taken. And, then, I would examine the patient to try to get some further information about what's going on with the patient.

Q: Okay. And you stop there after the examination?

A: No. After the examination and their history is taken, then I would make a determination as to whether further testing needed to be done and whether further treatment at that point was indicated.

Q: Okay. Well, I was talking about a patient where you suspected cardiac ischemia, okay?

A: Yes.

Q: Okay. So, would it be true that after the history and after the physical in a patient with potential cardiac ischemia you would do an EKG?

A: That is a possibility.

Q: And you would probably order blood work to determine whether or not there was something that may have occurred in the form of a heart attack, right?

A: That's a possibility, also.

Q: Because enzymes will show that, right?

A: Well, enzymes are a part. They won't necessarily show it all of the time.

Q: I understand that. But if it's a more recent bit of damage to the heart, the cardiac enzymes will show up as abnormal on the blood work, right?

A: They can, yes.

Q: And, likewise, an EKG is going to show if the patient has an abnormality from past damage that left some scar in the heart or acute ischemia at the time of the EKG, right?

A: That's a possibility. It is not 100 percent.

Q: And I'm not suggesting that it's always 100 percent. Part of what you do when you're talking to the patient and getting this history is to also assess risk factors to whatever extent you can, right?

A: In relation to a patient that's presenting with cardiac symptoms, is that your question?

Q: Right, yes.

A: Yes, that's correct.

Q: And on the admitting form pain in the chest is one of the complaints that's listed, correct?

A: It's one of the complaints. There are multiple complaints.

Q: Okay. Pain in the arms, pain in the back, pain in the chest and vomiting, right?

A: That's correct.

Q: I assume the complaint would be what amounts to the chief complaint of the patient for the visit, right?

A: That's right.

Q: Now, when you were taking care of Mrs. Simmons in the emergency room—I understand she comes in and the nurse sees her and does a nursing assessment of the patient, right?

A: That's correct.

Q: And this is done before you even see the patient, right?

A: Yes.

Q: And, then—and this nursing—just so the jury is oriented, this nursing assessment sheet is what's been on the board and we have talked about here that lists at the very top the chief complaint, back pain, chest pain, vomit, arm pain, timed at 5:05, correct?

A: Yes.

Q: And then gives this history of the present illness about what brought her there in the first place, correct?

A: Yes.

Q: Now, this is prepared by the nurse before you ever see the patient, correct?

A: Yes.

Q: And it's available for you before you see the patient to go in—before going in to see the patient, the material—or this sheet is there for you to review if you so choose, correct?

A: Yes, I will see that. I'll pick it up, I may review it just before going in to see the patient. I may review it as I'm going in to see the patient.

Q: You also have the option of talking to the nurse directly and conversing a little bit about what this patient—what is going on with this patient and so on, correct?

A: Yes, I do.

Q: At no time did you ever talk to the nurse about her evaluation or assessment of this patient, correct?

A: I don't believe that I did.

Q: So, the only information you would have had available would be the documentary information from the chart which would include this nursing assessment sheet?

A: Yes.

Q: Correct?

A: That's right.

Q: Now, from your review of the nurse's assessment sheet, which I assume you did look at before you saw her, correct?

A: Yes.

Q: Okay. From your review of this sheet, you were certainly aware that she had awakened from a sound sleep with back pain, chest pain, vomit and arm pain, right?

A: Yes.

Q: Doesn't say anything in there, in that history about her having been awakened from a cough, does it?

A: No, it doesn't.

Q: As a matter of fact, you don't remember ever having gotten a history when you talked to this patient directly about coughing being the cause of her being awakened, right?

A: I was able to obtain a history of the cough. I don't have any documentation that it was the cough that woke her up.

Q: Okay. What she did do when she woke up is she took Motrin, an over-the-counter painkiller, right?

A: That's right.

Q: Now, Motrin is not the kind of medication that you would take for a cough as a layperson, is it?

A: No.

Q: Motrin is the kind of a pain—or a medication you would take for pain that you were experiencing; I mean, that's typically what people use it for, right?

A: That's correct.

Q: So, you would agree with me at least in the mind of your patient that she had a severe pain that caused her to take Motrin and not a cough for which she would have taken something like a cough medicine, right?

A: No. I elicited a history that she did have a cough, but I would agree that she took the Motrin for the pain that she was having at that time.

Q: Now, when you saw this patient, you also took a history yourself, right?

A: That's correct.

Q: And that history ultimately was dictated by you, correct?

A: Yes.

Q: The very first thing you show is that the chief complaint that morning was chest pain, correct?

A: Yes. I also included the other two complaints that she had initially which were coughing and vomiting.

Q: I understand that. The fact is the very first thing you listed in this case as a complaint of this patient was chest pain, right?

A: The order of those complaints is not significant. She had all three complaints as her initial assessment.

Q: Okay. Well, you would agree with me that chest pain is often associated with a cardiac problem, isn't it?

A: It is a possibility.

Q: Now, you asked her about the intensity of her chest pain?

A: I did not ask her that specifically. The intensity of the chest pain was documented on the nurse's notes.

Q: And that's the thing that shows that she had an intensity that was eight out of ten, correct?

A: That's right.

Q: Now, eight out of ten is a very severe degree or level of pain, isn't it?

A: Yes, it is.

Q: Have you—are you familiar with pain scales? I'm sure in medicine you have dealt with a lot of different pain scales, right?

A: Yes.

Q: And are you familiar with the description that is typically given to describe an eight out of ten on a pain scale?

A: I'm not sure I understand the question about description.

Q: Well, obviously, the more—the higher the number the more severe your pain?

A: That's right.

Q: So, if somebody has got a two, it's a lesser degree of pain; if somebody has got an eight or a nine or a ten, it's a more severe degree of pain, right?

A: That's right.

Q: So, there are characterizations that are given for pain scales so that people know whether they fall into the five, the six, the three, the eight, kind of scale, correct?

A: Yes.

Q: Would you agree that an eight would have—is characterized—or can be characterized as physical activity severely limited; you can read and converse with effort; nausea and dizziness set in as factors of pain on occasion?

A: It sounds to me like you're reading that from a text. Could I—

Q: I'm reading this from a pain scale called Mankoski Pain Scale, okay, just pulled off the internet. Do you have any reason to disagree with that pain scale description for an eight out of ten?

A: No, I don't.

Q: Now, you never even asked about—you didn't ask about the intensity. You also didn't ask about the duration of the pain, correct?

A: That's correct.

Q: It would be something that would be important to know, isn't it?

A: Depending on the presentation of the patient, yes.

Q: And that's something which is helpful to make a diagnosis, isn't it?

A: It can be.

Q: And would you agree that if a patient has chest pain for more than five minutes that they should go to an ER for evaluation and assessment?

A: That is not necessarily true. It would depend on what other symptoms the patient is experiencing and what the context of the chest pain is.

Q: You never asked about the intensity or the duration and the fact is you cannot remember why you didn't ask her more detail about her chest pain, do you?

A: I'm not sure I understand that question.

Q: Well, do you know why at this—as you sit here and after you have evaluated this case in your mind for years, why you didn't ask her more detail about her chest pain? You don't remember that, do you?

A: Well, the presentation of the patient was fairly straightforward when I asked her the questions in the history.

Q: Do you know if this patient ever had chest pain in the past? I don't mean now. I mean when you were seeing her. Did you know on November 6th, 2002, at the end of that visit whether she had ever had chest pain in the past?

A: I don't know. Or I didn't know at that time.

Q: Right. You know now, obviously.

A: Yes.

Q: But at that time, you didn't know, right?

A: Right.

Q: And that's because you didn't ask her, right?

A: That's correct.

Q: You also didn't ask her about any family history of heart disease, did you?

A: That's right. And the reason that I didn't was—

Q: I didn't ask that, sir. You can give that later. The fact of the matter is you didn't ask about prior chest pain; you didn't ask about family history; and you didn't know anything about her brother being 32 at the age of his MI and death, right?

A: At that time, no.

Q: Okay. That sort of information in a patient who presents with chest pain as a complaint would be important to know, wouldn't it?

A: It would be important depending upon the history and physical exam that was taken initially and on the context of the presentation of the patient.

Q: Now, the other thing that this history tells us when she says she's awakened from a sound sleep with the symptoms including chest pain is that that chest pain by definition is unstable angina, right?

A: No. That is not necessarily true.

Q: Okay. Is there, in fact, a definition of unstable angina that means you get chest pain at rest or without exertion?

A: That is a definition of unstable angina.

Q: And unstable angina, at least as defined in that context, is dangerous, is it not?

A: Yes, it can be.

Q: Because it can lead to an MI or a heart attack, can't it?

A: Yes, it can.

Q: And now as we sit here, we know that indeed occurred, correct?

A: No, I don't think that can be said. I mean, eventually the demise of the patient was due to an MI; we can say that.

Q: Well, again, I think what you're trying to tell the jury is that this woman had absolutely no cardiac problem at all when she was in the emergency room on the morning of the November 6th, right?

A: No. I'm not saying that at all.

Q: Okay. So, would you admit that on the morning of November 6, 2002, when she was in the emergency room with a chest complaint that she had a cardiac problem?

A: She—from the—in hindsight from the pathology report we understand that she did have cardiac disease. I'm not denying that.

Q: Okay, you're not suggesting that she was without any cardiac problem at the time of the emergency room visit but sometime in the next 12 hours there was some migration of a clot to her left anterior descending, are you?

A: No, I'm not.

Q: Now, one of the things you ordered for her was Tylenol, right?

A: Yes.

Q: And that, I guess, would be for pain, right?

A: That's correct.

Q: You also ordered a chest x-ray, correct?

A: Yes.

Q: And you—when she ultimately went to get the chest x-ray in the radiology department, she actually was made to walk there, right?

A: Yes. She did walk to the radiology department to get the chest x-ray done.

Q: Would it be your practice to send somebody with chest pain and a potential cardiac problem to another department in the hospital, have them walk there as opposed to going by wheelchair?

A: Not if they came in with a clear-cut cardiac problem. This patient presented with cough, post-tussive vomiting. The cough was productive. She coughed so hard she was vomiting. That is not a presentation of a patient who has cardiac ischemia. Therefore, both my assessment and the assessment of the nurse on this presentation was such that the patient was able to walk to the radiology department to get her chest x-ray.

Q: Well, were you relying on the nurse's assessment?

A: I take that into consideration.

Q: Well, okay, we will get to that. You say if there are clear-cut cardiac problems or symptoms you wouldn't have them walk; you would have them go by wheelchair; is that what you said?

A: What I'm saying is if a patient comes in with heavy chest pain complaining that this is a terrible pain that they have in their chest; they can't breathe; it gets worse when they exert themselves; that is a patient that I would not send to the radiology department. I would get a portable chest x-ray.

Q: Well she had severe pain in her chest as well as her back that was rated eight out of ten, right?

A: And if you read in the nurse's notes it says in the second line that most of that pain was between the shoulder blades and radiating down the right arm.

Q: Right. Where is your heart?

A: It's in the—it's actually a little left of the center of the chest.

Q: A little left of center in the chest, but it's—

A: Yes.

Q: —between your chest and your back, right?

A: That's correct.

Q: It's not out in the front with nothing in the back, right?

A: That's correct.

Q: So, it lines up pretty much between the shoulder blades as to where it's physically located, correct?

A: That's right.

Q: And the severe pain that she has between her shoulder blades, based on all the history she gave you, there was nothing to say that that could not have been the heart that was exhibiting the pain in her system, correct?

A: But if you will—

Q: Correct? Correct?

A: That is—

Q: Correct?

A: That is a possibility.

Q: Okay.

A: Can I answer further?

Q: You'll have your opportunity to explain your side. I'm just trying to get something through here. You have—in addition to that eight out of ten, you have chest midsternal pressure—pressure. Now, would you agree with me that pressure or tightness in the chest can be a sign of a cardiac problem?

A: It is a possibility. It can also be a sign of multiple other problems that are going on including respiratory type problems.

Q: Right. And—so, respiratory; it could be bronchitis?

A: Yes.

Q: Could be perhaps pneumonia?

A: Yes.

Q: Could it be a PE?

A: Yes.

Q: And it could be a heart problem?

A: That's in the line of possibilities.

Q: Now, somebody could have a heart problem that could be fatal, right?

A: Yes.

Q: What's it take to order an EKG?

A: I would have to circle the order and give it to the secretary to get ordered.

Q: Okay. And the secretary gives it to the nurse, and the nurse puts the 12 leads on the patient, plugs them in and runs off the strips to determine what the EKG is showing for that patient's heart, right?

A: That's correct.

Q: And this is a fairly—this is a—totally risk free to the patient, isn't it?

A: Yes.

Q: And it is inexpensive, correct?

A: I don't know the cost.

Q: Okay. Cost certainly should not be a factor that you would take into account, right?

A: Right.

Q: Okay. And it is reliable in the sense that it can give you information, more information about the status of that person's heart and heart rhythm, right?

A: That's correct.

Q: And it doesn't take very long to do, does it?

A: No.

Q: And it's all right there in the ER. I mean, they can do it with no difficulty at all in the ER. It's not like you got to go across the street or I didn't ask about certain risk factors around the corner. Right?

A: That's right.

Q. Isn't it true, Doctor, that you never even considered ordering an EKG?

A: I did not consider ordering an EKG because was not indicated in this presentation.

Q: Well, you keep talking about presentation, and I'd like to ask you about that. Isn't the patient's presentation based in part on your observations and the information you gather?

A: Yes, it is.

Q: As a matter of fact, that's a large part of the presentation, as you call it, right?

A: Yes.

Q: So, if you don't know anything about certain risk factors or history in that patient—for example, the risk factors she had for coronary artery disease—that's because you didn't ask about it, right?

A: I didn't ask about certain risk factors because of the complaints, the history and physical and the nurse's notes that were obtained in the department that morning.

Q: In other words, because she came in complaining of chest pain you decided not to ask her about a history of CAD or heart disease or chest pain?

A: She was not only complaining of chest pain, but if you take the entire context of her complaints, it was not a cardiac presentation.

Q: My point being, Doctor, that presentation is dependent on you and what you do or say to a great extent, right?

A: To a great extent.

Q: And you can't necessarily rely on a patient to offer information about her history or her prior episodes of chest pain or her prior family history, you can't rely on a patient because the patient doesn't know what is important for you to evaluate, correct?

A: That's correct.

Q: That's why it's up to you to gather the information and ask the questions to get this stuff so you can put it in the context of what's going on with that patient, right?

A: Yes. And those questions that are asked are guided by the examination and the interview or the history obtained from the patient.

Q: And it's your testimony in this case that that presentation, as you call it, didn't fit the diagnosis of something that could be cardiac in nature, right?

A: That is right.

Q: Well, what does the term rule out mean in medicine?

A: Rule out means that you consider something and then do further testing to say that that diagnosis or that disease is not present.

Q: Okay. So, it's an evaluation and testing to exclude a particular thing as the source of the problem?

A: That's right.

Q: Okay. For example, if somebody has a biopsy and it comes back negative, they don't have cancer; I mean, it's a way of saying, okay, we have tested, and we found that there's no cancer in this patient or in their liver or whatever it may be, right?

A: Yes.

Q: And for heart problems, the cardiac catheterization seems to be, I think you would agree the gold standard for the testing and evaluation of whether somebody has coronary artery disease, correct?

A: Yes.

Q: So that would be an example of a test that rules in or rules out cardiac problems or coronary artery disease in a patient, right?

A: Yes, it is.

Q: But in your practice, you certainly don't order the cardiac catheterization as the first line of testing for a cardiac problem, do you?

A: No, I would not.

Q: The fact of the matter is the first thing you would do is get an EKG, right?

A: If it was indicated, according to the patient's presentation, then, I would, yes.

Q: And then you would follow that or at the same time get blood studies done to evaluate whether or not there is any evidence of a cardiac enzyme elevation, right?

A: Yes.

Q: Now, are you capable of interpreting an EKG?

A: Yes, I am.

Q: And I'm sure that you have probably ordered thousands of EKGs in the emergency room in your career, right?

A: Yes.

Q: And an EKG is certainly a test that can help to rule in or rule out a potential cardiac problem, right?

A: Yes, it is.

Q: And if a patient has past damage to their heart, some damage in the form of a scar or necrotic tissue from some other event previously, an EKG can show that abnormality, right?

A: It can. It does not always.

Q: I understand. Depends pretty much on how significant that is, right?

A: Yes, that's right.

Q: And whether it interrupts or affects the conductivity of the heart electrically on the EKG, right?

A: Yes.

Q: Likewise, if somebody has ischemia, acute ischemia, they come in, and they have got chest pain, they have got chest pressure, and they have got what amounts to closing or narrowing of the arteries, the coronary arteries, that's going to show up in an EKG, isn't it?

A: Not all the time, but it can.

Q: But it certainly can?

A: Yes.

Q: And if it does, it gives you another piece of the puzzle to say we better look further on that, correct?

A: Yes.

Q: And if that EKG came back in a positive or abnormal fashion, regardless of the enzymes, you may go to yet another test, like a stress test, correct?

A: Are you saying I would go to a stress test if there were abnormalities on the EKG, is that the question?

Q: If there are abnormalities in the preliminary testing for EKG and enzymes, one or the other, particularly the EKG, it may result in going to the next level which would be a stress test?

A: It may.

Q: All right. And it may lead to a cardiac catheterization, which would be diagnostic of CAD, right?

A: That's correct.

Q: Now, would you agree as a general proposition that people who experience chest pain for any period of time should, in fact, get it evaluated; that's a good piece of medical advice to the general public?

A: Yes, it is.

Q: Why is it important for a person with chest pain to go to the hospital?

A: To have that chest pain evaluated.

Q: Is it also to determine what that physical condition is that's causing the chest pain?

A: That would be part of the evaluation.

Q: Is it also because chest pain can be a sign of something that is more serious that could occur?

A: It depends on the context of what's going on at that time, but it can be an indicator of something more serious going on.

Q: And it's also because chest pain and whatever it represents can be successfully treated, right?

A: Yes, it can.

Q: And if it is chest pain caused by ischemia, for example, that would be a harbinger or something that would perhaps be more serious later on like an MI, right?

A: That's correct.

Q: And if it's caused—if the chest pain is caused by ischemia, would you agree that it can be successfully treated, and an MI or heart attack can in many instances be avoided altogether?

A: Yes, that's right.

Q: Now, as I understand it, your hospital has a chest pain protocol; is that right?

A: I believe you're referring to a nursing protocol if I'm correct.

Q: The hospital gives emergency room nurses a protocol saying if somebody comes in with a chief complaint of chest pain this is what you should do?

A: They have multiple protocols for different presentations. Chest pain would be one of those.

Q: Okay. And all I'm talking about right now is chest pain, not appendicitis or anything else. And is Exhibit 26 a complete copy of the guidelines of care for—or protocol for chest pain?

A: Yes, it is.

Q: And you say this applies to nurses because they need to have this to guide them through their work; is that right?

A: I'm not sure you can say they need to have this. This is present so that if they have a patient presenting with this complaint, then they will have guideline that they can use to guide their work-up that patient in the emergency department.

Q: Right. And would it be fair to say that from your perspective anyway you don't think this applies to physicians?

A: No. This applies to the nursing staff.

Q: And I assume that it applies to nurses because they are not as well trained as doctors so they may need a little bit of guidance to deal with the potential risk associated with a complaint of chest pain, right?

A: Well, I wouldn't say that the nurses are less trained. I would say they are trained in a different venue. So, these guidelines are to help them in the work-up of that patient.

Q: But isn't it true, Doctor, that if appropriate you even follow these guidelines?

A: I'm not sure I understand the question. Are you saying that I should — I'm bound by these guidelines?

Q: No, I didn't say that. I said, isn't it true that you, in fact, follow these guidelines if appropriate under the circumstances?

A: I don't follow nursing guidelines.

Q: I'm sorry?

A: I don't use nursing guidelines in my work-up of patients.

Q: Well, I'm going to draw your attention to page 23 of your deposition at line 12. It says, guidelines—I'm sorry, line 11: That you are to follow those guidelines? That was the question.

A: Guidelines are guidelines. They're used as a reference. So, if you—if you are saying, well they're binding, and you have to follow them, that's not correct.

Q: But it is suggested by the Clinic Health System that you consult those and follow them if appropriate; is that right?

A: If appropriate, that's correct.

Q: That's what you testified to under oath in this case, did you not?

A: In that deposition at that time, you were referring to physician guidelines from the Clinic. I don't believe that you were referring to the nursing guidelines that were talking about.

Q: I'm sorry to differ. One of the things you also do in your work is give courses, every once in a while, to emergency medical technicians; is that right?

A: I don't give courses. I do continuing medical education for paramedics.

Q: All right. I'm sorry I called them courses. You give talks that are substantive for the benefit of emergency medical technicians, correct?

A: That's correct.

Q: And I assume that you talk to them about a variety of subjects, correct?

A: Yes.

Q: And I assume you also tell them about how to deal with a patient that has chest pain complaints, right?

A: Yes.

Q: And I assume you also are aware of the fact that emergency medical technicians do EKGs on these patients even in their homes or in the truck or on the way to the hospital, correct?

A: Yes.

Q: Do you tell emergency medical technicians if there's chest pain you don't always have to do an EKG?

A: No, I don't tell them that.

Q: Okay. The fact of the matter is you teach them that if there's a chest pain complaint get an EKG as a matter of course, correct?

A: No. They—paramedics do not always get an EKG. They do have monitors on the trucks, and they will typically place the patient on monitors, However, emergency medical technicians and paramedics are guided by a set of guidelines according to their training.

Q: Their guidelines are different than physicians?

A: And nurses.

Q: Okay. Now, when Mrs. Simmons checked in, her chief complaints, as we said, was back pain, chest pain, vomiting and arm pain; and I believe you indicated that you got a history of cough and post-tussive vomiting; is that right?

A: That is correct.

Q: Now, was the coughing the reason why you elected not to get an EKG on Mrs. Simmons for her chest pain complaint?

A: Coughing was part of that, in my judgment, but I took in context all of the complaints and all of the history that the patient was giving me at that time; and as a result of that, I, I did not elect to get an EKG at that time.

Q: What about a cough rules out a cardiac problem in a patient?

A: Cough in itself does not rule out a cardiac problem.

Q: As a matter of fact, Doctor, you're not suggesting to this jury that a person who has a cough can't have a heart attack or can't have heart disease, are you?

A: No, I'm not,

Q: Well, was another one of these various reasons the fact that there was yellow sputum that she apparently had coughed up, was that another part?

A: That is another part in the history that the patient gave to me.

Q: Is yellow sputum something that rules out or excludes a cardiac cause for the complaints of chest pain?

A: No, it does not.

Q: A person who has a cough and productive yellow sputum certainly can still have a heart attack or heart disease, right?

A: That is a possibility.

Q: Was it the pain that was between her shoulder blades that led you to believe that this complaint didn't need or require an EKG?

A: Pain between the shoulder blades is an atypical type of presentation for cardiac ischemia or coronary artery disease, but that in itself did not lead me away from getting an EKG.

Q: Well, but pain between the shoulder blades certainly doesn't rule out a heart problem, does it?

A: No, it doesn't.

Q: And a person can have an MI or heart disease and still have pain between the shoulder blades, right?

A: Yes, they can.

Q: As a matter of fact, you talk about it as an atypical presentation for heart disease; is that what you said in so many words?

A: That's exactly what I said.

Q: Well, you are aware of the fact that women more often present with atypical or different kinds of presentations than men, right?

A: Yes, women can.

Q: Was it the cervical spine scoliosis on x-ray that caused you to think that this was not cardiac in origin?

A: No. It was part of the entire work-up, history and physical exam that I did. That was part of it, but that in itself did not eliminate me from getting an EKG.

Q: And I didn't say in itself. This is one of a list of things that you believe pointed you in a direction other than her heart?

A: But what you're doing is taking each one specifically and singling it out; and I'm saying that I took all of those in context as an entire presentation of the patient and as such did not order an EKG.

Q: Well, wouldn't it be fair to say that for all of those things that we have just listed, put them altogether, that a patient who has all of those things still can have a heart attack?

A: That's a possibility. All things are possible.

Q: And they still can have heart disease?

A: Yes, they can.

Q: And the chest pain they present with can be perfectly consistent with heart disease or heart attack?

A: Are you referring specifically to this patient?

Q: I'm talking about a patient who comes in with those things that you said pointed away from cardiac despite the presence of chest pain.

A: She had chest pressure. Most of her pain was between the back and down the right arm.

Q: Which as you acknowledged earlier can be from the heart, right?

A: It's a possibility.

Q: None of the things that you found as factors leading you away from chest pain would rule out cardiac as a cause, would they?

A: That's correct.

Q: And anyone of these or all of these things could be in a person who still has heart disease or is going through a heart attack, right?

A: Yes, it can.

Q: So, what about this patient's presentation makes it okay not to do an EKG?

A: Well, you're saying that with this presentation that I'm obligated to rule out a cardiac origin. I'm saying that that is not the case. The patient presented with these symptoms, and I'm saying that there's no evidence in those symptoms that the patient had ischemic cardiac disease. The presentation was one of bronchitis and an infectious upper respiratory disease; and as such, I'm not obligated to rule out a cardiac origin.

Q: Well, let's just see. The log sheet that you have up there shows as one of her complaints chest pain, correct?

A: That's correct.

Q: And the hospital patient information sheet shows chest pain as one of her chief complaints, correct?

A: That's correct.

Q: And your listing as the first chief complaint or one of the chief complaints is chest pain, correct?

A: That's correct.

Q: And the nurse noted from the assessment chest pain as one of the chief complaints, right?

A: Yes.

Q: And described chest pressure and pain in the history, correct?

A: Yes. Can I make a clarification?

Q: And then there is further an order for the chest x-ray and the clinical history given for that is chest pain, correct?

A: Yes. Can I make a clarification about that?

Q: About which?

A: About the multiple areas of chest pain that you're talking about.

Q: Sure.

A: The—let's just take the last one for instance. The order for the chest x-ray as indicated as chest pain that is put in by a clerk in the emergency department who's taking the information off of the nurse's notes. The log is entered by a registrar who is in the front of the emergency department and is again taking that information off of the nurse's note. So, most of this is coming from one source which would be the nurse's notes or my chart. It's not significant that each of those different individuals are getting a history of chest pain from the patient. That is not the case.

Q: And I never said that, Doctor. The fact of the matter is it's coming from the medical people who have taken the history and recorded the chief complaints, that's you and the nurse?

A: That's correct.

Q: And two of the references we identified here are from your record and the nurse's record and they say the chief complaint includes chest pain, right?

A: Yes. And you're taking that totally out of context as chest pain itself.

Q: All right. Up there in signs and symptoms, what does it say?

A: Where are you pointing to, sir?

Q: Signs and symptoms. What does it say here for signs and symptoms relating to this patient?

A: Pain in chest. And, again, that—

Q: Thank you.

A: —is entered by the clerk who puts the order for the chest x-ray in, yeah.

Q: Now; if all of these things that we have talked about caused you to conclude that an EKG really didn't have to be done on her, tell me this: What does a patient need to have at a minimum to get an EKG when they come in with chest pain if you're the one covering the ER?

A: Well, the patient certainly wouldn't present with a productive cough, that she coughs so hard she would be throwing up and causing the chest pain. That is not the presentation that would lead me to get an EKG.

Q: Can a patient who comes in with a productive cough that's coughing hard, coughing enough to vomit, can that patient still have a heart attack?

A: All things are possible.

Q: Can they still have heart attack or heart disease when their complaints include chest pain?

A: Yes, they can.

Q: And that's pretty important to rule out if you have a means of doing it so easily accessible to you in the emergency room, isn't it? Isn't it?

A: To order that test, you need to have an indication as to why that test needs to be ordered and that was not present in this case.

Q: Truth is, Doctor, you never even thought or considered a cardiac cause for your patient's chest pain complaints, did you?

A: It was in the differential when I initially evaluated the patient; but as I got further history and physical exam, it went further and further down the list, and I did not work that part of the differential up.

Q: Isn't that failure to even consider it the reason you don't even remember if she was on a heart monitor in the emergency room that morning?

A: I'm not sure I understand that question.

Q: Well, haven't you already testified in this case that you don't even remember if she was on a heart monitor that morning?

A: That's correct. I don't recall that.

Q: And isn't the reason you don't remember she was even on the heart monitor that morning is because it wasn't even in your thought process that she could have a cardiac problem at the core or the root of her chest pain complaints? Isn't that's the reason why you don't even remember if she was on a heart monitor?

A: No. That has nothing to do with it.

Q: And isn't it also the case that you don't ever remember ever looking at any heart monitoring strips or heart monitor information about her heart rate, heart rhythm, things that would show up on a heart monitor?

A: That's correct. I testified to that previously.

Q: In fact, Doctor, isn't it true that once she mentioned the fact that she had been to her family doctor and had a diagnosis of bronchitis some weeks before that you presumed the same diagnosis and operated accordingly? Isn't that true?

A: No, absolutely not. I based my treatment upon my interview with the patient, upon the history that obtained, upon my physical exam and the treatment of the patient in the emergency department. I did not base my—I do not base my treatments and evaluations upon another physician.

Q: Doctor, you learned about this poor woman's death not long after it happened, right?

A: That's correct.

Q: In fact, you got a call at home from the ER—or ED director, correct?

A: Yes, that's right.

Q: And that call concerned you quite a bit, didn't it?

A: Yes, it did.

Q: And isn't that why you requested a copy of the autopsy from the coroner's office only days later?

A: Yes, I did.

Q: And in that letter, didn't you indicate to the coroner that this was your patient?

A: Yes, in the emergency department.

Q: And you have reviewed the autopsy since then, haven't you?

A: Yes, I have.

Q: You don't have any reason to disagree with the coroner about what her cause of death was, do you?

A: No, I don't.

Q: And you have looked at that autopsy?

A: Yes, I have some time ago.

Q: And you are familiar both from your review as well as the other testimony in this case that Mrs. Simmons was not found to have any bronchitis on autopsy, right?

A: I don't know that that was specifically looked for in the autopsy. I may be incorrect about that.

Q: Do you have anything to tell this jury that says that there was evidence of bronchitis on autopsy?

A: No, I don't.

Q: So, there is no reported pathological basis to say this patient had bronchitis on autopsy, right?

A: That's correct, but they may not have investigated that during the autopsy.

Q: Doctor, is it true and you agree that cardiovascular disease is the number one killer of women in the United States?

A: Yes.

Q: Thank you very much.

Disposition of the Case

Both the hospital and PCP settled the claim. The ER doctor took it to trial where the jury returned a verdict in his favor. However, a poor jury instruction misled the jury and the case was reversed and remanded on appeal. Subsequently, the ER doctor also settled.

BIBLIOGRAPHY & ACKNOWLEDGMENTS

August, Albert. Excerpted from *Cross Examination of Timothy Madison, MD*, at http://embouncebacks.com. Alterations have been made for the purposes of brevity, readability, and clarity.

Kowalski v. Marymount Hosp. Inc., 2007-Ohio-828.

Personal thanks to Michael B. Weinstock, MD, of embouncebacks.com for his help and contributions.

CHAPTER 13

The Physician's Defenses
– Legal Armor and Operations Plan for Trial –

THE GAME PLAN

Too many doctors suffer from the misconception that malpractice cases are often brought thoughtlessly on a whim or on impulse. The occasional bizarre and sensationalized malpractice case in the news fails to contradict that impression. If doctors had any idea of the amount of time and money attorneys risk losing in this type of litigation, they would have a better understanding of the high degree of careful screening, diligence, and investigative work that is completed before filing such an action. No sensible attorney will spend hundreds of hours and $30,000–$60,000 for records, experts, depositions, transcripts, etc., on a case without significant potential for a recovery. One or two losing malpractice claims like that could easily put an attorney out of business. In addition, there are severe civil penalties for filing frivolous lawsuits.

Many physicians do not fully appreciate the seriousness, bona fide legal grounds, and strong factual substance involved in bringing such cases. They mistakenly believe that their defense will be a slam dunk or foregone conclusion—this is not so. If you find yourself in this situation, your defense firm will need your undivided cooperation and attention. Be prepared to invest substantial time and effort in your own defense. Start by educating your own lawyer on the medicine at issue. This may include not only the relevant anatomy, physiology, and pathology, but a guide of pertinent literature and identification of thought leaders in the field.

Malpractice insurance is the first key to a solid defense. Should the insured physician be served with a malpractice complaint, the carrier will hire a top-flight defense firm to represent both the doctor's and the carrier's own best interests. Doctors should also be aware that they are not required to accept the assigned attorney or firm should a personality conflict arise owing to poor chemistry or a difference of opinion.

The following is not meant as a comprehensive guide, but rather should be seen as an overview of some of the available defenses against a malpractice lawsuit, depending on the circumstances.

Affirmative Defenses

An affirmative defense is one that provides a defense without having to contest the plaintiff's accusations or charges. It avoids liability through acts or evidence that are not addressed in the plaintiff's complaint. Sometimes called excuse defenses, they can limit, excuse, or avoid liability without arguing the rights and wrongs of the case. The following are examples of some arguments a defense attorney may use to protect a doctor from improper or insufficient charges.

Motions are often filed to dismiss charges and may cite some of the following reasons.

1. **The complaint fails** to state a claim in whole or in part, upon which relief can be granted.

2. **The complaint further fails** to state facts sufficient to constitute a legal cause of action against the defendant.

3. **Inadequate service of process**—There has been an insufficiency of process and service of process so that this court lacks jurisdiction over the person of this answering defendant and therefore cannot render a judgment in this case.

4. **Improper venue**—The case was not filed in the county where the defendant works or lives or where the incident took place and therefore must be dismissed.

5. **Statute of limitations**—The plaintiff's case and claims are barred due to the expiration of the applicable statute of limitation.

6. **Assumption of the risk**—A person cannot recover damages if they have voluntarily exposed themselves to the risk of harm. This defense often applies in risky activities such as football, skydiving, or skiing, where dangers are well known but people choose to participate in them anyway.

   The doctrine of "assumption of the risk" means that the patient understands the possibility of unpreventable known risks and complications, and knowingly consents to the treatment. Therefore, if any of the advised consequences develop, the plaintiff's express or implied assumption of those risks negates recovery. For example, a patient is aware of the possibility of vertebral artery damage in a competently performed anterior neck fusion operation and voluntarily accepts that risk. The consent may negate a claim of malpractice in the event that complication materializes. This is one reason why well-written informed consent forms are so important for every doctor's medical practice.

7. **Contributory negligence**—This is when conduct on the part of the plaintiff contributed to the injury or harm. This means that some of the injuries and damages were caused or were contributed to by the plaintiff's own negligence.

   The legal principle at work here is that no one should be able to collect for any self-inflicted damages. As such, contributory negligence is a complete bar to collecting any damages. Basically, the defense is that "your injury is your own fault."

   However, the results of the contributory negligence defense in practice could be unduly harsh and unjust. For example, a female patient has cataract surgery but due to non-sterile technique develops an infection. She does not keep her follow-up appointments and her eye suffers permanent injury. Should she be denied any recovery because of the delay when she may not have been aware of the seriousness of her situation?

   As a result, most states have abandoned this legal defense.

   When the affirmative defense of contributory negligence does arise, it is often in terms of the patient's failure to disclose information that contributed to or caused the injury. This encompasses erroneous, incomplete, or misleading information from the patient. For example, a doctor testifies that he would not have prescribed Pitocin (due to the risk of perforation and scarring of the uterus) if the patient had disclosed that she had undergone three prior abortions.

   Patient non-compliance, according to Erin McNeil Young, JD, is evidence of contributory negligence. If proven, in those jurisdictions that allow contributory negligence as a defense, the patient could not collect damages even if the defendant doctor had clearly breached the standard of care.[1]

---

[1] See "Prove Patient's Non-Compliance: A Defense Verdict Might Result," *Physician Risk Management* (Nov. 2012): 49–51.

8. **Comparative negligence**—This is a partial defense that reduces the amount of damages by the percentage of fault by the plaintiff.

   When the patient does not cooperate with the doctor, this defense is often raised. An example of this would be a doctor recommending regular cervical Pap smear screenings, but the patient neglecting to have the tests done on a regular basis. That patient may or may not be at fault, but will have any judgment or jury verdict reduced by her percentage of fault or even vacated (in states that recognize contributory negligence) if she is later diagnosed with cervical cancer. The same is true if a patient fails to take medications as prescribed or fails to follow post-surgical instructions. There are a host of other scenarios as well. Again, a well-documented and honest medical record, demonstrating such non-compliance in an objective manner, is your best defense.

9. **Third party negligence**—When the injuries and expenses, if any, of which a plaintiff complains were caused by the acts or omissions of another or others whose conduct the Defendant had no reason to anticipate and for whose conduct the Defendant is and was not responsible. This means that, aside from the doctor's conduct, another individual was the real cause of the injuries. This might be another doctor who cared for the patient, or a nurse, a tech, or any other person. For example, this would be the case if a second hospital treats a patient after the first hospital failed to diagnose an acute abdomen. Following successful surgery at the second hospital, the patient is administered excess fluids, leading to death from congestive heart failure. Administering excess fluids in this case was both negligent and not foreseeable by the first hospital as part of its own negligence. Therefore, the first hospital is off the hook even though their conduct harmed the patient. Lawyers often call this an "independent intervening or supervening cause."

10. **Sole negligence of co-defendant**—When more than one doctor is named as a defendant, it's possible, but inherently dangerous and often unwise, to blame the other doctors.

11. **Related or identical litigation**—There are two types, either the same case or the same issue.

    A. **Same case, *res judicata***—If it's the same case as one that has already been litigated, the plaintiff's claims are barred by *res judicata*. *Res judicata* means "a thing already decided." As a legal concept it basically says that a person gets one, and only one, day in court on a matter. The law will not allow a party or person to have two bites of the same apple. It bars, or precludes, relitigation of a matter that was already decided.

For example, in Ohio a physician was sued for medical malpractice. The patient failed to present evidence that the doctor had failed to comply with the applicable standard of care and the court dismissed the lawsuit. Later, a loss of consortium claim was filed by the patient's husband. The court determined that a successful claim relied upon a claim of malpractice by the physician, which was already decided in the doctor's favor. Thus, the claim was dismissed under the doctrine of *res judicata*.

B. **Same issue, *estoppel*—**The term *estoppel* is a legal principle meaning "stopped" or "blocked." *Estoppel* bars a person from adopting a position in court that contradicts his or her past statements or actions. This effectively prevents relitigation of the same issue. Let's say a man is found to be the father of a child in a paternity suit. Later, if he is sued for child support, he cannot deny his paternity. Since the issue of paternity has already been decided, that person is blocked or stopped from trying to deny it.

As a further illustration, let's assume that a doctor is sued for failure to diagnose the sexual abuse of a child. The doctor defends himself/herself on the grounds that a family court has already determined that no sexual abuse ever occurred. The lawsuit against the doctor is likely to be dismissed in most states under the doctrine of *estoppel*. Thus, *estoppel* prevents a person from denying the truth of a fact already determined in a court or administrative hearing.

In *Thompson v. Wing* 70 Ohio St.3d 176 (1994) the plaintiff sued a doctor for the delayed diagnosis of cancer. The Court ruled in favor of the patient. Later the patient died, and the heirs brought a wrongful death suit. The court dismissed the suit since the same malpractice issue had already been litigated and therefore barred a later wrongful death action by her beneficiaries.

Estoppel can also be used offensively to extend the time one has to file a lawsuit. In one case, a man was diagnosed with hepatitis C after a cardiac bypass operation. Since he did not receive any blood products during surgery, he contacted the chief of infectious diseases at the same hospital. The patient was told that this was a case of transmission by unknown means. He did not pursue any legal action. Later it was discovered that the chief of infectious diseases knew that the patient's surgeon had hepatitis C and that several of his patients were infected. Thereafter, the patient sued the hospital. The suit was filed after the legal deadline and the hospital requested that the case be dismissed as a result. Because the chief of infectious diseases had misrepresented the facts to the patient, the hospital was blocked from claiming the suit should not proceed since it failed to provide the known facts that would have allowed the patient to investigate a claim. See *Putter vs. North Shore Hospital* 2006 NY Court of Appeals Slip Op 08281.

12. **Waiver**—This means that someone voluntarily gives up a right or privilege. A patient may sign a waiver of claims as a separate document or as part of consent to undergo a procedure. Waivers do not prevent a lawsuit from being filed and litigated.

13. **Good Samaritan statute**—Ordinary negligence damage claims are barred by statutes granting immunity from negligence to anyone rendering emergency assistance or care.

14. **Unforeseeable damages**—The damages of which plaintiff complains were the proximate cause of the progression of a disease or condition that was not reasonably foreseeable and were not caused by any act or omission of this answering defendant.

15. **The plaintiff failed to join** certain necessary and indispensable parties without whom complete adjudication cannot be had, as a result of which plaintiff's complaint must be dismissed.

16. **Contractual limit of duty**—A health care provider's duty may be limited by contractual agreement.

17. **The plaintiff failed to mitigate** or limit his damages as required by law.

Substantive Defenses

"Substantive" means that it is not merely a matter of procedure but goes more to the heart of the matter. The following is a list of examples.

1. Failure to allege proximate cause or failure to allege an actionable breach of duty.

2. Plaintiff failed to comply with statutory requirements, including conditions precedent or notice requirements, prior to filing the action.

3. Plaintiff has failed to allege a legal relationship between plaintiff and the health care provider who allegedly caused plaintiff's injury that would give rise to any duty or liability on the part of the defendant.

4. No proximate cause or causation between defendant's conduct and the injury. (See "Lack of Causation Themes" below.)

5. Plaintiff's acceptance of workers' compensation benefits bars this action.

6. Plaintiff is barred from recovery because plaintiff has released the original tortfeasor (wrongdoer) and has alleged that the acts of this defendant merely aggravated the injury caused by the original tortfeasor.

7. Any damages awarded must be reduced by the proportional amount of the patient's fault in causing or contributing to the harm. The plaintiff is barred from any recovery if their level of fault reaches 50% or 51%.

8. Plaintiff's damages must also be reduced by the amount that plaintiff has received from collateral sources, such as insurance.

9. Plaintiff's recovery for non-economic damages is limited by law.

10. Another defendant or others were careless and negligent. It is this carelessness and negligence that proximately contributed to the damages referred to in the complaint. This negligence either bars or proportionally reduces any potential recovery.

11. Plaintiff consented to all conduct of this defendant.

12. Plaintiff's claim for punitive damages is improperly pled and plaintiff has not established that there is a substantial probability that she will prevail on the claim.

13. The doctor properly withdrew from the patient's case and displayed due diligence in the care.

14. The negligent employee was acting outside the course and scope of their employment, also known as "frolic and detour." The employee's conduct served only the employee's personal interest and was not part of their employment duties. Thus, the employer cannot be held responsible.

Lack of Causation Themes

Lack of causation is often the most viable and effective defense in a malpractice lawsuit. Some of these themes can offer reasons explaining or excusing the result. Others indicate that even if the doctor's care was not in sync with what some experts would recommend, such an oversight had little, if anything, to do with the claimed injuries and was warranted under the circumstances. Such themes not only humanize the defendant doctor but focus the jury on the real-life medical dilemmas from the physician's perspective and may include the following.

1. Any decision a doctor makes is a judgment decision under difficult circumstances and the doctor should not be faulted for using his or her best judgment.

2. The patient waited too long before seeking medical advice.

3. The natural course of the patient's illness or disability was the sole cause of the injury that this patient allegedly suffered.

4. The patient signed a waiver and was informed of the risks and dangers of the procedure, which the patient voluntarily accepted.

5. Plaintiff suffered from other illnesses or disabilities that were the sole or substantial cause of the injury that the patient allegedly suffered.

6. The patient failed to provide accurate and complete information about present complaints, past illnesses, hospitalizations, medications, and other matters regarding his or her health.

7. The patient refused to take the advice of the doctor and/or failed to follow the course of conduct recommended by the physician. That is a contributing cause or the sole cause of the injury. The patient must bear some responsibility for his or her own injuries or bad result.

8. The patient's injury was not a reasonably foreseeable outcome of the doctor's acts.

9. There was no direct cause between the doctor's decisions and conduct, and the reported injury.

10. The doctor followed a medically recognized and accepted procedure or course of care.

11. The patient's injury is one of the accepted normal and/or known risks and complications of the procedure and the plaintiff did not need to be warned of those possible complications.

12. A different treatment or procedure would not have made any difference.

13. An unforeseeable anatomical anomaly or congenital abnormality was present, making the area vulnerable to injury, and as such was respon-

sible for the poor surgical outcome. Through no fault of the surgeon, scar tissue from a previous surgery masked the affected structure, thus preventing the doctor from fully identifying it owing to the abnormal anatomy.

14. Earlier diagnosis/treatment would not have made a significant difference.

15. It was a clinical judgment call within accepted medical standards.

16. No negligence occurred. The patient's ultimate outcome in terms of medical difficulties cannot be shown by the attorneys to have been affected, or brought about, by an error or malpractice.

17. If negligence did occur, it's a moot point—there are no damages. The patient was already ill through no act or fault of the doctor.

18. A specialist was consulted and relied upon. Therefore, there is no liability to the treating doctor.

19. A subsequent intervening cause that was not the fault of the defendant was the source of the patient's real difficulty. For example, the patient first acquired an infection which compromised his health, and then the patient required further surgery for an unrelated problem which further weakened his condition to the point that his organs began to progressively fail.

20. The patient was quite sick. Higher risk procedures were necessary to attempt to save the patient's life, although those procedures had more inherent dangers.

21. There was adequate treatment and diagnosis, but a poor result despite the doctor's efforts.

22. The patient had an atypical presentation, which masked his actual condition from this or any other doctor.

23. There was such a limited role for this defendant physician in the patient's care that no liability or blame can attach.

24. 20/20 hindsight defense. There was no way at that time for the doctor to reasonably suspect the obscure condition, diagnosis, or problem that the patient was having with its unusual presentation. The diagnosis would have been difficult to make even for the best and most experienced doctors.

25. Doctors cannot guarantee results. It is wrong for a plaintiff to sue for breach of a guarantee that was never given.

26. The disease/injury predated the treatment by the defendant, therefore the defendant cannot be held responsible.

27. There was a low index of suspicion that the working diagnosis was incorrect.

28. The treatment provided by the health care provider was an acceptable alternative form of treatment.

29. The "respectable minority defense"—In this case, a respectable minority of doctors find the decisions that were made to be part of an acceptable course of action in giving good care to the patient.

30. The nurse did not adequately communicate the change in status to the doctor.

31. There was no chance for nurses to communicate symptoms or changes to the doctor, or it's not the doctor's fault that nurses gave him imprecise information, e.g., a faulty sponge count.

32. The "zebra defense"—In this case the diagnosis is so obscure that it did not deserve to be considered in the differential diagnosis, i.e., "When you hear hoof beats you look for horses, not zebras."

33. This patient had no risk factors, so the doctor had no reason to include that specific "condition" in the differential diagnosis.

34. The signs and symptoms were patently atypical for the condition, so the doctor had no reason to entertain the diagnosis of "this condition" in his work-up.

35. The patient had multiple conditions, so that the second or third condition obscured the first.

36. The patient was already in the process of having an MI, stroke, etc., so the doctor wouldn't have been able to prevent the damage regardless.

37. Even if the patient had lived, he or she would have had a shortened life expectancy battling morbidity, so any damages should be appropriately reduced.

38. "Stuff happens" and the doctor is not necessarily responsible for a bad outcome. In other words, "results vary" for a multitude of reasons.

39. It's unfair for the plaintiff to judge the doctor's conduct, since he or she lacks the more extensive knowledge and education of a doctor.

40. Doctors or other health care providers are ordinary people. No one is perfect. They are fallible and make mistakes, and making an innocent and well-intentioned mistake of judgment is within accepted standards. It happens every day.

41. It was a rare and difficult case to diagnose, even for a specialist.

42. No doctor is required to insure the accuracy of his diagnosis any more than any doctor can guarantee the success of treatment. The patient was entitled to a careful and thorough examination according to his or her condition as attending circumstances permitted and that is precisely what the doctor did.

43. There is a notable absence of any incriminating notation in the medical record that specifically shows any medical mistake or error. This means that the plaintiff cannot prove what happened or that it is in any way directly related to any mistake by this doctor.

44. Touching upon the standard of care, the doctor might testify that "I and all the other doctors I know in my field do it this way, so it is customary medical practice."

45. The doctor made the best decision possible for this patient's benefit under the circumstances.

46. The magic fingers defense, i.e., the doctor originally felt a lump, but it was moveable and soft, with smooth contours, and was not in the exact location of the lump at issue in this case.

47. It is just a difference in opinion among experts. That is not malpractice.

48. Considering the plaintiff's state of health and the limited options available, the doctor's conduct did not make a difference because the outcome was inevitable.

49. According to statistics, the patient was not likely to improve significantly anyway.

50. Under the circumstances, the patient is lucky to have had the outcome that occurred.

51. Clinical alterations or innovations were necessary to achieve established goals.

LEGAL DEFENSES TO LACK OF INFORMED CONSENT

Emergencies

Serious medical emergencies are a complete defense to a physician's failure to obtain informed consent, i.e., when the delay necessary to obtain informed consent would result in serious harm or may be life-threatening to the patient.

Therapeutic Privilege

Therapeutic privilege occurs when complete disclosure may have detrimental effects on the physical or psychological well-being of the patient. If these are the facts, then the doctor has no duty to disclose the risks. When a doctor has a special relationship with the patient, this not only vests the doctor with responsibility of disclosure, but also requires him to exercise discretion in prudently disclosing information in accordance with the patient's best interests. In this situation, to disclose more than what is absolutely necessary would run counter to the responsibility assumed through the doctor-patient relationship.

Known Risks

Commonly known risks, e.g., risk of pain after a tooth extraction, need not be disclosed. This defense creates a presumption that the patient has knowledge of the risk. Remote risks when the procedure is simple, and the complications are commonly appreciated, also negate the need for informed consent.

The Patient Refused Information

When a patient refuses the information and consents to treatment regardless of the risks, or when the patient does not wish to know the risks, the physician may safely proceed with treatment without informed consent. These circumstances create a legal waiver for consent. The doctor's attempt to supply informed consent and patient's response should be well documented.

Unknown Risks

If the doctor does not know of a material risk in the exercise of ordinary care, obtaining consent is usually not necessary.

Unforeseen Risks

Situations in which the harm to the patient was not reasonably foreseeable do not generally require consent.

Third Parties

In most jurisdictions, a health care provider has no duty under the informed consent statute to disclose risks to third parties.

INFORMED CONSENT SUMMARY

If the patient signed a medical consent form, the emphasis will be that the patient knowingly assumed all the risks and complications by asking the physician to perform the procedure. (See "Chapter 6: Informed Consent" and "Chapter 9: Consents and Releases.")

CONCLUSION

In the unfortunate event of a lawsuit, every doctor needs a persuasive, effective malpractice defense. Your malpractice carrier through your legal team will do most of the heavy lifting for your defense. That includes legal and medical analysis of the case, how you likely adhered to the standard of care, finding errors in the plaintiff expert's opinions, exposing the lack of causation, reducing damages, securing a top-flight expert on your behalf, and finding or producing illustrations, videos, charts, diagrams, etc., to make a powerful presentation of the medicine to a jury.

BIBLIOGRAPHY

For the Defense. Defense Research Institute.

Gladwell, Malcolm. *Blink*. Little, Brown and Company, 2005.

King, Joseph. *Law of Medical Malpractice in a Nutshell*. Nutshell Series, 1986.

Mello, M.M., and C.H. Williams. "Medical Malpractice: Impact of the Crisis and Effect of State Tort Reforms." *The Synthesis Project* 10. Robert Wood Johnson Foundation.

Schoenbaum, Stephen C., MD, MPH, and Randall R. Bovbjerg, JD. "Malpractice Reform Must Include Steps to Prevent Medical Injury." *Annals of Internal Medicine* 140, no. 1 (Jan. 2004): 51–53.

Shandell, Richard E. *The Preparation and Trial of Medical Malpractice Cases*. 1981.

Wojcieszak, D., J. Saxton, and M. Finkelstein. *Sorry Works!: Disclosure, Apology and Relationships Prevent Malpractice Claims*. 2008.

CHAPTER 14

Make Your Testimony Shine in Deposition and in Court

There are three things you must do absolutely alone in this world—
be born, die, and testify
—Jimmy Walker (1881–1946), former mayor of New York City

INTRODUCTION

In the past, doctors, nurses, and therapists could go through their entire careers without having to testify in a courtroom. Today, however, it is commonplace for health professionals to be summoned as witnesses in some form of legal proceedings, whether these arise from traffic accidents, work injuries, child custody battles, abuse cases, and/or alleged medical malpractice.

Going to court is stressful. On one hand, doctors are comfortable making difficult decisions regarding the diagnosis and care for a great variety of patients on a daily basis. On the other hand, a courtroom is likely to be well outside the sphere of a physician's comfort zone. It's foreign territory with an entirely different set of rules and standards.

Most doctors will be called upon from time to time to testify on behalf of their patients. Some doctors will be used as expert witnesses to testify on standard of care or damages in personal injury or malpractice suits, or they may serve as advisors to help prepare the plaintiff's or defendant's attorneys.

EXPERT OPINIONS

Expert testimony must be founded on expert knowledge which has been obtained through education, training, and experience. As such, the opinions expressed by medical experts are properly supported by facts. These facts can be established by the evidence or by facts that are generally known and/or used by experts under similar circumstances. A strategic point to remember is that in malpractice defense, the treating doctor often becomes an extra expert witness, which is both a potential advantage and an unadulterated risk.

Whether appearing on the plaintiff's or the defendant's behalf, the expert will likely be asked questions from unusual angles, often out of logical sequence and in terms that are unfamiliar and confusing. Deposition and trial questions are at times intrusive, personal, and offensive. My advice is to get over it.

Experts must expect questions that:

- Test the depth and breadth of their recall.
- Limit their qualifications/credentials.
- Determine whether education, training and experience are relevant and meaningful.
- Ask about their litigation history.
- Probe the witness' general knowledge of the chosen professional field, methods, equipment, standards, science, and literature.
- Examine the doctor's general knowledge of the case.
- Ask what information the doctor relied on or assumed in forming the opinions.
- Delve into facts underlying the expert's opinion.
- Inquire into the legal and professional standards complied with in all areas of care.
- Ask what journals the witness reads regularly.
- Request the title and journal of the last article read on the subject of the trial.
- Probe whether the witness will change his or her mind. This is done with hypothetical questions in which some of the assumptions or facts are altered. Then the doctor is asked how those facts, if true, would change the opinion. For example: "Doctor, I want you to assume that the defendant doctor failed to make notes regarding any review of this patient's prior medical records. Let's also assume that the doctor never looked at or reviewed the patient's prior medical history. Here's my question: Wouldn't you agree that the failure to review the patient's prior medical history is a departure from good and accepted medical practice?"
- Ask if the expert is 100% certain of being correct, and whether the facts are true and accurate and how that's known.
- See if the expert demonstrates bias—via literature, prior depositions, etc.

- Ask the expert to divulge fees, income, etc.
- Probe into any past negative actions with regard to the doctor's reputation and license, including the number and types of complaints filed.
- Determine how the expert got into the case, e.g., when the expert was first contacted and by whom, what was asked of him or her, and if the expert advertises his or her own services or goes through an expert agency.
- Insist on seeing past and current advertising and promotional materials.
- Make the expert explain reasons for differences in opinion with other experts.
- Make the expert explain whatever he may have said on his website, his publications (if any), or anyplace that the public and, therefore, the plaintiff's counsel can see.

Although the process is inconvenient, most doctors quickly acclimate to depositions and trials that involve their patients. Few things, however, cause doctors as much anger, anxiety and frustration as testifying on their own behalf in a medical malpractice suit. The doctor will feel that he or she is definitely not in control.

ATTORNEY GOALS
For the Deposition

Attorneys have six central goals during a deposition. The first is to commit the doctor to a set of facts. The second is to discover all the facts, arguments, potential theories, and opinions that will be presented in the courtroom. The third is to gain valuable information and testimony to use for summary judgment of the case. The fourth goal is to uncover inconsistencies that can be used at trial. This includes inconsistencies between yourself and other experts or witnesses and also inconsistencies between your deposition and your trial testimony. The fifth is to obtain favorable admissions from you about the case.

The sixth and final goal is to give the attorney an opportunity to size you up and assess your strengths and weaknesses with regard to knowledge, communication skills, and demeanor as a witness. The deposition gives malpractice attorneys important information such as how impressive you are as a speaker and witness or how well you can explain clinical concepts to a lay audience (an indication of your powers of persuasion), what the defense's or plaintiff's case is based upon and how strong or weak it is, whether you are easily confused or intimidated, and how well you think and react under pressure.

Depositions are part of the discovery phase of a legal proceeding. Other than a jury trial, a deposition is probably the most stressful litigation event a doctor will face.

The doctor's deposition is often the single most important pre-trial event.

For Trial

At trial, the opposing attorney's one primary purpose is to discredit you. This includes your abilities, your judgment, your opinions, and your entire testimony. In the movie *Enemy of the State* (1998), the character played by Jon Voight illustrates this point effectively when he says, "Credibility is the only currency that means anything on this kind of playing field. I want his credibility...I want people to know he's lying before they hear what he says."
—Thomas Reynolds in *Enemy of the State* (1998)

To help accomplish this goal, the lawyer will ask questions that may indicate that the doctor is not telling the whole truth; is uncaring, i.e., didn't listen, didn't follow up, resents the patient; or is incompetent. Attorneys like to devise questions that make the witness's answer unimportant or irrelevant, no matter what their response may be. For example, "If this problem is not diagnosed, it can have bad consequences for the patient?" In this case, answering "Yes" agrees with the attorney and casts a shadow of suspicion on the doctor's diagnostic abilities, while answering "No" makes the witness appear foolish. A good plaintiff's attorney will likely attempt to demonstrate that the patient faithfully fulfilled his or her part of the doctor-patient contract, but the doctor did not. (See also "Chapter 2: The Doctor-Patient Contract.")

Doctors naturally resent being sued. They resent the patient for suing them and are often loath to admit that they did anything wrong. Even if they did something wrong, they are likely to deny that this action or omission had any negative effect on the outcome. These can be points of vulnerability in deposition or at trial. You should definitely consult your defense attorney about these points.

TRIAL PREPARATION

"There are two sides to every story and then there is the truth." —Court TV

Trials are not about the actual *truth* but what *appears* to be the truth. That's probably why there are so many television shows on the subject. The following is hard-won advice on how to prepare for trial.

Attire for Deposition or Court Proceedings

Look dignified. When giving testimony, dress as well as you would for a day at work or when visiting your house of worship. This shows respect for the court and jury. Do not dress to impress. Conventional wisdom recommends keeping it classy, but not flashy, in general accordance with the following:

Men

- A dark blue, black, or gray single-breasted suit for men helps convey credibility.
- Light blue or pastel shirts are more accepted than stark white shirts.
- No jewelry except for a wedding ring.
- Overly casual or flashy clothing will distract the jurors from the substance of your actual testimony.

Women

- A dark business suit is usually best. Pulled back hair is optional.
- The general rule is no jewelry, although a string of pearls or a neck scarf will draw attention to the face, thus encouraging jurors to look directly at the testifying doctor.

Understand "Attorney Talk"

Attorneys use words and language in different ways from the general public and doctors. The following are some examples.

"AUTHORITATIVE"

If you admit that any book, article, journal, publication, or author is "authoritative," "reliable," or "standard" (depending on the state), you can be cross-examined from those books or articles. (See "Bonus Tips for Deposition," p. 240.) Most witnesses are understandably reluctant to admit to any literature as authoritative. Don't, however, throw away your common sense. If the attorney asks if *Gray's Anatomy* is authoritative, you may look silly by trying to deny its authority. Of course it's authoritative. It would be fair, though, to point out that the science of anatomy continues to expand and that newer findings may not be included in the text. Also keep in mind that *Gray's* is a textbook of normal anatomy. You are rarely in court to testify about "normal anatomy." A trauma or injury usually involves a departure from normal anatomy, so *Gray's* will likely not be directly relevant to the case at hand. Better still, find a textbook or two that corresponds to your way of thinking. Discuss this with your attorney first, however, as the texts may contain material potentially damaging to the defense. Doctors appear dignified and scholarly when they can base their opinions on published medical literature. In this way, you can solidly support your opinion with the existing published literature and leave yourself less open to criticism.

"MEDICAL PROBABILITY AND MEDICAL CERTAINTY"

The law recognizes an element of uncertainty in every medical opinion. Medical probability only means "more than 50% likely" or "more likely than not." Medical certainty is a bit more nebulous. How certain is anything in medicine? It would seem that a likelihood of something greater than 80% would clearly indicate a degree of medical certainty, or predictability, on any practical scale. In some states, medical certainty means the same thing as medical probability, i.e., that something is more likely than not. As a legal term, attorneys would like it to imply 100% certainty. Medical certainty is the law's way of showing that the doctor's opinion is not speculation, guesswork, or a mere theory.

Either way, there is nothing wrong with saying, "I do not understand your question. Would you explain it, please?" After all, doctors do not communicate with each other in such terms.

Minimize Nervous Habits

Remember that jurors expect physicians to be surefooted and fearless. Constantly clearing your throat makes a witness appear evasive and nervous. Any hint of condescension should be avoided. Ask your defense firm to videotape you while answering tough questions. Your pre-programmed unwanted habits, gestures, and facial expressions will be glaringly apparent, and you will be able to address them before your appearance in court.

Be Accurate About Previous Conversations

In testimony about prior conversations, specify whether you are paraphrasing or are quoting the person directly. If you recall only the gist of the conversation rather than the precise words, make that clear.

Recalling the Events

When certain events, patient advice, or a course of care are not specifically documented in the record, the doctor should admit to any lack of specific recall. The doctor can testify as to his or her clinical customs and habits of care to explain any seeming deficiency in documentation. For example, "It is my custom and practice in these situations to order standard screening tests. There was no need to make a note about this action since I knew what I would always do and needed no reminder of the course of action I would take for this, or any other, patient's benefit. Unfortunately, this particular patient failed to obtain those tests."

Explain the Patient's Outcome

The time to tell your story is at trial. Every malpractice case involves a poor medical outcome, so the doctor must be prepared to offer a plausible explanation as to why the patient had a poor outcome.

Don't Act "Smart"

A frequent mistake made by physicians in malpractice cases is attempting to impress the jury with their education and training as a testament to how smart they are. Instead, physicians should try to show the jury that they were caring and compassionate by being attentive and that they took all the time required with the patient. Jurors are already laboring under the false impression that most doctors unduly rush when seeing or treating their patients.

Make Your Testimony Shine

Attorneys rightly fear physicians since they are not easy witnesses to cross-examine. They are intelligent, and it takes minimal effort to make them well-prepared witnesses. Physicians know far more about the medical facts and science of the case than attorneys, and most jurors have a profound respect for doctors. If the jury sees you as a teacher, the members will likely appreciate your efforts to explain complex topics. If a concept requires technical language, be sure to offer a simple definition. If you don't, your lawyer should elicit one before moving on to any other topic.

Lawyers also have a duty to prepare witnesses with regard to their testimony, how the law applies, requirements of proof, and improving phrasing even to the extent of suggesting specific particular words to make the meaning clearer. An attorney is forbidden to encourage testimony that is false.

In a malpractice trial, the defendant doctor will likely be limited in testifying to the care and treatment provided and whether it was necessary under the circumstances.

If you are called upon to testify, have your records with you, sit erect with hands relaxed on your lap or table, speak slowly, clearly, and audibly, look at the jurors when answering questions, be alert, and consider the following as sound advice.

Core Principles for Testifying Doctors

1. Listen to the question.

2. Make sure you understand the question. Never answer a question you do not understand. You have the right and obligation to tell the lawyer if you don't fully understand the question. Ask the attorney to rephrase it or say, "Your question makes no sense to me as you asked it." Do not answer any question until you fully understand it.

3. Pause briefly before answering a question. Think before answering. By taking a moment to deliberate before answering you will not sound rehearsed or careless in your consideration. Even if you know the answer immediately, take a breath while you replay the question in your head. Think about exactly what was asked, not what you thought they would ask.

4. Answer only the question that was asked. "A good witness is one who has the knack of only answering what was asked." —Tierney, *How to Be a Witness*

   Give a straightforward answer in the form of the shortest, clearest, most accurate direct answer you can to the *exact question asked* and then stop talking. Brevity is not only the soul of wit, but the heart of clarity.

   Witnesses are anxious to prevent attorneys from trapping them. At times we all think we know where the lawyer is going, and we want to cut off his water, so to speak. Thus, there's a tendency to jump ahead to a question you anticipate being asked and cut it off by offering an explanation. This is a poor strategy.

   Giving an explanation in place of the answer to the question actually asked will confuse and alienate the jury while making the witness appear evasive and defensive. Give a brief explanation if you must, but do not offer excuses; then give a solid and simple answer to the question as asked. Dodge & Fitzer (2009) provide the following example.

Q: Yes or no, the patient's lab reports were never put into the chart?

A: I called the lab and was told the results, but no they were not put in the chart.[1]

5. As a corollary to number 4, don't open Pandora's box. Never volunteer information of any kind. Additional cross-examination questions are often the children of volunteered facts or unduly long answers. The purpose of your testimony is *not* to teach or educate the plaintiff's attorney. Avoid the temptation to show off your knowledge. This is not a social conversation; don't treat it as one. For example, consider this exchange.

Q: Do you know the time?

A: No.

Q: Do you wear a watch?

A: No.

Q: Do you keep track of time?

A: Yes.

Q: How do you track time?

A: I have a cell phone.

Q: Well, what time is it?

A: I don't know.

Q: Could you look at your cell phone?

A: Yes.

Q: What time is it?

A: 11:15 AM.[2]

This witness was able to resist the temptation to give the time, as we would do in a conversation, and just answered the questions that were asked.

If an attorney asks you an overly broad question that invites you to volunteer information with a long answer, ask the attorney to be more specific or simply provide a short answer, as in the following example.

---

[1] Angela M. Dodge and Steven F. Fitzer, *When Good Doctors Get Sued: A Practical Guide for Physicians Involved in Malpractice Lawsuits*, 3rd ed. (Dodge Consulting & Publications, 2009), 95.

[2] Ibid.

Q: Tell the jury what happened on the patient's first office visit.

A: The patient told me her symptoms, I took a medical history, and I performed an examination.[3]

6. The most fundamental testimonial rule is to tell the truth. You just took an oath to tell the truth. The honest answer is always the best answer, so tell it simply and directly. If you tell the truth, no one can trip you up.

7. Be prepared! As Louis Nizer said, *"Preparation is everything! It makes the stupid man bright, the bright man brilliant, and the brilliant man steady."* Know the facts of the case, brush up on anatomy and authorities in the field, and review conflicting theories of the case. Above all, know your own chart backwards and forwards. Take the role of being an expert witness seriously.

8. Jurors expect physicians to be confident and unafraid. Express competence, confidence, and compassion while you are on the witness stand. Resist the temptation to clam up on cross-examination. If you spoke freely on direct examination, then you should speak just as freely under cross-examination. This strikes a balance that will not be lost on the jury. Do not suddenly limit, qualify, or weaken your opinion by turning quiet, uncertain, and sheepish during cross.

9. Never ever exaggerate. At deposition or trial this includes avoiding the frequent use of intensifiers such as "very" or "incredibly." This maxim further extends to your resume. On the negative side, overstating your achievements is undermining to your credibility. The upside is that an up-to-date and accurate CV with nothing inflated is a benchmark of your forthrightness and honesty.

10. Know your attorney's central theme of the case and reference the medical records to actively support that theme.

11. Expect surprises and tests. You'll get them in either case. The more important your testimony is to the case, the more the other side will test you.

12. Maintain a professional attitude, i.e., be respectful, pleasant, good humored, and modest. If the lawyer scolds you or yells at you, respond with a smile and a soft, measured answer. Attorneys hate that.

---

[3] Ibid., 93.

13. Real people testify with some feeling. Avoid testifying like a pedantic professor whose sterile learning experiences have left him with the mere shell of a human personality and little genuine emotion. Testifying in a dull, robotic, and disinterested way may lead the jury to think you are well-rehearsed or even lying. Use expression. It adds spice.

14. Remember, "If a good witness you would be, do not agree when you disagree." If you disagree with *any part* of the question posed, the proper answer is "No." We have all had the experience of agreeing with someone or yielding a point in the interest of being sociable and not wanting to appear too stubborn or inflexible. Social graces are for social occasions, which your testimony is certainly not. When necessary, disagree courteously, but, by all means, disagree.

    Q: Why didn't you refer this patient to a specialist when you were unable to diagnose the problem she was developing?

    A: At that time, I was still in the process of gathering information and test results to make a diagnosis. I made a diagnosis and a referral as soon as the tests indicated this patient needed a specialist.[4]

15. As an addendum to the previous principle, if you disagree with any specific word or phrase in the question, then speak directly to that point as the focus of your response.

    Q: This patient had a *serious* spinal problem when you first saw her, didn't she?

    A: She was *concerned* about the pain in her lower back.[5]

    If the attorney is successful in letting the word "serious" pass unnoticed, it would be used repeatedly to the doctor's detriment.

    Q: Didn't this patient make *multiple* requests for more medication to control the pain?

    A: As I recall, she made *one or possibly two requests.*[6]

    Q: Wouldn't you agree that this patient had an *unacceptably poor* outcome?

    A: She had a relatively *rare and unfortunate* outcome.[7]

    Q: How do you explain these horrific results?

---

[4] Ibid., 63.
[5] Ibid., 62.
[6] Ibid., 62.
[7] Ibid., 90.

A: I wouldn't describe it that way.[8]

Q: How could you allow an untrained resident to play doctor in such a delicate and crucial surgery?

A: Please clarify your question.

Q: Is it possible that...?

A: Anything is possible in theory, but here in the real world, I don't think that's possible.

16. Do not memorize an answer or answers. As the saying goes, "You can teach a parrot to say anything, but he won't know what he's talking about." You will sound rehearsed. Likewise, you are likely to be caught and become embarrassed. Aim to convince by listening to and responding to the question asked, rather than memorizing canned responses. Persuade listeners by educating them and satisfying their minds. Prepare by responding to practice questions with clear and related ideas that you can draw on regardless of the question.

17. The doctor should attempt to enlighten the members of the jury without burying them under a mass of technical mumbo jumbo. Avoid technical language if possible. Boil down complicated material into understandable pieces of information. Keep your testimony conversational. Refer to a model, prop, picture, exhibit, or diagram whenever possible to make your testimony memorable. Use analogies. We all love analogies where the inanimate comes to life.

Hairsplitting distinctions are unconvincing and rarely work. Speak plainly and simply. Movie fans may recall *The Verdict* (1982) for examples of this principle under the tutelage of James Mason as defense attorney Ed Concannon.

18. Don't guess! You cannot know all the facts. If you don't know the answer, simply say "I don't know." "I don't know" is an appropriate and complete answer and can be a sign of both wisdom and honesty. It's okay to approximate or estimate, but do not guess.

19. We all forget important facts, dates, and details at times. If it happens to you, just say "I can't remember" or "I don't recall."

20. If confronted with a yes or no question that you think you cannot answer honestly, say to the attorney, "If I limit my answer to yes or no, I will not be able to give factual testimony" or "If I must answer yes or no, it

---

[8] Ibid., 60.

will be misleading to the jury. Is that what you want?" You can also say, "Yes/no under certain circumstances" or "As I understand your question the answer is yes/no."

21. Never answer before the lawyer finishes the question; the last word of his question may change its whole meaning.

22. Be comfortable with delays and silent moments. Attorneys are.

23. Shun the knee-jerk reaction to match the tone and pace of the cross-examining attorney's questions. It makes the witness look like the lawyer's powerless puppet.

24. Never get angry. Stay calm. Never shout. The first one to raise his voice loses. Any sports coach worth his or her salt will tell you that an angry player makes mistakes. The same is true during your cross-exam, under any circumstances. For example, if a lawyer stings you in cross-examination, maintain eye contact and do not flinch. Flinching will tell others that a good blow has been struck. Be steady. Maintain your composure and dignity at all times during your response. Also, if a lawyer is disrespectful to you while you remain calm and collected, jurors will resent the lawyer and favor you.

25. Do not argue with the attorney. Jurors perceive arguing as being disrespectful. If the attorney is disrespectful and overly aggressive, the jury will dislike him and sympathize with you.

26. Never be sarcastic, flippant, or attempt to be cute. It rarely impresses a judge or jury. Act like the professional you are.

27. Never allow yourself to be interrupted before you finish answering the question. If you are interrupted, ask the court reporter to read the question back and politely insist on finishing your answer. The question was important enough for the attorney to ask, so you should be given the chance to respond fully. Like a remark taken out of context, a partial answer can be misleading and come back to hurt you later.

28. If you are shown or asked about any document, *read that document completely and with care* and at your own reading speed. Don't let the lawyer provide you with only portions of a document. Demand a complete copy and the time to review it entirely, if he wants your opinion.

29. Correct a prior answer if necessary. We all admire a person who can admit to an error and correct it.

30. Stop when an objection is made. Listen! Your attorney may give an important clue about an unfair or trick question. For example, "Object,

to the form of the question." This is the signal for you to ask the attorney to rephrase the question.

31. Stick to the facts. Testify only as to what you *personally know*, not what you think or surmise or have heard from someone else.

32. Don't look for cleverly laid traps in every question. It can make you look hesitant, apprehensive, or even worse—stupid.

33. Be objective and impartial. Don't be afraid to admit that your opinion is not absolutely conclusive, but do not be directed away from the fact that your opinion is well-founded. Ask yourself and your attorney what unfavorable facts you can safely admit to in the case. Admitting to a fact or two that are not in your favor makes you look thoughtful, well-balanced, and fair. Also ask your defense attorney what the other side's weak points are and how best to exploit them.

34. Consult your records and reports as necessary and take all the time you need.

35. If the doctor is a testifying expert and not simply a fact witness, then he must also answer hypothetical questions. For some hypothetical questions, e.g., "What would you have done if…?," a fair and honest answer might be, "I would need to know more facts and circumstances before I can answer" or "I do not find your hypothetical believable, so I am unable to respond to it."

36. At all times, simply be reasonable, rational, and logical. This is especially true when giving your opinions. This enhances your trustworthiness.

37. Try to avoid repeating the same standard phrases and words in your responses. It compromises credibility because it makes you sound robotic as a witness.[9]

38. If possible, avoid agreeing to a negative or answering in the negative.[10] Examples:

     Q: You failed to order the blood test at that time, didn't you?

     A: No, I didn't order that particular test. (negative)

     A: I ordered the tests I thought were appropriate at that time. (positive)

---

[9] Stanley L. Brodsky, *Coping with Cross Examination* (Washington, DC: American Psychological Association, 2004), 86.

[10] Constance G. Uribe, MD, *The Health Care Provider's Guide to Facing the Malpractice Deposition* (CRCCC Press, LLC, 2000), 118.

A: I would never start treatment without first obtaining consent. (negative)

A: It is my practice to obtain written and verbal consent from every patient before starting treatment. (positive)

39. Beware of misdirection. Attorneys like, and frequently use, misdirection to accomplish their goals. Verbal misdirection often involves using generalities as applied to this patient. For example, "Can arthritis cause any of the symptoms this patient was experiencing?" The response should be a request for clarification.

40. There are few certainties in science, but in court all experts must be positive and certain. Your opponent's expert will be. Act accordingly.

41. Be nice! In the movies don't you want the nice guy or girl to win? As the jury watches this legal drama unfold, the witness who is not only knowledgeable, trustworthy, and confident, but also likable has a much better chance of winning at trial than one who is distant or "difficult."

42. Tell the truth. This bears repetition because it is so important. In every case there are acts or omissions in your care and treatment or aspects of your opinions that are questionable. Complete honesty means that you may have to concede the obvious and admit weaknesses. Such candor only enhances your credibility. No case is perfect. Don't be afraid to admit the truth and don't allow anyone to bully you into a departure from the truth.

For additional examples of trial questions and answers and targeted advice, I recommend Dodge & Fitzer's *When Doctors Get Sued* (2009), from which many of the above examples have been drawn.

Bonus Tips for Depositions

At deposition, just answer the questions asked. Nothing good can come from your testimony at a deposition. In fact, this is your best chance to lose the case before a trial ever gets started. So your deposition is *not* the time or place to tell your side of the story or to fully explain things or to defend your actions. That is what your trial is for.

Be brief and to the point. Answer the question asked and stop. Don't embellish or offer examples, comparisons, or analogies. Understand that every question the opposing lawyer asks is intended to harm you and your case in some way. This is why it is so important to give the shortest honest answer you can and then stop talking.

Do *not* volunteer any information so that the proceeding can end as soon as possible. Make the opposing attorney work a little. Try not to work for him.

In answering questions, you need to appear to be knowledgeable and competent without being overly wordy. Therefore, some questions will require a thoughtful explanation. However, a number of other questions put forth in a deposition can be answered truthfully with one of five responses:

- "Yes."
- "No."
- "I don't know" (Doctors are expected to know most of the facts regarding their own patients, so use this answer only when you absolutely do not know.)
- "I don't recall" or "That's all I can recall at this time."
- "I don't understand the question."

If, in fact, you do not have a vivid specific recollection of this particular patient, the deposition will likely be shorter, less stressful, more accurate, and easier to defend.[11]

Never offer or volunteer to draw or sketch anything and resist any invitation to do so.

Do not bring notes, diagrams, books, documents, or other materials to the deposition unless ordered to do so by subpoena or asked by your attorney.

Do not cite the medical literature in a deposition unless you are asked. This only tips off the opposing attorney and allows that lawyer to prepare to rebut the material at trial. If you have done a literature search, the opposing attorney will insist on having a copy of that search.

If you agree that a textbook, journal, or another doctor is an authority in a specific area, it's an admission that you would look to this book, journal, or person for the truth and accept it. Recognize that such an admission extends to every syllable of every published page or opinion, and that opposing counsel will consider himself at liberty to apply every statement in the publication to your case willy-nilly, as he wishes.

In a malpractice case in which you are the defendant, if possible, never criticize a co-defendant. You will likely create another expert against yourself in the process.

---

[11] Susanne Moore, RN, JD, *Deposition Dissection: A Handbook for Doctors Facing Deposition* (Tucson, AZ: Lawyers and Judges Publishing Co., Inc., 2005), 50.

There is one question you may hear at deposition that you will rarely, if ever, hear at trial and that is "Why?" Even at the very beginning of the deposition, you may be asked a highly pointed question such as "Why didn't you operate on this patient within a few hours of this medical emergency?" Don't be thrown off the medical witness ride in the first eight seconds. Be ready for a surprise opening.

VIDEOTAPED DEPOSITIONS[12]

Avoid videotaping if possible, but if it must be:

- Dress appropriately.
- Turn off cell phones and pagers.
- Avoid eating or drinking.
- Look at the camera, not counsel, when answering questions.
- Hold exhibits up to the camera.
- Be aware of your negative or defensive body language.
- Immediately look down at your files during objections or conversations between the attorneys. This allows you to appear comfortable and composed. Otherwise, the natural tendency is to look at each attorney as he speaks. The appearance of your eyes ping-ponging back and forth on video can make you look like a crazed and confused deer in the headlights.

CONCLUSION

Depositions and trials are stress-filled events. At times you can almost feel the red laser dot on your forehead as the opposition focuses his sights on you. Still, some individuals seem to thrive in that environment as though they were born for it.

A modicum of practice and experience in this area is invaluable. Have you ever heard an experienced coroner give testimony? Their statements are well-measured, reasoned, and said with precision. Fear and trepidation do not have to be the coin of the realm; after all, you know your specialty better than any attorney possibly could. In the end, the best expert witness is one who is knowledgeable, composed, principled, and reasonable.

---

[12] Eeric Truumees, MD. http://www.aaos.org/news/bulletin/oct07/managing3.asp. (Site no longer available.)

BIBLIOGRAPHY

Cohen, Kenneth S. *Expert Witnessing and Scientific Testimony: Surviving in the Courtroom*. 2007.

Dodge, Angela M., PhD, and Steven Fitzer, JD. *When Good Doctors Get Sued*. 3rd ed. 2009.

Lubet, Steven, and Elizabeth Boals. *Expert Testimony: A Guide to Experts and the Lawyers Who Examine Them*. 2009.

Personal notes.

CHAPTER 15

Core Malpractice Concepts
– Controversial Issues to Consider –

Controversial and unsettled issues seem to regularly infiltrate and degrade otherwise relatively factual deliberations regarding malpractice.

The following represent likely plaintiff's bar positions on some of the core issues. Physicians should be roughly familiar with these stances and some of the facts that support them. These brief informational vignettes are not meant to be conclusive, but rather serve to give the reader a broader understanding of how plaintiff lawyers approach malpractice. Although the examples are based on facts, there is clearly room for other opinions in addition to other sources of factual information that can be valuable.

Physicians will be better prepared for trial if they understand the underpinnings of the typical plaintiff arguments made in malpractice suits and will be able to articulate more clearly why they disagree with arguments that are not persuasive or have questionable sources.

TORT REFORMS

In the recent past, a number of news pieces appeared in the press regarding excessive numbers of malpractice lawsuits, runaway juries, frivolous lawsuits, excess verdicts, and concerns that doctors were being driven out of practice by the so-called malpractice crisis. As a result, in the early 2000s, state legislatures responded vigorously, giving special treatment and protection to doctors on a number of those issues.

Traditionally, reforms attempted to alter the medical malpractice landscape in one of three ways: (1) allowing fewer lawsuits by creating barriers to filing, (2) creating artificial limits on plaintiffs' compensation by imposing damage caps for non-economic damages such as pain and suffering; or (3) changing the method of paying out settlements to plaintiffs (payments over time versus large lump-sum settlements).[1]

---

[1] See http://journalofethics.ama-assn.org/2016/03/pfor6-1603.html.

Newer, more narrow limits on the legal rights of plaintiffs for the time allowed to bring their cases, made it more costly and difficult to file a case. Artificial limits or caps on how much can be collected in damages were put into place as well as curbs on joint and several liability. Public funds have also been made available to pay malpractice claims in some states.

Tort reforms such as caps were passed under the guise of lowering physicians' liability premiums and health care costs. However, for the most part, this did not happen.

Caps have done nothing to lower malpractice insurance rates. Although insurers do pay out less money when damage awards are capped, they do not pass those savings on to doctors by lowering their liability premiums. Caps may also represent an unfair discrimination. A person who was injured by a negligent doctor or health care provider would have the amount of his actual damages limited. A person injured by anyone else would not have such fabricated legal limits. As former senator Mary Landrieu from Louisiana summed it up, "The high price of health care in this country is a serious issue that demands serious attention. Putting limits on damages have little or no effect on skyrocketing malpractice insurance rates."[2]

Moreover, "extensive research, including some done by the Congressional Budget Office and Government Accountability Office, has shown that tort reform has had little to no influence on health care costs."[3] The state of Texas, for example, has some of the strictest caps, but also has some of the highest health care costs in the country.

Physicians in states with caps, including Texas, have suffered substantial premium rate increases even while insurers have enjoyed a slowdown in their payouts. In fact, median medical malpractice insurance premiums over an eleven-year period rose over 48% in states with caps as compared to 36% for states without caps.[4]

Recent legal reforms, however well-intentioned, may have been both misguided and misdirected. Reforms have done nothing to curb malpractice

---

[2] http://www.quotesinspirational.com/quotes.

[3] Steve Cohen, "Do Big Malpractice Awards Really Increase Medical Costs?" *Insurance Journal* (Aug. 25, 2013). http://www.insurancejournal.com/news/national/2013/08/25/302803.htm. Copyright 2015 Bloomberg. See also Tom Baker, *The Medical Malpractice Myth* (University of Chicago, 2005).

[4] Martin D. Weiss, Melissa Gannon, and Stephanie Eakins, "Medical Malpractice Caps: The Impact of Non-Economic Damage Caps on Physician Premiums, Claims Payout Levels, and Availability," *Weiss Ratings, Inc.* (June 2, 3003). https://www.ncbi.nlm.nih.gov/pmc/articles/PMC2690332/.

premiums, lower health care costs, or prevent patient injuries. Present ill-considered legislative safeguards have failed to yield the desired effects for physicians or patient safety.

DEFENSIVE MEDICINE

Defensive medicine refers to the process of ordering extensive tests and procedures that may or may not be medically needed because doctors are presumably afraid of missing a diagnosis and possibly becoming the target of a lawsuit as a result.

First, this type of medicine is essentially unsafe for patients. Because all tests and procedures carry risks, medical studies that are unnecessary force patients to confront and undergo needless dangers. Potential perils to patients might include harm or injury from hospital procedures and admissions such as increased radiation exposure, severe allergic reactions from contrast dye, nosocomial infections, or adverse reactions from unnecessary prescriptions. In other words, risks can outweigh potential benefits from nonessential tests, procedures, and treatments.

Additionally, some tests may lead to false positives, thereby indicating a disease process that the patient does not actually have. Any misdiagnosis inevitably leads to unnecessary treatment. Thus, doctors who routinely utilize defensive medicine are not practicing good medicine. Paradoxically, they increase their patients' risks of harm and their own risk of subsequent malpractice claims.

Second, the practice of ordering unnecessary tests and procedures increases health care costs without just cause or good reason.

Third, and perhaps worst of all, a number of doctors practice defensive medicine because it generates extra income. Tests and procedures that are ordered are either medically necessary or not. If they are medically necessary, it is not defensive medicine. However, if tests or procedures are unnecessary, then such methods can be considered poor medical practice, unjust enrichment, or fraud. The practice is both unsafe and illegal. In a recent example, eleven cardiologists and a hospital in London, Kentucky, were charged with conspiring to perform unnecessary surgeries on their patients to defraud insurance companies in an effort to improperly enrich themselves.[5]

---

[5] Peter Waldman, "Kentucky Hospital Settles Claims that Doctors Cracked Chests for Unneeded Heart Surgeries," *Bloomberg Business* (Jan. 29, 2014).

Meanwhile, there is no hard evidence that such practices actually reduce or eliminate accusations of malpractice. Defensive medicine fails to protect the patient and is itself a liability issue since it expands physician liability. For these reasons, defensive medicine is seen as neither advisable nor a good option for practicing physicians. Despite these examples, the phenomenon of defensive medicine does not mean that most doctors are in constant fear that patients will sue them. Rather, it suggests that physicians should develop and establish systematic and thorough procedures in the best interests of their patients which coincidentally are also in their own best interests.

In conclusion, ordering unnecessary tests (defensive medicine) is practicing outside the standard of care and will not limit liability or decrease malpractice exposure. Also, with the rise of managed care and a focus on cost containment, the days of ordering needless tests and rendering unnecessary care may be short-lived.

EXCESSIVE NUMBER OF LAWSUITS?

Despite claims that lawsuits are rampant, there has been a steady decline in the number of medical negligence court filings in recent years.[6] Reports of excessive numbers of malpractice lawsuits persist, but simply do not add up.

The 1999 Institute of Medicine Report listed an annual number of 44,000–98,000 deaths from medical errors. Even at the time, this report was considered by many to be a considerable underestimate.

Indeed, a more recent study from John Hopkins University that was based on earlier reports estimated that 251,000 hospital deaths each year was closer to the actual number. The authors believe this figure still understates the actual number of deaths due to the limits of the previous reports.[7] Classen et al. calculated over 400,000 deaths due to medical mistakes take place each year in hospitals.[8] Likewise, James reported an incidence of 210,000–400,000 deaths in hospitals from preventable oversights,[9] which is echoed

---

[6] "Court Statistics Project," National Center for State Courts (2013), http://www.courtstatistics.org/~/media/Microsites/Files/CSP/Highlights/18_1_Medical_Malpractice_In_State_Courts.ashx

[7] Martin A. Makary and Michael Daniel, "Medical Error—The Third Leading Cause of Death in the U.S.," *BMJ* 353 (2016): i2139.

[8] D. Classen, R. Resar, F. Griffin, et al., "Global 'Trigger Tool' Shows that Adverse Events in Hospitals May Be Ten Times Greater than Previously Measured," *Health Aff* 30 (2011): 581–589. DOI: 10.1377/hlthaff.2011.0190.

[9] J.T.A. James, "A New, Evidence-Based Estimate of Patient Harms Associated with Hospital Care," *J Patient Saf* 9 (2013): 122–128. DOI 10.1097/PTS.Ob013e3182948a69. pmid: 23860193.

by a *Consumer Reports* estimate of 440,000 deaths per year.[10] In addition to the number of deaths reported as a result of preventable medical errors, the Institute of Medicine reports that hundreds of thousands more suffer non-fatal injuries.[11] Interestingly, only one in eight preventable medical errors committed in hospitals was reported to result in a malpractice claim.[12]

So, compared to the number of deaths and injuries reported, the number of patients actually bringing a lawsuit is quite small.[13] Despite the perception of a sue-happy society, the vast majority of patients think very highly of their doctors and most strive to avoid confrontation and conflict. Overall, most patients are reluctant to file a lawsuit even if they have suffered real injury and loss.

In his popular book, *Blink* (2007), Malcolm Gladwell opines that, "The overwhelming number of people who suffer an injury due to the negligence of a doctor never file a malpractice suit at all."[14] Gladwell further implies that patients are much more likely to file malpractice lawsuits if they have been wronged or insulted *in addition to* any mistakes that may have been made in their treatment. In other words, if insult has been added to injury.

POORLY PERFORMING PRACTITIONERS

A relatively small percentage of doctors are known to be responsible for the majority of malpractice lawsuits. Still, little seems to be done to stop the small number of doctors in each state who repeatedly commit malpractice. Recently analyzed data from the National Practitioner Data Bank found that 2%–5% of doctors in the U.S. account for more than half of all medical malpractice payouts.[15] These problematic practitioners must be rooted out and stopped, instead of routinely allowing them to continue practicing.

In addition, hospitals appear reluctant to take action against incompetent physicians. According to Harvey Wachsman, MD, JD, a recent article in the *New York Times* provides a poignant example. The article reports on

---

[10] *Consumer Reports Magazine* 81; 5: 31–43 (May 2016)

[11] National Institute of Medicine, *To Err Is Human: Building a Safer Health System* (2000).

[12] Harvard Medical Practice Study Group, *Patients, Doctors and Lawyers: Medical Injury, Malpractice Litigation, and Patient Compensation in New York* (1990).

[13] Summary, "Hospital Incident Reporting Systems Do Not Capture Most Patient Harm" Report (OEI-06-09-00091), Office of Inspector General, Department of Health and Human Services (Jan. 6, 2012).

[14] Malcolm Gladwell, *Blink: The Power of Thinking Without Thinking* (Back Bay Books, 2007).

[15] Robert E. Oshel, "What You Don't Know About Your Doctor Could Hurt You," *Consumer Reports* 81; 5: 31–43 (May 2016).

a surgeon who caused the death of a patient by tying off the wrong duct during gall bladder surgery. After an autopsy revealed the cause of death, the hospital was aware of the mistake, but did nothing. A few months later, the same surgeon made exactly the same mistake, resulting in the needless death of yet another patient. Inexplicably, the hospital failed to take action again. The victim's family was never told, and the doctor was not prevented from operating on other patients.[16]

Not even the doctor was informed of his mistakes, so there was no attempt to prevent similar tragedies in the future. Perhaps inevitably, it happened again a few months later. The physician was finally reported to the state board, but not until three patients had died within six months from what should have been routine surgery.

When doctors place patients in needless danger or fail to take care not to harm them, it is both unethical and unprofessional. Nevertheless, five out of six serial physician offenders with five or more malpractice payouts have not been disciplined by their state medical board in any way.[17] For the most part, poor practitioners do not lose their licenses, they do not lose hospital privileges, and they typically do not pay more for malpractice insurance.

Thus, it appears that some physicians are not held accountable, either professionally or ethically.[18]

Making sure that incompetent doctors are not allowed to practice is essential. The first filter in this process is the licensing and examination requirements. In addition, the disciplinary authority of the licensing board must hold all physicians accountable and appropriate consequences for repeated malpractice should be strictly enforced.

ATTITUDES ABOUT MALPRACTICE

Misconceptions and distortions are present in all emotionally charged issues. Malpractice is no different. Whether we like it or not, inaccuracies and distortions help shape our actual beliefs perhaps as much as hard facts. One reason is that we tend to remember the stories, but not whether the sources of those stories were reliable. The following statements are typical examples that we have all likely heard and that may influence our attitudes about malpractice.

---

[16] Wachsman, 117–118.

[17] National Practitioner Data Bank (Sept. 1, 1990–Sept. 30, 2002).

[18] For a more recent review of this persistent problem see "What You Don't Know About Your Doctor Could Hurt You" by Rachel Rabkin Peachman, *Consumer Reports* 81; 5: 31–43 (May 2016).

Malpractice Lawsuits Are Frivolous

Despite oft repeated claims of frivolous lawsuits, researchers at the Harvard School of Public Health examined more than 1,400 closed medical negligence claims and found that 97 percent were meritorious.[19] In fact, a General Accounting Office report showed that plaintiffs have an injury that could be regarded as insignificant less than 10% of the time.

Doctors Are Fleeing from Medical Practice[20]

There is a long history in this country of sensationalized stories of doctors leaving the medical profession because of lawsuits or malpractice premiums, among other reasons. As far back as 1851, the *Medical Examiner* asserted that, "Mischievous prosecutions for some years have alarmed medical gentlemen in various parts of the country to such a degree that many have concluded to let all surgical patients go unassisted for their afflictions."[21] Of course this account was greatly exaggerated. Along the way, similar claims have been made.

In reality, physicians are not fleeing the profession. There are more doctors now than at any previous time in the nation's history and the number of doctors is increasing faster than population growth. The number of physicians has increased in every state, regardless of the presence or absence of caps, or other special limitations on the injured patient's right to sue.[22]

Attorneys Are at Fault

Finally, in spite of the alleged avarice of ambulance-chasing attorneys, contingency fee lawyers actually reject a significant number of potential cases. These lawyers evaluate cases in terms of the risks involved and the potential returns associated with those risks. Lawyers must reject all cases that do not potentially yield a satisfactory risk/return ratio. It is well known that some medical malpractice attorneys reject as many as 80% or more of the requests they receive for representation.[23] The bottom line is that attorneys are very careful to investigate claims, mainly because they are so expensive

---

[19] David M. Studdard, Michelle M. Mello, M. Phil, Atul A. Gawande, et al., "Claims Errors, and Compensation in Medical Malpractice Litigation," *N Engl J Med* 354 (2006): 2024–2033.

[20] *Medical Malpractice: Characteristics of Claims Closed in 1984* (Washington, DC: General Accounting Office, 1987).

[21] Wachsman, 161.

[22] "Five Myths About Medical Negligence," report from The American Association for Justice on Medical Negligence (Nov. 2009).

[23] https://www.propublica.org/article/patient-harm-when-an-attorney-wont-take-your-case.

to take to trial. As David Berry with Corboy & Demetrio in Chicago puts it, "What people don't realize is that firms like ours protect physicians whose care is reasonable from litigation way more often than we sue people. For every lawsuit I file, I probably protect 25 doctors from getting sued."[24]

Often, cases with real injuries but with lower damages are abandoned despite their merit because of the time expenditures and high costs required to bring a case with a questionable return to trial.

Runaway Juries Are the Problem

Although reports about runaway juries that award huge and unjustified amounts in certain cases surface from time to time, the National Association of Insurance Commissioners (NAIC) reported that malpractice payouts dropped more than 50 percent in a six-year period. However, more recent data indicates that payouts are on the rise again.[25]

Considering that approximately 80 percent of medical malpractice lawsuits involve death or serious injury,[26] some large verdicts are to be expected, but no cause and effect relationship between jury verdicts and insurance premium costs has ever been demonstrated.

AN ACTUAL MALPRACTICE SOLUTION

Anesthesiologists used to pay some of the highest malpractice premiums in medicine. Adverse outcomes from serious brain injuries or death due to anesthesia were frequent occurrences.[27]

As a result, the American Society of Anesthesiologists conducted a broad-based assessment of the causes of injuries to patients. Anesthesia procedures were reviewed and improved to include better training and limits on the number of consecutive hours an anesthesiologist could work without rest. In addition, medical hardware was redesigned and outfitted with improved safety devices.[28]

Within 10 years, the mortality rate from anesthesia dropped from 1 in 6,000 to 1 in 200,000 administrations. Anesthesiologists' malpractice insurance rates fell to among the lowest of any specialty. In other specialties

---

[24]"Physicians Shouldn't Rely on 'Code of Silence'," *Physician Risk Management* (Nov. 2012), AHC Media: Continuing Medical Education Publishing. http://www.ahcmedia.com/articles/77235-want-to-prevent-lawsuit-chart-decision-making.

[25]https://www.leveragerx.com/malpractice-insurance/2019-medical-malpractice-report/. Accessed Mar. 21, 2020.

[26]Cohen (supra)

[27]Ibid.

[28]Ibid.

(e.g., obstetrics and gynecology) reforms have led to malpractice awards falling. For example, at New York Presbyterian Hospital awards fell from $50 million dollars to $250,000 thousand dollars per year.[29]

The lesson here is that doctors themselves should act to investigate, scrutinize, and improve safety in their own practices. This can dramatically reduce the need for attorneys to deter unsafe practices by means of lawsuits.

CONCLUSION

As we have seen in this chapter, an isolated fact or statistic cited to support plaintiffs' positions is not necessarily valid, accurate, or proof of anything. Physicians and their attorneys should be prepared to refute any exaggerated claims or misrepresentations that can unfairly influence the way many people perceive malpractice suits.

Every doctor, attorney, and politician is encouraged to read *The Medical Malpractice Myth*[30] by Tom Baker for a straightforward factual analysis of which malpractice issues are legitimate and the key problems underlying policy making.

BIBLIOGRAPHY

Baker, Tom. *The Medical Malpractice Myth*. University of Chicago, 2005.

Born, Patricia H., J. Bradley Karl, and W. Kip Viscusi. "The Net Effects of Medical Malpractice Tort Reform on Health Insurance Losses: The Texas Experience" *Health Economics Review* 20177, 42. https://healtheconomicsreview.springeropen.com/articles/10.1186/s13561-017-0174-2.

Hyman, David A., MD, JD, and Charles Silver, JD. "Five Myths of Medical Malpractice." *CHEST* 143, no. 1 (2013): 222–227. https://www.americanbar.org/content/dam/aba/administrative/medical_liability/five_myths_of_medical_malpractice.authcheckdam.pdf.

Vidmar, Neil, Paul Lee, Kara MacKillop, and Kieran McCarthy. "Uncovering the 'Invisible' Profile of Medical Malpractice Litigation: Insights from Florida." *DePaul Law Review* 54, no. 2, "Starting Over?: Redesigning the Medical Malpractice System" (Winter 2005).

---

[29] Ibid.

[30] Tom Baker, *The Medical Malpractice Myth* (University of Chicago, 2005).

CHAPTER 16

Achieve Maximum Malpractice Protection
– Start This Forty-Two Point Plan Now! –

No one can promise absolute immunity from lawsuits. It is incumbent on every physician to embrace solid protection strategies and proactive measures to discourage and deter lawsuits, minimize liability, properly and efficiently manage malpractice claims that do arise, improve testimonial skills, and increase the chances for a successful outcome, as well as better protect personal and professional assets. Why not minimize the downside as much as possible in the face of a potential lawsuit?

FORTY-TWO ACTIONS FOR MAXIMUM MALPRACTICE PROTECTION

1. Establish a sound business foundation to help maximize your protection. The first step is to select the optimal practice structure for your individual circumstances as described in Chapter 7.

   Obviously, the organizational form that has the most advantages and fewest disadvantages for a doctor's individual situation is the best. A business attorney's advice would be indispensable. The wisdom of this course of action will be readily apparent when your taxes are reduced, and personal assets are not at risk amidst the stress and chaos of a lawsuit. Whether you are in private practice or the employee of a large corporation, the right business structure is the first essential step in protecting personal and professional assets.

2. Start an asset protection plan through a skilled and experienced attorney to safeguard both personal income and possessions. Asset protection is an area of the law that seeks to insulate acquired assets from lawsuits or creditor claims legally without concealment, fraud, or tax evasion. The list of assets that can be absolutely shielded from creditors and lawsuits is short, but very important. It includes property interests,

life insurance plans and annuities, retirement plans, such as 401(k) or Keogh plans, asset protection trusts, and also interest(s) in a limited liability company or limited partnership. Asset protection is distinct from limiting liability. Both approaches should be utilized to broaden the safeguards for professional and personal assets.

3. Because taxes are the biggest threat to savings, assets, and wealth accumulation, you need to implement an organized and goal-oriented tax plan that will yield benefits year in and year out for an entire career and beyond. Consult a reputable tax attorney.

Here are some examples:

- Have a tax advisor minimize your reportable income and maximize deductions. As part of minimizing your taxable state and federal income, consider purchasing triple-A (AAA) or double-A (AA) rated general obligation tax-free municipal bonds or a bond fund as a safe and sound investment.

- Remaining taxable income should be decreased as much as possible through uppermost contributions to 401(k) or Keogh plans. Also consider investing in appreciating assets, e.g., real estate, rather than income-producing assets.

- Take advantage of the 1997 Taxpayer Relief Act. The law excludes up to $250,000 in capital gains tax for an individual homeowner and up to $500,000 for joint return taxpayers. This exclusion is available once every two years.

- Give more tax-free gifts to your children, i.e., up to $15,000 per child from the father or mother, or $30,000 per child from married couples, and keep those assets in the family.

4. Follow these commandments in practice:

- Prevent patient injury. *Primum non nocere* or "first do no harm" is the first commandment of medical practice and is as old as medicine itself.[1] There are some patients that medicine cannot help, but there are none that cannot be harmed; so be careful and cautious on behalf of your patients. Be especially wary of increasing the risk of harm to a patient unless there is good reason to do so and, if there is, then document that reason.

---

[1] Richard E. Anderson, *Medical Malpractice: A Physician's Sourcebook* (Totowa, NJ: Humana Press, 2005), 92.

- The second commandment is to preserve the patient's dignity at all times.[2] For example, prior to the physical examination, every patient should have the courtesy of meeting their doctor in private while fully clothed. The physical examination is the most awkward and potentially embarrassing aspect of receiving medical care. Therefore, a knock on the door and pausing a few seconds before entering is a welcome courtesy.
- The third commandment is based on the following: "Treatment is what a doctor does for a disease. Medical care is what the doctor does for the patient."[3] Whenever possible try to render more care than treatment.

5. Physicians must faithfully fulfill their part of the doctor-patient contract (see "Chapter 2: The Doctor-Patient Contract") and document if a patient does not perform their part. For example, a patient fails to provide accurate information, misses appointments, or doesn't follow instructions possibly leading to underdosing or overdosing, etc.

6. Take care not to inadvertently begin an unwanted doctor-patient relationship, especially through a website or social network page. If a person is relying on the doctor for advice that will not be forthcoming, the seeds to a lawsuit are unintentionally being planted. Ask your personal counsel to analyze your site for potential legal pitfalls and perils.

7. Do not abandon an established patient. That is, do not sever the relationship while there is still a need for continued medical attention. This includes securing physician coverage while you are away and not overbooking your patient caseload to the exclusion of some patients in need. With regard to patients who have more immediate and pressing needs, do not inadvertently suspend the relationship in their time of need, e.g., do not, for any reason, leave a patient unattended for any length of time who is pregnant and in active labor, having a possible impending MI, or is in a different potential crisis situation.

8. Follow good, current, safe, and accepted practices for taking a proper history, performing a thorough examination, using appropriate diagnostic tests, and administering care demonstrating ordinary caution. Providing necessary and appropriate care is the best way to minimize the possibility of being sued. (See also "Chapter 5: How to Commit Malpractice Without Trying.")

---

[2] Ibid., 92.

[3] James E. Schutte, *Preventing Malpractice Suits. A Handbook for Doctors and Those Who Work with Them* (Seattle: Hogrefe & Huber Publishers, 1995), 7.

9. As much as possible, avoid making a diagnosis and/or prescribing treatment over the phone. If the physician chooses to make a diagnosis under those circumstances, then the caller should be informed that the diagnosis is presumptive and must be confirmed via an office visit for a physical examination or other testing. If medications are prescribed, they should be for symptom relief with the least harmful medicine at the lowest dosage possible until an OV can be arranged.[4]

10. Understand both the medical and legal causes of malpractice as outlined in Chapter 5. Be guided by the medicolegal rules and recognize the roads to potential medical errors in order to actively avoid them.

11. Perform a brief risk analysis whenever patient care takes a new direction. (See also "Chapter 5: How to Commit Malpractice Without Trying.")

12. Maintain true and reasonably accurate, timely, and complete medical records to the extent required by the standard of care. Explain the course of medical decisions in the record and document any reason to deviate from standard treatment or care guidelines.

    If possible, give an explanation for every complication. Document patient non-compliance, if it occurs, honestly and objectively. Make customary corrections with care. Never, never, never improperly alter the medical record. (See also "Chapter 8: The Medical Record.") Altering the record may result not only in shame and embarrassment, but also a reservation of rights letter, losing the court case, and possibly voiding your liability coverage. Because altering medical records can be evidence of fraud and spoliation, additional charges may be brought.

    In the event of litigation, the medical record is the most crucial piece of evidence at trial. The preservation of that original well-documented record without alterations is absolutely vital in the defense of any malpractice claim.

13. For inpatient care, be certain to review the hospital chart. As obvious as this advice seems to be, misadventures such as failing to read the nurse's notes do happen and more than occasionally. Every physician has good cause to take extra care in scrutinizing the entire hospital chart. "In a jury's view, the attending physician would have to have a very compelling reason for ignoring any information in those charts."[5]

---

[4] Anna B. Reisman and Davis Stevens, *Telephone Medicine*, American College of Physicians, American Society of Internal Medicine (2002), 63–64.

[5] Schutte, 113.

Events in a hospital account for 70%–80% of all malpractice claims. Therefore, extra attentiveness and care must be taken. If in reading the nurse's notes you find an error, point that out to the author and ask him or her to correct it properly.

14. For all elective treatments and procedures, the use of hazardous drugs, and for all invasive or complicated procedures with significant risks, **informed consent is mandatory**. It is also highly recommended for off-label prescriptions with significant potential side effects. (See "Chapter 6: Informed Consent.")

Be certain to **disclose all material risks** to the patient. Since courts have different rulings on what constitutes a material risk, confer with counsel. Pending specific advice, the default position should be that all serious risks, however remote, be disclosed and that all unpleasant and inherent risks be disclosed for an elective procedure.

Provide the patient with educational materials on the condition, disease, or procedure. Consider underlining or highlighting relevant phrases in the documents provided. This will effectively demonstrate that the doctor not only provided these teaching materials to the patient but went over it with the patient. If you take this step, make a record of what brochures, facts, or data you provided.

Finish informing the patient with enlightenment about realistic expectations regarding the treatment or procedure.

Finally, **secure the patient's verbal consent** in addition to using an informed consent document. Record the consents as well as the educational materials in the daily notes of the medical record.

Even on routine patient visits, **don't just recommend** that patients, e.g., "stop smoking" or "need to lose weight." Instead, educate them about their increased risks of having a heart attack or stroke and document that in the record. This brand of good medicine is a strong point in defense of any physician if a patient claims that the doctor never told them about the possible serious medical consequences of their condition.

15. Study after study has found an inverse correlation between patient satisfaction and the filing of lawsuits. Develop a better bedside manner that demonstrates kindness and caring as well as courtesy and respect. Good eye contact, a smile, and a clear two-way conversation are key elements in effectively interacting with patients.

In striving for good communication, listen to patients carefully, ask their opinions, and be comfortable sharing medical information.

Educate patients regarding reasonable expectations and try to treat every patient like a friend.

When obtaining information from the patient, practice the art of active listening by asking, "What is the problem that you came in for today?" Following the patient's explanation, consider rephrasing the response, e.g., "If I understand you correctly, you said that…" or "Tell me more about…" After making recommendations, consider inquiring, "What do you think about the procedure I've just described?" During the examination process, let patients know in general terms what you are doing and why. For example, "I'm going to look at and listen to your abdomen, then check it for tenderness" or "I'm going to examine you and then talk over the results with you."

Near the end of the visit consider asking your patient, "Is there anything else?" No one feels rushed or unduly hurried if that question is asked. Seeing the doctor can cause anxiety, so the patient may forget to ask important questions. Encourage him or her to write down those questions and bring that list on his next visit.

Following the visit, communicate any discharge instructions orally and supplement them with written instructions for the patient to take home. It is critically important that discharge instructions state the signs and symptoms to look for, when to follow up, and the reasons to seek emergency room care or return to the office.

16. Few things look better for the physician in the medical record than consults with other experts. Medicine has become more complex. Do not unnecessarily delay or hesitate to refer a patient to a specialist, sub-specialist, or other practitioner, for a second opinion and then follow the advice of that consultant. This is especially true in difficult, challenging, non-responsive, or complex cases.

While it is often helpful to obtain another doctor's opinion, it can be damaging to the patient (and to the doctor's defense during a lawsuit) if that advice is rejected.

If two consultants were utilized and they disagree, then obtain a third opinion. Physicians should always make referral decisions and interact with a specialist in the best interests of the patient. Follow up with both the patient and the specialist after making a clinical judgment for a referral because liability can extend beyond simply connecting the patient with an expert.

When selecting a physician to provide a consultation, be reasonable. When making a referral to a newer colleague a reasonable referring doctor would first verify that the consulting physician:

- is licensed in that state
- has not been disciplined by the board of medical examiners
- is board certified in their specialty
- has full hospital privileges[6]

If a referred patient "no shows" for a consultation:

- document the no-show in the chart
- notify the referring physician
- clarify that the referring physician will follow up with the patient
- verify the conversation by sending a fax or an e-mail to that referring doctor

17. Embrace available technology and modern resources when reasonable to do so. Polypharmacy, or the administration of multiple drugs, is increasingly prevalent in our aging society because of co-morbidities and multiple treating physicians.

When such a patient presents with a new complaint, look first to his most recent medications. For example, a patient presents with hypertension and the doctor prescribes amlodipine. Shortly thereafter, leg edema develops. To counter the swelling, furosemide is added, but that leads to hypokalemia. Therefore, the patient is put on a potassium supplement. The potassium supplement causes heartburn, so a proton pump inhibitor is prescribed.[7] A different antihypertensive could have easily prevented all the ensuing problems and eliminated needless polypharmacy.

Polypharmacy in the elderly is associated with an increased risk for adverse drug events (drug-drug and drug-disease interactions), reduced functional capacity, geriatric syndromes, and increased mortality.[8]

Deprescribing for older patients is suggested as a simple method for reducing polypharmacy with demonstrated benefits. For example,

---

[6] Schutte, 116.

[7] D. Cooney and K. Pascuzzi, "Polypharmacy in the Elderly: Focus on Drug Interactions and Adherence in Hypertension," *Clin Geriat Med* 25, no. 2 (2009): 221–233.

[8] Kathryn McGrath, Emily R. Hajjir, Chandrika Kumar, Christopher Hwang, and Brook Salzman, "Deprescribing: A Simple Method for Reducing Polypharmacy," *Journal of Family Practice* 66, no. 7 (July 2017): 436–445.

deprescribing can improve cognition while deprescribing proton pump inhibitors reduces the risk for fractures, clostridium difficile, and pneumonia. Deprescribing statins improves quality of life in patients with limited life expectancy and still benefits the patient for at least 5 years.[9]

Many hospitals and other medical facilities employ computerized medication monitoring programs to help prevent or minimize medication errors, and/or adverse drug reactions, drug-drug interactions, and drug-disease interactions. Such programs are readily available for doctor's offices as well. Unfortunately, however, these programs are associated with "alert fatigue." Numerous and overly detailed medication alerts that are irrelevant to the patient or standard clinical practice, such as "check pregnancy status" alerts for male patients, slow down productivity and cause the majority of physicians to override most of those so-called alerts.

In addition to computerized prescribing aids, doctors can invest in automated systems for electronic health records that include medical history, allergy checks, lab test tracking, and scheduling or rescheduling patients and procedures, etc. When employing electronic health records, be certain to use the EHR in a standard non-customized way.

18. In the event of an unexpected bad result, practice extreme honesty. This includes answering "I don't know" when it is true. Do not avoid the patient or hide facts.

Avoiding the discussion of a complication can make the physician appear guilty of wrongdoing. The patient may interpret this as having been misled or may assume that the physician is refusing to be truthful about the incident in an attempt to hide something or cover it up. Explain any known reasons for the complication and the future options and be empathetic with respect to the patient's disappointment and misfortune. This helps keep the patient from having to seek answers at a law office.

If the physician is unable to identify a clear reason why things did not turn out well, Chicago attorney David R. Barry Jr. recommends telling the patient just that, but in terms like, "I did things the way I always do them, and we ended up with this outcome, and I don't know

---

[9] Ibid.

why."[10] This way, the doctor's testimony matches what the patient says in deposition or trial, and the doctor's credibility increases.

Apologize? A recent trend that has met with some success is for doctors to offer a medical apology. The upside with an apology is that demonstrating humanity and empathy often consoles the patient, demonstrates professional responsibility, adds credibility to the physician's honesty and helps to satisfy the patient's desire for an explanation.

As a caveat, it must be noted that in common law, an apology is allowed as evidence as an admission against one's own interest. Thus, although a medical apology is an acceptable legal option in some states, in other states an apology can be considered an admission of guilt for committing malpractice. Only in states that have enacted legislation specifically changing this rule of evidence can one make an apology without taking on serious and unnecessary legal risks. Saying "sorry" can be a good and effective form of risk management, but if it is done it must be done judiciously. Always seek legal advice from personal counsel, your risk manager, and/or your liability carrier before engaging in a formal apology. Insurance companies, in particular, can often provide guidance about proper medical apologies that console patients and their families, offering the desired explanation/closure, while also helping doctors avoid admissions that could lead to a malpractice claim.

19. Follow all patient complaints to a diagnosis, where reasonably feasible.

    Adequately investigate any potentially ominous signs and symptoms to prevent a possible catastrophe. Don't ignore patient comments with regard to any symptoms the patient is feeling. (See also "Chapter 5: How to Commit Malpractice Without Trying.")

20. Have strong, up-to-date, and comprehensive office policies. To the extent you insist on writing down your procedures, do so in such a fashion that maximizes the probability that a reviewing court will agree that the documents are not discoverable. Confer with legal counsel on this matter.

    Existing office policies should cover areas such as patient care, equipment maintenance and certification, records, etc. An office employee

---

[10] "Physicians Shouldn't Rely on 'Code of Silence,'" *Physician Risk Management* (AHC Media: Continuing Medical Education Publishing, Nov. 2012), . http://www.ahcmedia.com/articles/77235-want-to-prevent-lawsuit-chart-decision-making.

should be specifically designated to make sure that all office equipment is properly maintained and that information is well-documented and current.

Devise a mechanism to improve the likelihood that the doctor reviews, initials, and dates all reports before filing them. Devise mechanisms to improve the chances that patients will follow up in a timely fashion and will be advised of all lab/test results and other time-sensitive medical recommendations promptly. One approach might be to so arrange matters that charts of patients with abnormal test results are not refiled until the patient has been contacted and informed of the results.

Use follow-up communications that can be verified, such as e-mails or correspondence by certified mail. If needed, develop procedures to follow up on missed or canceled appointments, or on patents who have not undergone recommended testing, by contacting those patients and asking them to reschedule.[11]

Review existing procedures on a regular basis and have those procedures audited, preferably by someone in malpractice risk management.

Conscientiously follow all policies whether set forth in your hospital or office-based practices policy manual. If they do not reflect what you as a physician actually do, then change those policies. Not following your office or institution policies can be devastating if these procedures are discoverable.[12]

21. To decrease the risk of medication malpractice claims, physicians must pay reasonable attention to adverse effects, warnings, and contraindications for drug use. If not, plaintiff's counsel will likely allege that an apparent failure to heed known dangers in the prescription of medications is substandard medical care.

   In short, drug indications have little, if any, significance in malpractice cases, but failing to pay reasonable attention to warnings, contraindications, and adverse effects can grow legal and medical troubles faster than bacteria in the blood stream.

22. Avoid distractions and sleep deprivation prior to performing a complicated procedure. If you feel inordinately fatigued, then postpone and reschedule the procedure for another time or with a colleague.

---

[11] Schutte, 178.

[12] G. Joshpe, *Pearls and Pitfalls of Medical Malpractice* (2010), 8–10.

23. A physician can never take too much care in selecting, training, and supervising staff.[13] In an office setting, the private practitioner sets the hiring standards, such as education, skills, experience, professionalism, and preferred personality type required. Staff should be helpful without waiting to be asked and be courteous even when the patient is not. After all, patients who feel bad tend not to be friendly, particularly patient, or polite. Once they know how to do it properly, staff should document all telephone and written communications with patients through standard phone log forms.

    Additionally, the employee files should contain the disciplinary records for every employee so that they are complete and unabridged without additions having to be made. (See also "Preventing Employee Negligence," p. 70.) Keep all such files strictly segregated from your patient charts. Consult counsel about the best ways to maximize the probability that such employee files are not discoverable.

24. Be careful about aggressive attempts to collect unpaid balances. Overly assertive collection practices can trigger lawsuits, particularly from disgruntled patients who may feel that the doctor took little interest or effort in addressing their problems or was indifferent to repeated reports of continuing pain. Frustrated or angry people are not patient or forgiving.

    If a patient complained about or was openly dissatisfied with their care or the result of that care and is thereafter sued for payment, a real and imminent risk of a counterclaim for malpractice exists. No doctor should push that patient into collection litigation and certainly not prematurely.

    If a patient is clearly unhappy with his condition or outcome, the doctor may ponder reducing or canceling the bill. If so, check with your medical group's or health facility's legal counsel or a personal attorney to be certain that waiving medical fees is not an admission of negligence in your state. Even a patient who has no legitimate beef can file a claim, purely as a way to avoid paying. He may think—not without reason—that the physician or facility will abandon collection efforts as a way to settle a potential malpractice claim.

---

[13] Carl Horn III, Donald H. Caldwell, and D. Christopher Osborn, *Law for Physicians— An Overview of Medical Legal Issues* (American Medical Association, 2000), 41.

In light of the above scenarios, seriously consider implementing an office policy whereby any patient who drops out of care with a significant balance owing toward the doctor's services not be sent to collection or summoned to court until the statute of limitations on filing a malpractice claim has run in your state. Consult your friendly neighborhood attorney for specific legal advice in your state and under the individual patient's circumstances.

25. Stay abreast of new developments in your practice area. Today's accepted standard of care can quickly become tomorrow's outdated impropriety.

    It is generally sound advice to avoid being the first to adopt a new standard, and to also avoid being among the last to accept it.

26. Advocate for the patient and his needs and consistently maintain the standard of care. These days, there are often conflicts between the physician's preferred course of treatment and the level of care authorized by the patient's HMO. If restrictions on the physician's treatment autonomy are too great, or if the scope of care to be provided to patients is too narrow, the physician ought to pass on that company's business instead of bearing the liability risks.[14] In the meantime, physicians should seek changes in the law to provide relief for this dilemma that, in the zeal to cut costs, doctors have been pushed into.

27. If you feel somewhat out of control owing to the consumption of alcohol or drugs, you should immediately contact your attorney for advice on the wisdom of approaching the state medical society for help.

28. Do not slip into a routine or fall victim to overconfidence. Doctors have seen the same symptoms thousands of times and may assume a specific diagnosis without a full medical history or adequate testing. No physician can predetermine which symptoms are minor and which are serious. Avoid complacency as a result of clinical "tunnel vision" for failing to look at the big picture.

29. Studies have shown that operating rooms often have communication problems and less than optimal teamwork. Both these factors have been linked to poor postoperative developments, which are a prescription for poor outcomes and pending lawsuits.

---

[14] Ibid., 45–47.

Implementing a pre-surgical checklist and/or medical team training are demonstrated to reduce both medical errors and postoperative mortality.[15,16]

Surgeons should dictate operative notes shortly after completion of the surgical procedure. Otherwise, it may invite accusations of inaccurate memories, faulty record-keeping, poor patient care, or altering the actual facts.

30. Be extra cautious in your approach to possibly practicing defensive medicine.

Weigh the purported protection it may offer against possible risks, such as charges of fraud, insurance investigations, increased state board scrutiny or other administrative agency inquiries, and conceivably more patient injuries leading to more malpractice lawsuits. (See also "Chapter 15: Core Malpractice Concepts.")

31. Do *not* go bare. The downside with loss of hospital privileges, inability to participate in MCOs, and hanging on an unstable hook of potential financial ruin is just too steep. Obtain and maintain an affordable but solid malpractice insurance policy through a reputable carrier.

Secure an ample level of coverage and add an umbrella policy, if available, since it can provide an extra layer of coverage in addition to your malpractice policy. Contact your employer or insurance carrier to see if an umbrella policy is currently in force or if one can be obtained. (See also "Chapter 10: Malpractice Insurance.")

Think about attending risk management classes offered by your malpractice carrier. Liability insurers often couple attendance with modestly discounted premium costs. Do not be afraid to get a second or third opinion when deciding which attorney or law firm to hire for your defense. If possible, consider hiring your own attorney to work with the carrier's defense firm. This is especially true if you have received a "reservation of rights" letter, or the claim exceeds your coverage, or there is

[15] J. Neily, P.D. Mills, Y. Young-Xu, B.T. Carney, P. West, D.H. Berger, L.M. Mazzia, D.E. Paull, and J.P. Bagian, "Association Between Implementation of a Medical Team Training Program and Surgical Mortality," *JAMA* 304, no. 15 (2010): 1693–1700. DOI: 10.1001/jama.2010.1506.

[16] A.B. Haynes, T.G. Weiser, and W.R. Berry, et al., "Safe Surgery Saves Lives Study Group. A Surgical Safety Checklist to Reduce Morbidity and Mortality in a Global Population," *N Engl J Med* 360, no. 5 (2009): 491–499. PubMed.

a disagreement about a possible settlement. The attorney you hire has a fiduciary duty to you alone and has no allegiance to the insurance company.

32. Consider securing malpractice coverage under a corporate or company name, including an LLC, if possible. By having corporate policy coverage only, doctors might decrease their chances of being named individually in a lawsuit and in case of a negative verdict the NPDB report will be in the business name and not that of the physician.

    Unfortunately, beyond filing suit and taking discovery, opposing counsel most likely will not know whether you have any individual exposure or not, and so is likely to name both you as an individual and your business entity in the lawsuit. If opposing counsel can be satisfied that dropping you as an individual is not inconsistent with his duty to the plaintiff, he might be willing to do so. Keeping your name out of the NPDB is one of the best things you can do to preserve your reputation.

33. Because physicians are more likely to be sued personally for traffic collisions, premises accidents, and other mishaps, you should maintain office premises liability insurance coverage, as well as significant personal liability in homeowner's and automobile coverage with policy limits high enough to provide adequate protection for your nonprofessional activities. Have your policies reviewed by an insurance professional.

    Physicians are also at significantly higher risk to suffer a period of disability for a length of time from disease or injury than to have an early demise. So, while it is prudent to have adequate insurance coverage for life, disability, and health, the most important priority of the three is to secure adequate disability insurance.

34. Monitor your website and other marketing materials for accuracy regarding your skills, credentials, experience, and any clinical representations. Do not confuse, mislead, misinform, or misdirect patients. The state board will find you. Post a privacy policy and a set of "terms and conditions." Consider asking a risk manager or your lawyer to evaluate your site for risks.

35. If you receive a notice or believe there is the threat of a lawsuit or a complaint:

   a) Call your malpractice insurance carrier immediately. Depending on the circumstances and the carrier's advice, you may also need to contact your medical facility, risk management department, or medical administrator.

      Most insurance carriers have a "claims repair" procedure to assist the insured health care provider in trying to resolve claims or potential claims in the early stages.[17]

   b) Once a claim has been filed, do not alter your patient's records in any way, and caution your staff to be similarly circumspect.

   c) Do not discuss the case with anyone except your attorney, personal physician (if needed for treatment), insurance carrier, defense firm, clergyman, or spouse.

      If a physician discusses the lawsuit with anyone else, including a colleague or close friend, the other side can call that person and grill them about the conversation, most likely to that doctor's detriment.

   d) Confer with your lawyer and ask him if it would be useful to make a list of all the efforts you made to avoid or lessen any possible harm to the patient. If he asks you to write a summary of events, treat it confidentially, mark it as such, and keep it in a separate place from other documents. While it may not be relevant to the specific allegations in the complaint, this action may have valuable crossover effects. Such a list can show a pattern of concern and safety-minded clinical customs demonstrated by the physician, and may well enhance credibility regarding the doctor's habits and usual procedures on behalf of patients.

   e) Do not perform library or computer searches on any issues in the case unless specifically instructed to by your attorney. Only then are the results confidential.

36. Be completely forthcoming with your defense attorneys. Do not hold back. Your attorneys cannot prepare for what they do not know. Be well aware of your defense discovery plan and litigation strategy. This will educate you as to what facts are necessary to prove the four elements

---

[17] Carl Horn III, Donald H. Caldwell, and D. Christopher Osborn, *Law for Physicians— An Overview of Medical Legal Issues* (American Medical Association, 2000), 52.

of negligence in your case, as well as any defense that you as the doctor may assert.

Teach your defense team all there is to know about the medical aspects of the case. This will educate your lawyer about the complexity of medical decisions involved.

37. Consider requiring or strongly urging that a pathologist be included as a medical records reviewer. A pathologist, as Cyril Wecht, MD, JD, suggests, helps to ensure that all material facts in the case are fully explored and that every possible explanation is provided. The pathologist can compare the defendant physician's conclusions against the findings presented by the records and determine the appropriateness of both the diagnosis and the treatment. The pathologist can usually provide information that will correlate the various laboratory test data and provide insight as to whether such data supports or does not support the clinical diagnosis. A pathologist can also determine the appropriateness of the selected tests and evaluate the results.

    Furthermore, he or she can provide information that can relate the laboratory findings to the actual disease process and suggest other possible diagnoses that should have been considered. If necessary, tissue slides, cytology slides, peripheral blood smears, blood marrow biopsies, etc., can be evaluated for a missed diagnosis or misdiagnosis.[18] A pathologist can be an invaluable wellspring of information in a medical malpractice case.

38. Politely but firmly insist that someone at your defense firm fully prepares you for direct and cross-examination, or hire an attorney or consultant for that specific purpose. It's worth it. Movie fans may know that *The Verdict* (1982) gives piercing insight into this process.

39. If your case goes to deposition or trial, pivot the odds in your favor. Your lawyer may want you to testify as a fact witness only for your best defense. Or, if your lawyer agrees, you can be an additional expert in your own defense. As such, you would be the only expert with firsthand knowledge of the events. In either case, follow as closely as possible your attorney's instructions and strategies as well as the rules for testifying in Chapter 14.

---

[18] Cyril Wecht, MD, JD, FCLM, "Clinical and Forensic Pathology," *The Medical Malpractice Survival Handbook* (Philadelphia: American College of Legal Medicine, Mosby/Elsevier, 2007), 317–318.

40. Jurors usually give more weight to written records than to witnesses. Make certain that your testimony is consistent with those records and with your attorney's theme of the case. Know your chart cold.

41. Do what you have to do, when you have to do it, whether you are in the mood or not, and do it well. That is the definition of being a professional.

42 Appreciate and enjoy your patients, most of whom think the world of you. Treat them well.

BONUS TIPS

Schedule a meeting with a reputable business/tax attorney after reading this guide to:

- Establish a business structure in a way that gives the most liability protection and tax advantages, yet minimizes regulatory requirements, accounting fees, paperwork, expensive attorney input, and other costs. (See also "Chapter 7: Practice Structure.")

- Set up an asset protection plan to safeguard your earned income.

- Enact an effective tax strategy to minimize reportable income and maximize deductions on your yearly federal and state taxes.

- Shelter tangible assets such as property, equipment, and vehicles, etc., and protect future income assets.

- Engage in estate planning to exempt property passed to your spouse or children from tax liabilities and to exclude federal estate taxes on the first million dollars.

- Have your consent and release forms reviewed for effectiveness in order to achieve the maximum breadth and depth of their protective effects, as well as assuring full compliance with state laws. (See also "Chapter 9: Consents and Releases.")

- Request your attorney to review your office policies manual and employee files and to minimize the chances of their being discoverable.

- Meet with an insurance specialist to ensure that your professional and nonprofessional policies provide adequate protection.

- Analyze your website and social network pages to avoid legal problems, including the start of an unwanted doctor-patient relationship.

CONCLUSION

Physicians should try to run their practices in such a way that they can honestly say they took their time and gave their full attention to each patient's needs. To point out the obvious, doctors should be warm, caring, honest, and open. That's the kind of doctor everyone wants. At times that may mean being forthright by expressing empathy or apologizing for an adverse outcome. It goes without saying that doctors should not be overly rushed, curt, or domineering—satisfied patients are far less likely to sue.

A solid physician-patient relationship, valid comprehensive consents, and accurate, legible, clear, complete, and timely medical record documentation are critical for successful risk management and malpractice defense. The medical record, consents, and consultations help demonstrate that the physician acted prudently and exercised sound judgment in evaluating the patient, as well as weighing the risks and benefits of potential treatment plans.

BIBLIOGRAPHY

Belli, Melvin M., Sr. *Belli for Your Malpractice Defense*. Oradell, NJ: Medical Economics Co., 1986.

Gladwell, Malcolm. *Blink*. Little, Brown and Company, 2005.

Horn, Carl, Donald H. Caldwell, and D. Christopher Osborn. *Law for Physicians: An Overview of Medical Legal Issues*. The American Medical Association, 2000.

King, Joseph. *Law of Medical Malpractice in a Nutshell*. Nutshell Series, 1986.

Mello, M.M., and C.H. Williams. "Medical Malpractice: Impact of the Crisis and Effect of State Tort Reforms." *The Synthesis Project* 10. Robert Wood Johnson Foundation.

Reisman, Anna B., and Davis Stevens. *Telephone Medicine*. American College of Physicians, American Society of Internal Medicine, 2002.

Schoenbaum, Stephen C., MD, MPH, and Randall R. Bovbjerg, JD. "Malpractice Reform Must Include Steps to Prevent Medical Injury." *Annals of Internal Medicine* 140, no. 1 (Jan. 2004): 51–53.

Shandell, Richard E. *The Preparation and Trial of Medical Malpractice Cases*. 1981.

Walston-Dunham, Beth. *Medical Malpractice Law and Litigation*. West Legal Studies, CENGAGE Delmar Learning, 2005–2006.

Williams, Alan J. *Physician, Protect Thyself*. Denver, CO: Margol Publishing, 2007.

Wojcieszak, D., J. Saxton, and M. Finkelstein. *Sorry Works!: Disclosure, Apology and Relationships Prevent Malpractice Claims*. 2008.

APPENDIX

Complications Connected with Common Medical Procedures

Every doctor has an affirmative duty to reduce the risks, if possible, of known complications associated with a medical procedure or treatment. Complications associated with common medical procedures include the following.

Name of Procedure	Associated Complications
Adenoidectomy	Bleeding, nasal speech, nasal regurgitation of food or liquids
Anesthesia, general	Abnormal reaction to drugs, aspiration of stomach contents, injury to vocal cords or throat, injury to teeth, lips, and tongue, brain damage, malignant hyperthermia
Arteriography, cerebral	Injury to the arteries entered, bleeding at the catheter entry site, stroke, paralysis, blindness or brain damage, emboli to the brain, allergic reaction to the injected contrast medium
Arteriography, coronary	Injury to the artery, damage to the heart, myocardial infarction, possible need for open heart surgery, irregular heartbeat, bleeding at the entry site, clotting, allergic reaction to or kidney damage from the injected contrast medium
Angioplasty	Paraglegia, loss of an extremity, bowel infarction, renal failure
Aortic dissection	Stroke, renal failure, bowel infarction, paraplegia, death
Aortic graft	Bleeding or infection or emboli, kidney failure or loss of limb, inadequate blood to bowel or spinal cord, myocardial infarction, sexual dysfunction, death
Appendectomy	Infection, bleeding, intra-abdominal abscess, leakage from colon requiring colonostomy, hernia in the incision

Name of Procedure	Associated Complications
Arteriovenous shunt for hemodialysis	Bleeding or infection, damage and risk of rupture to blood vessels, recurrent thrombosis, severe edema of extremity, inadequate blood supply to extremity, inadequate blood supply to nerves.
Blood transfusion	Fever, kidney failure, hepatitis, AIDs
Breast augmentation	Scar formation around implant causing hard breast, deflation of implant, loss of sensation to the nipple and breast, persistent pain in breast, distortion of breast mound, leakage of implant contents (Silicon gel risks are omitted from this list.)
Breast biopsy, excisional	Infection and/or blood clot, failure to obtain accurate diagnosis, disfiguring scar, failure to locate and remove abnormality
Cardiopulmonary bypass	Stroke, respiratory complications, kidney failure, death
Carotid endarterectomy	Blood clots, infection, stroke, nerve injury causing mouth throat and tongue problems, myocardial infarction, death
Cataract surgery	Loss of vision or decrease of vision, bleeding inside or behind the eye, painful eye, droopy eyelid
Catheterization, central venous	Hemorrhage into chest cavity or elsewhere, pericardial tamponade causing compression of the heart, cardiac arrest or stroke, collapse of lung, damage to blood vessels, infusion of fluid into the chest cavity
Cervix removal	Uncontrollable leakage of urine, injury to bladder, injury to the bowel or intestinal obstruction, ureter injury, sterility, pulmonary embolism
Childbirth	Injury to bladder, injury to rectum, fistula between vagina and rectum, hemorrhage possibly requiring hysterectomy, brain damage to fetus
Cholecystectomy	Pancreatitis, injury to the bile duct, retained stones in the bile duct, narrowing of the bile duct, injury to the bowel

Name of Procedure	Associated Complications
Coarctation of the aorta	Quadriplegia or paraplegia, permanent hoarseness, leakage of body fluid from intestines into chest, loss of bowel and/or bladder function, impotence in males
Colon surgery	Infection of the incision, intra-abdominal abscess, leakage from colon and possible colostomy, injury to other organs and blood vessels, diarrhea—possibly permanent, formation of scar tissue causing intestinal blockage, hernia in incision
Colonoscopy	Infection or bleeding, perforation of colon or rectal wall, cardiac arrhythmias
Dental implants	Infection, bleeding, failure to heal, permanent and disfiguring scarring, premature loss of implant, loss of bone, numbness of face and mouth, fracture of jaw, injury to adjacent teeth or sinus
Dilation and curettage	Hemorrhage with possible hysterectomy, perforation of the uterus, injury to the bowel or bladder, sterility
Ear tubes	Persistent infection, perforation of eardrum or cyst behind the eardrum, need to surgically remove the tubes
Endoscopic Retrograde Cholangio Pancreatogram (ERCP)	Infection, perforation of esophagus, stomach or intestines, cardiac arrythmias, pancreatic inflammation
Endoscopy, intestinal	Puncture of the bowel or blood vessels, abdominal infection, operation to correct surgery, injury to ureter or bladder
Epidural, spinal	Abnormal reaction to drugs, leakage of cerebrospinal fluid with severe headaches, epidural blood clot or abscess, broken needles or catheters, incomplete analgesia, back pain and/or paralysis
Femoral bypass grafts	Bleeding requiring operation, necrosis of skin around incision, thrombi or emboli, limb loss, nerve damage, myocardial infarction, death
Fibroid removal	Uncontrollable leakage of urine, injury to bladder or ureter, intestinal obstruction or injury to the bowel, sterility, pulmonary embolism

Name of Procedure	Associated Complications
Gastrectomy or pyloroplasty	Infection in the abdominal cavity or of the incision, bleeding requiring transfusion, leakage from stomach, inability to maintain weight, chronic vomiting after eating, diarrhea and need for vitamin B12 injections, recurrence of condition for which surgery was done.
Hemodialysis	Hypotension, hemorrhage, sepsis, cardiac arrythmias, allergic reaction to tubes and dialyzer, pulmonary edema, air bubbles in the bloodstream, seizure, hypothermia, fever, metabolic disorders, viral infections such as HIV, cardiac arrest
Hemorrhoidectomy	Bleeding, post-operative pain especially with bowel movements, temporary or permanent difficulty controlling bowel movement or gas, recurrence of hemorrhoids, narrowing of the anal opening requiring repeated dilations
Hernia repair	Infection, bleeding, recurrence of hernia, injury to or loss of testicle or spermatic cords, nerve injury resulting in numbness and chronic pain
Hysterectomy, abdominal or vaginal	Uncontrollable leakage of urine, injury to bladder and/or ureter, injury to bowel and/or intestinal obstruction, painful intercourse, ovarian failure requiring hormone administration, formation of fistula between vagina and rectum
Kidney stone lithotripsy	Bleeding in or around kidney, obstruction of kidney by stone particulars, failure to completely fragment stones, high blood pressure, loss of kidney
Liver biopsy	Bleeding, lung collapse, internal leaking of bile, puncture of other organs, aspiration pneumonia
Lumpectomy	Infection or blood clot, disfiguring scar, fluid collection in arm pit, numbness to arm, swelling of arm, damages to nerves of arm or chest, recurrence of cancer
Mastectomy, radical	Limitation of movement of shoulder or arm, swelling of arm, loss of skin requiring graft, failure to eradicate the malignancy, injury to major blood vessel

Name of Procedure	Associated Complications
Oral surgery	Infection, bleeding, failure to heal, injury to adjacent teeth, numbness of face and/or mouth, fracture of either jaw, opening between mouth and sinus or nose, tooth fragment in sinus, dry socket
Penile implant	Bleeding and infection, penile pain or numbness, injury to bladder or urethra, problems with implantable prosthetic
Prostatectomy	Bleeding and/or infection, injury to bladder, urethra, or rectum, impotence, retrograde ejaculation, bladder blockage, incontinence
Radial keratotomy	Loss of vision or decrease in vision, loss of eye, variable vision, radiating images around lights, over or under correction, cataract formation, retained need for glasses
Radiation therapy, head/neck—initial reaction	Altered sense of smell, taste or nausea, difficulty swallowing, weight loss, fatigue, hoarseness, cough, loss of voice, hearing loss, dizziness, dry and irritable eyes, increased risk of infection and/or bleeding, intensified by chemotherapy
Radiation therapy, head/neck—late reaction	Tooth decay and gum changes, bone damage in jaws, hair loss, scarring of skin, swelling of tissues under chin, brain, spinal cord or nerve damage, pituitary or thyroid gland damage, second cancers developing
Radiation therapy, thorax—initial reaction	Skin changes, hair loss on the chest, inflammation of the esophagus, heart sac, or lungs, bleeding or fistula from tumor destruction, intermittent electric shock-like feeling in the lower body, increased risk of infection or bleeding, intensified by chemotherapy
Radiation therapy, thorax—late reaction	Changes in skin texture, scarring, hair loss, lung scarring or shrinkage, narrowing of esophagus, construction of heart sac, damage to heart muscle or arteries, fracture of ribs, spinal cord or liver damage
Radical mastectomy	Limitation of shoulder or arm movement, swelling of the arm, loss of the skin of the chest, failure to completely eradicate the malignancy, decreased sensation or numbness, injury to major blood vessels
Renal biopsy	Injury to adjacent organs, infection, hypotension, bleeding from the kidney, intestinal perforation

Name of Procedure	Associated Complications
Rhinoplasty	Bleeding, infection, disappointing cosmetic result, impaired breathing through nose, septal perforation
Septoplasty	Bleeding, infection, injury to nerve of upper teeth, septal perforation, spinal fluid leak
Sigmoidoscopy/ proctoscopy	Infection or bleeding, perforation of colon or rectal wall, cardiac arrhythmia
Sinus surgery	Bleeding, infection, scar formation, spinal fluid leak, infection of brain tissue, blindness or eye damage, injury to sense of smell
Spinal manipulation	Soft tissue injury, rib fracture, stroke and arterial dissection have been reported on rare occasion with cervical manipulation, but no cause and effect has been demonstrated
Spinal operation	Pain, paralysis or numbness, weakness in extremities, loss of bladder function, loss of bowel function, unstable spine, recurrence of condition, injury to blood vessels
Thyroidectomy	Permanent hoarseness or impaired speech, low blood calcium levels requiring extensive medication, life long requirement of thyroid medication
Tonsillectomy	Bleeding, injury to nerves to tongue, nasal speech
Vasectomy	Bleeding and/or infection, testicular swelling or pain, spermatic granuloma (nodule in cord at site of surgery), reconnection of vas tube resulting in fertility
Ventriculoperitoneal shunt	Heart failure, infection in blood stream, occlusion of large veins in chest, blood or fluid collection around heart, blood clots in the lung
Ventriculoperitoneal shunt placement	Malfunction of shunt due to infection collection of blood or fluid between brain and skull, headaches, development of need for another shunt, blood clot in brain, blindness, seizures or epilepsy, leaks or separation of catheter

Source: The Association for Responsible Medicine

NOTE: The risks listed are taken primarily from the rules of the Louisiana Department of Health and Hospitals. The risks were defined by the Louisiana Medical Disclosure Panel and are required to be disclosed by physicians to patients. The Louisiana Medical Disclosure Panel Law requires that physicians tell patients: (1) the nature of the patient's condition, (2) the general nature of the proposed treatment/surgery, (3) the risks of the proposed treatment/surgery, as defined by the Panel, and (4) reasonable therapeutic alternatives and risks associated with such alternatives. It is always a good idea for patients to discuss these risks with their doctors and to ask how often these risks have occurred in his/her practice before undergoing any procedure.

BIBLIOGRAPHY

American Medical News. "Medicare Touts Audit Plan Success as Doctors Decry Bounty Hunters" (Dec. 18, 2006). "Medicare Audit Overreach?" (July 7, 2008).

Fabricant, Kalb, Hopson, and Bucy. *Health Care Fraud: Enforcement and Compliance.*

http://plaguelaw.umkc.eduxfilesx.258.htm.

Illinois v. Perkins, 496 U.S. 292; 110 S. Ct. 2394; 110 L. Ed 2d 243; 1990.

Klein, Jo-Ellen Sakowitz. *The Stark Laws Conquering Physician Conflicts of Interest?* 87 GOE, L.J. 499, 511, 1998.

LaFave, Wayne R., and Austin W. Scott, Jr. *Criminal Law.* 1986.

LaFave, Wayne R. *Criminal Law.* Hornbook Series, 2003.

Oregon v. Mathiason, 429 U.S. 492; 97 S.Ct. 711; 50 L. Ed 2d 714; 1977.

Rakoff, Jed S., and Howard W. Goldstein. *RICO: Civil and Criminal, Law and Strategy.* 1989.

Samaha, Joel. *Criminal Law.* Matthew R. Lippman, 2007.

Silverglate, Harvey A. *Three Felonies a Day.* NY: Encounter Books, 2009.

INDEX